A
HIGHER
KIND OF
LOYALTY

Also by Liu Binyan:

"Tell the World":
What Happened in China and Why
(with Ruan Ming and Xu Gang)

Pantheon Books New York

Liu
Binyan

A

HIGHER

A Memoir by

KIND OF

China's Foremost Journalist

LOYALTY

Translated by Zhu Hong

Originally published in China as *Liu Binyan zi chuan* by the
China Times Publishing Company, Taiwan.

Zhu Hong wishes to make grateful acknowledgment to the
Humanities Research Centre of the Australian National University
for generous support for the translation of this book.

Library of Congress Cataloging-in-Publication Data

Liu, Pin-yen, 1925–
    A higher kind of loyalty: a memoir by China's foremost
journalist/Liu Binyan.
        p. cm.
    ISBN 0-394-57471-0
    1. Liu, Pin-yen. 1925– —Biography.   2. Authors,
Chinese—20th century—Biography.   I. Title.
PL2879.P5Z466   1990
070'.92—dc20
[B]   89-42654

Book Design by Fearn Cutler

Manufactured in the United States of America

First Edition

Contents

Foreword

I was born a dreamer, shy and socially awkward. Under ordinary circumstances, I might have been a retiring poet or a scholar; neither my parents, my childhood friends, or I myself could have foreseen that I would be thrown into the turmoil of Chinese politics in my thirties and end up a political outcast. Still less could anyone imagine that thirty years after that, my fate would be repeated and that I would be thrown out of the Party a second time, again a political target.

Apart from short visits abroad, I have always lived in China; I am Chinese to the marrow of my bones. But there are few Chinese who have gone through a life like mine. I have done things that the ordinary Chinese would not do. But whatever I did, I was pushed to it by the tide: the political tragedies in my life have happened in important points in Chinese history.

Many compatriots pity me for my misfortune. But I consider myself lucky. When political misfortune first befell me in 1957, I was but getting an early taste of what was in store for hundreds of millions of my countrymen. Though my people have been through so many disasters, I have yet lived to see a profound force transforming China, pushing me forward as a witness and a recorder of the awakening of the Chinese people.

Looking back, I have no regrets. I have received much more from life than what I lost or had to give up. Many who consider themselves luckier than I are not able to write in their epitaphs, "Here lies a Chinese who had done what he should do, and said what he should say." Actually, there are many other Chinese who could say just this. I am more fortunate than most, however, in that I have survived, and hope to live to the end of the twentieth century and see the light of hope over China.

A
HIGHER
KIND OF
LOYALTY

chapter one

Life and Death

My earliest memory is of the assassination of the warlord Zhang Zuolin in 1928. I was three years old when the Japanese bombed his special train compartment in Huanguo village near Shenyang, where my family was living. The incident was a great shock, and people talked about it for a long time. I must have remembered the incident from hearsay, for I had no idea what a "special compartment" was; and because the Chinese word for *special* sounds like the word for *brick*, I always thought the bombed car was a compartment made of bricks.

In another time and place such an incident might have seemed an anomaly remembered for its strangeness rather than for its familiarity. But in the China of my childhood, such incidents were quite common, although they never lost their ability to shock; this was only the first of many such incidents that I remember. It was my introduction to death and the suddenness of death, and to a world in which very little seemed calm and stable.

As a little boy I became fascinated by the question of living and dying, and of the nature of death itself. Even as a small child, I wanted very much to see a dying person, having heard so much about them. I did see one, one day, a little boy, the son of a landlord, who had been in a car accident. He lay dying in the street, a trickle of blood coming from one ear, but otherwise unmarked, and I was surprised to see how calm his face looked.

When I was four my mother carried me in her arms to the scene of a murder. To this day I remember the row of five black coffins—two large ones and three small ones—lying in a spacious courtyard. The murderer had broken into the one-story gray building at night, axe in hand, and had attacked the master of the house, then his sleeping wife and children. The father had been newly appointed as the governor of a county and was about to leave for his post. It was said that the murderer did not touch any valuables in the house, which seemed to point to a case of revenge. I was particularly affected by the sight of the three little coffins, and I pictured the three little heads lying side by side on the edge of the bed as the axe came down on them.

Revenge against officials was not rare, but those three small coffins haunted me for years. Ghost stories were told about the murdered family. They became part of the folklore of the neighborhood. The legend went that each night they came out to buy snacks from the peddlers, who were startled to learn they had sold their goods to ghosts.

There was very little entertainment in the life of the Chinese people when I grew up—no music, little theater. Instead, it was as if the brutal realities of our daily lives were transformed into stage tragedy, as if we were watching from a distance, seeing a strange and frightening drama, compelling in its particularities and its passion.

Thus when I was still four my mother took me to a public execution. She had been to several of them; they were almost social occasions. Like many others, she was very curious about them. And the fascination with the mystery of death itself was something I shared with her. All I remember is the person to be executed—a young woman in her thirties, sentenced as a bandit. But the crowds did not see her as a criminal. In fact they repeated stories of her exploits, and were particularly impressed that she could aim and shoot a gun with either hand.

I do not really know how this custom of parading the condemned before execution came into being; perhaps the imperial dynasties fostered it as a means of combating crime. For whatever reason, such scenes were a common sight: standing on a horse-drawn cart with a policeman on either side, the condemned person would pass through the busy streets, escorted by armed carts in front and behind. The criminal—usually a strong-bodied man—would carry a placard on his back, bearing his name and offense, with a scarlet cross painted over his name signifying the death sentence. The few that I saw invariably stood proud and erect, and eyed the gaping crowd with condescension, fearless in the face of death.

I remember one in particular who sang a song in words that I did not understand, but it was interspersed with denunciations of the current regime. Those were his last words, so the authorities did not begrudge him the chance to have his say. What's more, the cart would stop at the condemned man's orders for him to accept gifts of food and drink from the shops lining the streets.

Not long after we moved to Harbin, my younger brother caught scarlet fever. We were very poor at that time and could not afford a private doctor. Mother took him to the public hospital, where he was placed in an isolation ward. He had big eyes and was a very handsome child of about four then. I remember the last time I saw him—I stood looking through a window, and saw him in Mother's arms, looking back at me through the glass with such mournful, tearful eyes.

Death then seemed everywhere. In the winter when I walked to school, I would regularly see the carts going slowly by, loaded down with the corpses of those who had died during the night—those who had starved or frozen to death, and opium addicts who had died on the streets. They were stacked one upon the other, stripped of their clothes. We called them "white stripes"—because they looked like the slabs of pork that hung in the butcher shops.

Further in the background were the constant reports and stories of fighting and military conflict. At the age of five, I first heard the sound of cannons when visiting my grandmother in northern Manchuria. My entire family was then taking refuge there, and we hid in the root cellars, where vegetables were stored; when we would leave the shelter to relieve ourselves, my mother's brother would point out the bullet holes in the window paper. Perhaps I had expected to hear that the battle was between Chinese and Japanese soldiers, for I remember being amazed that it was between rival Chinese military groups. Only in later years did I realize that fighting among Chinese was in some ways far more serious than that against foreigners.

Amidst such memories of death and turbulence are those of more idyllic moments. I still have a fleeting vision of my childhood years. For a brief time we lived in a little town called Yimianpo, a hundred miles from Harbin. It was a summer resort for the Russians. I remember the streets lined with trees and the clear, cool waters of the Mayan River that flowed down to the town from the green hills. My uncle would often take my older sister and me fishing, or we would watch him swimming in the river. Other times we would go out into the fields to pick wild strawberries, or catch worms in my grandfather's vegetable garden. Sometimes we would venture into his orchard. It was such a treat to eat the apricots and plums that seemed to drop straight into our mouths when we shook the trees. I would pick a peony and dig a hole in the ground with my little hands, where I would lay the peony, place a bit of glass over it, and then cover it up with earth. The next morning, I would uncover the flower to see whether it had grown and what had happened to it. These were among the very few months in my entire life that I lived close to nature as a normal human being.

My nickname was "Big Head" because my head was really rather large—the barber always maintained that I should pay full-price instead of half-price like other children. In the dialect of the Northeast, the term *big head* is used for someone who is easily fooled, or is somewhat of a simpleton. Yet at the same time, a large head was seen as a sign of intelligence. My big head was actually seen both ways. My schoolmates sometimes took advantage of me, because I was so innocent; other times they would ask for my help with their compositions, at which I was good.

I was born January 15, 1925, in Changchun, in Jiliang Province. Until I was six, when we settled permanently in Harbin, my family moved constantly. My father worked on the railway, and given his business trips and changes of assignments, as well as our taking refuge from war, I had already done a considerable amount of traveling by the age of four. At first we rode in a well-furnished second-class sleeping car, then in ordinary third-class cars—what we now call the hard-seat car. Eventually we ended up traveling in open cars used for transporting cattle or goods. Our deteriorating modes of transportation are an apt indication of our declining family fortunes.

Even by today's standards, I traveled more than most children. But the traveling and exposure to all kinds of people did not cure my innate shyness. I withdrew more and more into the world of my daydreams.

My childhood travels came to a halt in Harbin. Harbin is a very special city, unlike any other in China. A large segment of the population consisted of peasants who flocked to the city from Shandong and Hebei provinces to escape famine, while another part of the population consisted of exiled Russian aristocracy and tradesmen, and their descendants. The Russians lived in the former foreign-concession area, for the most part as comfortably as they had in prerevolutionary Russia; the Chinese lived however they could, in much more crowded areas.

When a peasant left his native place for the Northeast, he cut off ties to the family clan and broke away from feudal traditions. The opportunities that the vast expanses and the rich soil of the Northeast offered were there for anyone with the pioneer spirit. The people of the Northeast, especially of Heilongjiang Province, were descendants of these pioneers; they were more filled with the spirit of enterprise than their kinsfolk left behind on ancestral lands.

The urban population of Harbin also benefited from Russian and Chinese capitalism as well as from the progressive influence of Russian culture; thus, a more liberal atmosphere prevailed there. While Harbin's cultural heritage was perhaps not as rich as that of some of the other big cities, this liberal atmosphere helped to produce—in the space of two or three years in the early thirties—a dozen talented writers known across the nation. This was a claim that none of China's other cities, including Shanghai, could make.

My ancestors had been peasants in Shandong, and my grandfather left his native village at the turn of the century to settle near Harbin with his family. Instead of going to school, my father had to look after the children of wealthy Russians, from whom he learned Russian. During the First World War, China participated in the war effort by sending labor groups to Russia and France. My father was among those sent to serve in the eastern part of Russia from 1914 to 1921; he went to work on the Central Manchuria Railway as a Russian interpreter. He brought back the seeds of Russian liberalism from the Soviet Union, and he was influenced in many other ways by his years there. When he came back from a trip, he would embrace my mother in public, a very un-Chinese act. And he liked Russian literature. He lacked formal education, but he was always eager to study—when he came back from his years in the Soviet Union, he could neither write nor read Chinese, so he taught another person Russian, in exchange for lessons in Chinese.

Of the four children in my family, I was my parents' favorite and had perfect freedom to do whatever I pleased. And I seized this privilege to read and dream.

My father certainly encouraged, if not the dreaming, at least studying. I had to start learning Chinese characters when I was two, but soon felt more enjoyment than drudgery in my study. I would work in the house during parts of the day. In the early years, we had a house to ourselves and I rarely ventured out to join the other children. I was too shy, and I had a world of my own in which to dream. Though my father encouraged me to be a prodigy, he did not hold up any particular goal for me to pursue—he just wanted me to grow up to be a great man. Once, when we passed a store with a big car on display, father told me that if I worked hard, I might someday afford my own car. Nonetheless, it was his yearning for social justice that had the greatest impact on me.

My mother encouraged me as much as my father, and she, too, had a deep sensitivity to the poverty of others. I remember her making dumplings, a great treat for us. We were much poorer by then, living in Harbin; but although she knew how much I loved dumplings, and knew that I would gladly eat every one of them, she would always give some to our poor neighbors. My sister and I would protest that she gave too much away. "You should learn not to think only of yourselves," she would reply.

My older sister, Liu Fang, was the most unfortunate of us children. She was only four years older than I, but from early childhood, her fate was already cut out for her: she was to help with the housework and to look after me; as a result, she had to leave school. Still, she loved me dearly and was full of affection for the whole family, even though her whole life was spent giving up her own happiness little by little, as if she were repaying a debt.

I had always liked school, though I still could not get along well socially. And I liked to play ball, but felt too clumsy with my hands, too weak. The only time I was punished in public was the result of my basic naïveté. It was during my last year in primary school. That morning, the students in another classroom were doing their homework; their teacher, a young woman, supervised them while chatting intimately with a young male teacher. My class was having recess and my classmates egged me on to play a joke on the couple. I don't know where I got the courage, but I entered the room, walked up to them, and asked in a loud voice, "What are you two whispering about? Won't you let us in on your secret?" The class burst into laughter. The young woman paled with anger, and seizing the discipline ruler, she gave me six raps on the palm of my hand. She hit hard and it hurt so that I nearly cried. To this day, I don't know why I was such a fool that day. Certainly I had not done it to show off or to be a popular hero.

Those were the days of Zhang Xueliang's liberal rule. Life for me was peaceful and orderly, but the cloud of Japanese occupation gradually overshadowed our lives. I was ten, and I joined the older students in boycotting Japanese goods. I gathered all the Japanese manufactured articles I could lay my hands on—the plastic ruler, rubber running shoes—and took them to the big bonfire in the school yard. I also joined with students my own age and went from house to house, soliciting donations for the flood victims. Some people found my prepared speech amusing and would then make me sing for them before they donated their pennies. My teacher organized all these activities and I enjoyed them thoroughly.

The Japanese occupiers, however, soon arrived and Chiang Kai-shek ordered Zhang Xueliang's troops not to resist. I still remember the sight of their army caps with the blue-and-white badge of the Nationalistic armies, strewn about the fields as the army fled.

When I entered middle school in 1939, we had already lived under Japanese occupation for eight years. For many of those years the Japanese had remained in the background, preferring to work through the local Chinese forces subservient to them. It was only in middle school that I became aware of the growing Japanese control over education. Even the Chinese term *middle school* had been replaced by the Japanese term *national higher institution.* I went to middle school in search of knowledge, but my first lessons there repelled me.

Every morning, at the beginning of the schoolday, we had to sit up straight in our seats and add sums on the abacus to orders from a phonograph. Our main textbooks were the standard Confucian texts like *Book of Filial Piety, Analects,* and *National Morals.* I had already absorbed the influence of the new culture of the May Fourth movement; the aridity of the traditional teachings ran completely counter to my yearning for freedom and my spirit of rebellion. The teacher's methods, making us recite from memory all the time, also repelled me. (I had already learned better methods while studying Russian under my father's direction. The standard textbook of the time, with its endless repetitions—"What's this?" "It's a table." "Is this a table?" "Yes, it is."—bored me. I put it aside and went on to read a Tolstoy story directly from the original, even though I only understood about half. That way, I made more progress, and soon read Gorki's *Three Men* in the original.) I sat in the back row of the classroom, and would sometimes secretly read books of my own choice or play dice with the classmate sharing my double desk.

At school we also had to undergo military training under Japanese officers and spent hours endlessly marching back and forth. We also had to shave our heads and wear uniforms based on Japanese military models. The principal of my school was a Japanese man named Yoshita who always wore a uniform and sported a Hitler-style mustache. Every morning, he would stand on a platform in the schoolyard and harangue the gathered students. One morning, I did not stand where I was supposed to, and was ordered to kneel at the platform. It was my first taste of insult, which I never forgot.

There was one teacher I remember favorably: Mr. Li, a man with a strong social conscience who reminded us after class that we were Chinese. We should read classical Chinese poetry as part of our national heritage, he said, and he talked about Chinese national heroes. Even more, amidst a prevalent mood of despair, he insisted China would not dissolve; China would not die; it had to hold together. It was a stirring message at a time when every few days the Japanese would show pictures of their army standing atop the walls of yet another Chinese city they had captured, waving the Japanese flag.

I had some knowledge of Chinese history by this time from watching Peking operas. And my teacher's words resonated with the feelings I attached to the hero Yue Fei, the fighter against the northern barbarians. Before he set out to war, he knelt before his mother, and we saw four characters tattooed on his back: "Serve the country to the utmost."

The first question that rose in my young mind was, Why was there such injustice in life? Father said it was not so in the Soviet Union. Father often told stories about Lenin and the Russian Revolution to my little brother and me, and these especially stuck with me after I was seven and when our family fortune began to go downhill. In the Soviet Union, there were neither rich nor poor, he said, and the Soviet Union became a symbol of utopia in my dreams.

Surrounded by the struggle for survival, I began to see a way out of poverty and humiliation: I realized I would have to fight and persist. I buried myself in my studies. I saved my lunch money to buy or rent books. My reading interests began with works of modern Chinese literature and expanded to the ever-changing world situation. At the age of thirteen, I was already reading Japanese periodicals. I worried about the explosive situation in Europe, and I was baffled by the invasion of Finland and by the partition of Poland by the Soviet Union and Germany. How could a socialist country invade its weaker neighbor?

Because I could not afford to buy new Japanese periodicals, I would go and rummage through the many used-paper shops close to my school. Surreptitiously, I would open the tightly bound bundles of used paper, while keeping an eye on the owner of the shop. If I was lucky, I would come across a bundle of Japanese periodicals for a few cents per kilo. Once I opened a sack of used paper and found it was full of excellent banned publications—anti-Japanese books and magazines in Chinese! I opened a second sack, and found even more. I tried to hide my delight, and balancing my buying power with my ability to carry the papers, I took home half a sack.

In order not to alarm my parents, I waited until they were asleep before lighting a little oil lamp by my bed. Then I read *Save the Nation,* a paper published by the Communist Party, the *National News Weekly,* published by the Kuomintang, and *A Call to All Compatriots,* published by the Northeast Allied Army. Their message of national crisis deeply stirred me. I wept as I read. For several nights I was so moved by my reading that I could not sleep.

In my early teens, my ambition blossomed. First I wanted to become a famous Peking opera actor. In my mind, I pictured the poster announcing my performance, with the three characters of my name forming a bold triangle in the middle, and the names of my brother and another supporting actor placed on either side beneath mine.

The New Stage opera house was very close to where we lived. Of course I could not afford a ticket, but I often snuck inside. I was surprised at how bold I could be when it came to something I wanted badly. Not only would I sneak in, but I could put on a nonchalant air while doing so. I was always spellbound by the performances and identified with the characters in the plays. I worshipped the actors, never ceasing to marvel at their beauty and the spell they cast over the scene. As I made a habit of sneaking into the theater I grew even bolder and ventured backstage, peeping at the actors and actresses as they put on makeup, or as they undressed after the performance, trying to discover the secret of their charm. Of course I was more engrossed with the actresses; I adored nearly every one of them.

Later, I imagined myself as a famous writer returning to his home town in a blaze of glory; I saw myself walking through the streets while people greeted me from the houses. In the fall of 1938, Harbin's *Dabei Daily* sponsored a literary contest, and I decided to try my hand at writing. One night, using a chair as my table and a low stool as my seat, I sat underneath the single little bulb in our room, and began to write. The title of my piece was "The Heart of a Mother." The story took place one winter night. A young rickshaw-puller was trudging through the snow on his way to a gambling house. He lost again and again until all of his money was gone. Desperate for money, he robbed and accidentally killed a man. He was arrested and pronounced guilty. His old mother was overcome with grief, but since he was her only source of support, she had a right to take him back. Society, however, also had a right: to punish the criminal. What was to be done? I had never heard of such an incident; I simply made it up using the one source I had—the many poor people that I often saw and sympathized with.

Contrary to my expectations, my composition won third prize. When I received the twenty-yuan prize money, I treated my good friend Li Dan to dinner. Still, I was not particularly elated about the prize. In fact, I did not even save a copy of the issue with my story. Sixteen or seventeen years later, and again forty years later, when my works attracted nationwide attention, I took things very calmly as well. To this day I don't know the reason why. It is not that I am without vanity, but whenever I hear praise, I feel shy and undeserving. As a writer, I always feel my work is not good enough for publication; after it is published, I always feel it could have been better. I envy my more confident colleagues.

Shortly after winning this prize when I was fourteen, I began my friendship with the young writer Guan Muonan, then only twenty, who was making a name for himself in Harbin. My friend Li Dan and I had read his first book of short stories, *The Passage of Time*, and admired his style, which was similar to Lu Xun's, and we decided to call on him. At Guan's home, I was introduced to Marxist literary theory for the first time, and I also saw Guan's own notes. From then on, I visited his home from time to time and joined a study group he directed. It was made up of young leftist writers and poets and was, in fact, affiliated with the Communist Party.

While he was in his early twenties, Guan Muonan published two books at his own expense. And then it was permitted—whereas now, more than fifty years later, the luxury of publishing privately is still denied to us. Were the Japanese occupiers putting on a show of liberalism, to prove that the Manchurians were still the masters of Manchuria? Whatever the reason, books by progressive Chinese writers flowed freely into Manchuria, and were freely reprinted. Ba Jin's trilogy *Family*, *Spring*, and *Autumn*, for example, which had a revolutionary effect on an entire generation of Chinese youth, was reprinted in the occupied areas. While American films were later banned in the occupied area, German and French films were still shown. I still remember watching a French version of *Crime and Punishment,* while several decades later in liberated China this film was still taboo. Throughout the Japanese occupation, Marxist publications were available in the Japanese bookstores. I also remember a thick volume called *On the Anti-Japanese War,* which contained all of the anti-Japanese articles and speeches of the Chinese leaders at the time. In the late thirties and early forties, the Japanese journals were of course full of fascist propaganda, but opposing views were also printed, as were reports on the world situation. Evidently they made a distinction between writings that were politically subversive and those that were of pure ideology— although of course they also made a great display of ideology, their own brand of Confucianism.

By this point in my life, I had already wanted to be an actor, a writer, and a famous reporter in command of six languages. I had also wanted to join in the Anti-Japanese War. The narrowness of my life and the restrictions to my development had frustrated me. Middle school had also been a great disappointment. The textbooks had provided no answers to the questions I had about China and the world. The Confucian classics were stultifying.

So in the year 1940, I decided to go and join my sister, already married and settled in Beijing. There must be more freedom in Beijing than in Harbin, I thought. At least I hoped there would be.

chapter two

Original

Sin

Although I would have preferred to go to Shanghai, I went to Beijing when I left Harbin at fifteen. Many of my favorite writers had written their works in Shanghai, and in my mind, Shanghai was a symbol of freedom. Just as, forty years later, I preferred New York to other parts of the United States, so in 1940 I enjoyed the bustle and diversity of a great cosmopolitan city.

Beijing was the opposite of Shanghai; here everything felt stagnant. I disliked the uniform gray walls; both the noisy streetcorners and the quiet alleys with their courtyarded houses repelled me. For me, Beijing represented the past. It was, of course, one of the great cultural repositories of China, but I could smell the rot everywhere. And, like Harbin, Beijing was occupied by the Japanese.

But presumably I could still learn more there than in Harbin. While many of my classmates were supported by their parents, I could only turn to my sister Liu Fang, who was already married and living in Beijing. She agreed at once to my coming, and I set out.

My sister had married for love. Her husband, who had studied in Japan, was the son of a big landlord. Thus my sister had been able to insist on one condition for the marriage—namely, that her husband would help support our family, especially in paying for my schooling.

The marriage did not turn out to be a happy one; my brother-in-law drifted to womanizing and opium. Disappointed in her husband, my sister always believed in me and was sure that I would make a name for myself someday. Even when she realized that I had become a leftist and had chosen the path of revolution, she never opposed me. And later, when I was based in Tianjin and my comrades and I moved back and forth between Beijing and Tianjin, my sister would help us when she could.

Life in occupied Beijing was very bleak. My sister had to scrimp and save all the time, for besides supporting me in school, she occasionally sent money to our parents. During the week, I boarded at school, staying with my sister on weekends. The food at school was poor, so my sister always prepared something extra for me to take with me on Monday mornings. In my second year, inflation worsened, and I tried to economize too. I was used to eating a full portion of stir-fried, shredded pancakes for supper, but gradually I reduced it to half a portion. One night, I couldn't sleep, something that had never happened to me before; I realized finally that I had gone to bed on an empty stomach.

After a year and a half, the burden of paying for my schooling became too great for my sister. I left school but stayed on with her and began my own rigorous course of study. Every morning for about a year I would sit in a screened-off corner of my sister's sitting room to read Marxist theory and study foreign languages—mainly Russian and English, since my Japanese was already passable.

It was then that I decided to go to the liberated area of China and join the Anti-Japanese War led by the Communists. The Communists then seemed China's best hope for overcoming Japanese aggression, but I did not know how to go about joining the Party. Finally in September 1943, I was able to go to Tianjin with my childhood friend Deng Mai; from there we could travel to the liberated area.

In Tianjin, however, we learned that people were needed there for the underground struggle against the Japanese, and we were persuaded to stay. We joined the Federation of Resistance against Japanese Aggression, which consisted mostly of young people from eighteen to twenty years old who had not finished middle school. We were expected to support ourselves. In the beginning, there were no Communist Party members within the federation.

We began distributing anti-Japanese leaflets in Tianjin in 1943. We would scatter them from the top of the Commercial Center, one of the tallest buildings in the heart of the city, or squeeze handfuls of leaflets between the closed doors of passing streetcars and let the wind scatter them. Under cover of darkness, we would paste them up on walls or slip them under house doors. At my suggestion, we even distributed leaflets to the Japanese living in Tianjin. I took charge of this assignment: I drafted the message in Japanese, copied it onto forms I stole from the Japanese bank where I worked, and slid the copies under the doors of the Japanese residents.

At the time, we never discussed what we would do if we were arrested.

We knew no fear. All we felt was the exhilaration of taking risks.

When asked what the goal of our group was, we would give the obvious answer: to fight Japanese imperialism. But when questioned further about what we were fighting for, we were not so ready with answers. Freeing China from Japanese aggression would not solve all our problems. As for myself, I had joined the revolution mainly to liberate myself, to realize myself. I could not say precisely what this "self" was, but I had a feeling that there was something in me that, though still undeveloped, would eventually blossom, until one day I would do something very special. From my teens until the age of thirty, I had the conviction that although I was nobody at the time, someday I would be somebody. Within the federation I conscientiously fulfilled my assignments, and at the same time, I seized every opportunity to study.

We were taught that the true way to start on the revolutionary path was through self-abnegation. The first political term we learned was *bourgeois ideology*, which we were told was synonymous with *individualism*—although nobody could ever explain to me where rational self-interest ends and selfishness begins. At the time, faced with a common enemy, we lived in a spirit of comradeship. There was no petty malice or backbiting, but we were strict with each other—because we all had the "original sin" of individualism and had to repent. Of course, at the time, I did not realize that we as intellectuals were not the only ones who carried this burden of "sin," and that workers and peasants were not exempt from the task of "thought reform."

My particular problem, the comrades pointed out, was that I had "the airs of a decadent Russian aristocrat." Their criticism was not harsh; in fact it seemed somewhat playful. They cited my reluctance to use the public toilets and the fact that on long walks I was always thirstier than others. I admitted these shortcomings, but in my heart, I still could not swallow the comparison to a decadent Russian aristocrat. Perhaps I did look Russian, but why did I have to be called an aristocrat? But in the end, I had to admit that I was far from being a stolid proletarian worker or peasant. I do not know why, but throughout my life, I have never been truly content with myself or my environment; I have often felt a certain melancholy, as though something were missing.

Nonetheless, like my companions, I worked hard. I copied Mao's works word for word; I single-handedly printed and distributed them and other anti-Japanese leaflets—often surprised by my own audacity. The starkness of our living conditions was beyond anything I had ever endured: we subsisted on boiled cabbage and coarse cornbread, often only half-cooked. But I bore it all with good humor.

It was our job to disseminate progressive ideas, mostly to individuals or study groups. We went about it by giving them progressive works of literature, and then propagandistic documents published by the Kuomintang. In reality, such materials could be effectively used against the Japanese and the Kuomintang themselves. When we decided that our subjects were sufficiently advanced politically, we would then give them books published in the liberated areas, or our own reprints of the works of Mao.

We were very cautious in dealing with the people we were trying to influence. They were mostly the children of wealthy families; we would observe them carefully, weighing the good and bad points of each of them before we would admit them into our group. Consequently, although several years passed, membership in our federation did not grow significantly. And even members of the federation were not guaranteed admission to the Communist Party.

The years 1944 and 1945 were the last of the Anti-Japanese War, and the situation was very favorable for the activities of the Party. The Japanese concentrated their efforts on economic crimes such as black-marketeering, speculation, and transporting necessities into the liberated areas. We could easily have expanded our operations, since their repression of resistance was neither systematic nor very severe.

We were not very tolerant young men. A few of us roomed together at the house of our comrade Yang. Yang's father, a salt merchant, gave us financial support and allowed his house to be used as the base of operations for our federation. However, we did not at all understand the grave risks he was running for our sake. The situation did not last long. Under pressure from his father, Yang finally asked us to leave. From that moment on, we regarded him as a traitor, and we severed all ties with him. Ten years later, after liberation, Yang became the head of a primary school and a member of a local political consultative conference; in other words, he was accepted as a patriot. Still, when we met again, we never relented one bit in regarding him as a one-time traitor.

After we left Yang's place, we four young bachelors moved to the garret of a wooden building overlooking the entrance to a side street. The Japanese were incredibly careless: there we were, four young men living together, with many others coming and going at the most unlikely hours, and they never once bothered to check on us. Except for one disabled comrade, the three of us had occasional jobs, and some other comrades from wealthy families also gave us occasional help. Those were our only means of living. Life was hard, but we were not the least bit daunted; to us, everything seemed cast in an aura of romance.

In the spring of 1944, a momentous event took place in our little garret. The four of us took in a young woman. Her name was Jiang. She had been sold as a child, had endured indescribable suffering, and finally ended up in Tianjin as a dancer. A young man from a good family had fallen in love with her; they had lived together at first, and then married and lived with his family. But the man's parents refused to recognize her as his wife, and she finally had to leave. Out of pity, we took her in. We hung a sheet around a bed in the corner of the garret, and that became her room.

At the time, three of us happened to be employed, and only one, Comrade G., who was suffering from tuberculosis, was staying at home. Two years older than I, he was the leader of our group. The four of us were very close, like brothers, and Jiang, as the only woman, looked after Comrade G. It was a perfect arrangement.

Then suddenly one day, we were told that Comrade G. had seriously violated discipline, and that he must leave our ranks. He had fallen in love with Jiang and had slept with her. And what was more serious, he had divulged our political identity to her. Comrade G. soon left for Beijing, and then moved on to the liberated area in Jinchaji, in Hebei Province.

There was no written rule explicitly forbidding underground members from falling in love and getting married. Perhaps we considered the premarital sex immoral. Whatever the reason, we all accepted the decision to discipline Comrade G. Secretly, however, I wondered whether he had been punished too harshly. I did not think of the relationship between Comrade G. and Jiang as anything sordid: I thought it very natural, and I quite sympathized with them.

A few months later, four other comrades and I went to Fuping County to receive new assignments from the Urban Work Section. Just as we were walking westward through a wood in the Taihang Mountains, who should we see coming toward us but Comrade G. himself! I rushed up to him, and we shook hands. When I asked him how he was, he said he was studying at the North China Associated University. After he said goodbye and I rejoined the group, the leader, who had been in charge of disciplining Comrade G., roundly cursed me for having taken notice of the man! But how could he treat a comrade like that, I wondered—a comrade, not an enemy?

Later, I learned that when Comrade G. had left Tianjin for Jinchaji, his trip had not been arranged by the Party as I had imagined. No, he had been expelled from the organization and left completely destitute. Only through his own efforts had he made his way to the liberated area and joined the revolution again.

It was the first time that I found myself at odds with a decision of the Party. And it was also the first time that my own sentiments clashed with the dictates of the revolution. Of course, after the liberation, these clashes occurred more frequently. I had to remind myself continuously to keep my distance from "bourgeois" sentiments, to keep from becoming alienated from the dictatorship of the proletariat, a dangerous situation that I had to avoid. Gradually, I laid down a rule for myself: save your love and sympathy for the entire working class, rather than wasting it on individual suffering; beware of the words of any individual, but have absolute faith in the Party. In the coming years, I often found myself at war with this rule.

I joined the Party during this trip to the Taihang Mountains. We stayed at a village called Xibaipo, where the Urban Work Section of the Jinchaji branch of the Party was located. As soon as we arrived, we were told to wear gauze masks over our mouths so that we could not be recognized. Many young underground activists from Beijing and Tianjin were being trained at this base, and there was always the risk of betrayal if someone were arrested. Also, there was a chance that the place had already been infiltrated by enemy agents.

Two members of our group were representatives from the league head-quarters, and I had assumed that they were Party members, even veterans sent over from the base areas as special agents. As for myself, I had never thought I lived up to the standards of the Party, and never considered applying for membership, much less applying there in Xibaipo. As it turned out, these comrades who had come to Xibaipo with me had just been admitted into the Party and they had been waiting for me to make the request. Finally, they asked me whether I was willing to join. Of course I wanted to, and I filled out the application forms right away.

My other traveling companions left before me. I stayed behind, to wait for the formal approval of my Party application, and also to meet with the head of the Urban Work Section, Comrade Liu Ren, who was considering sending me to Harbin and wanted to talk to me. This plan never materialized, since Harbin was part of "Manchukuo," the puppet regime the Japanese had set up in 1932, as I was now nineteen, I would be sure to be drafted into the puppet army the moment I appeared there.

Soon, my Party application was approved. At the induction ceremony, I stood under the Party flag and repeated the pledge of allegiance to the Party. What left the deepest impression on my mind were the words "Never betray the Party."

The next morning I began the journey home to Tianjin. There I repeated the password "I was sent by Mr. Yu," which I had been given, to my superiors and was accepted as a member of the Party.

One day in March 1945, I walked into a classroom of Tianjin's prestigious Yaohua Middle School, clad in a long blue cotton gown. With my junior-middle-school credentials, I should have been sitting among the students, but there I was, a teacher, facing several hundred students. On the basis of a forged diploma from the Central University of Nanjing, I had become a geography teacher.

I was only twenty years old, six years younger than the age given on the diploma. In my attempt to appear older, I often lit up a cigarette to impress the others—and ended up with a lifetime habit.

I had to teach twelve classes. My students ranged from twelve to eighteen years old. The students were fascinated by me, for they had never come across a teacher so young and so casual in his teaching methods. The school had been built by Americans, and the buildings and equipment were quite modern. Social life on campus, however, was severely restricted. There was a very perceptible distance between the teachers and students; boys and girls had classes in separate buildings, and there was no communication between them, not even between brother and sister.

I spent hours preparing what I was going to teach the next day in class; otherwise, I would have had nothing to say. Since every class had only two hours of geography a week, I took over the geography courses for all twelve classes. I wasn't much older than the oldest boys.

Although I was always very shy, I did not have stage fright in the classroom. I discovered that teaching was somewhat like acting, that you had to captivate your audience and I found I could hold my students' attention. As a member of the underground, I found this ability to hold an audience very useful in drawing the masses to the Communist Party. It didn't matter whether there were dozens or hundreds of people, or even thousands; I could keep them listening for hours. At the same time, the support of the audience kept me going. The moment someone dozed off, or walked away, I would lose my hold. I thrived on the mutual reaching out of speaker and listener.

The students liked me for my sincerity, warmth, and relaxed manner. At the school, discipline was strict, and relations between teachers and students were very formal. I gave them a taste of something new. I was also quite forthright in discussing my political views during my lectures on world geography. The students were struck by the novelty, and impressed by my courage.

Several decades later, I am still known as a "babbler," so one can certainly imagine what I was like at twenty. I could never pretend to be something I wasn't, nor could I ever hide anything. Since government surveillance and control were quite lax during the latter part of the Japanese occupation, I decided there could not be any enemy agents among my students. I lost a sense of my mission in the underground and threw myself into teaching. The geography classes gave me the unique opportunity to tell the students what was happening in the world, and I held them riveted. Two or three of the older students did stand up and challenge me with hostile questions, but I took these confrontaions as boys' pranks and was not alarmed.

On August 9, 1945, a few days before the Japanese surrender, I received a telegram from Harbin. It said, "Mother passed away, return immediately." I was completely dumbstruck. I had never had a word of warning about my mother's poor health. What should I do? Harbin was part of Manchukuo, and you needed a visa to enter the city. And since I was carrying out a special political mission, I would also need Party approval. Mother was dead anyway, and so I wondered if there was any point in my going. Finally we decided that my sister, who was living in Qingdao at the time, and my father, who was staying with her, would go home for my mother's funeral.

That night I was overcome by bitter tears. For as long as I could remember, my mother's face had always been clouded with anxiety. My father was not a practical man, and the burden of supporting the family had fallen upon my mother's shoulders. The first time I left for Beijing to attend middle school, she saw me to the railway station and left me there. But the last time I left Harbin for Beijing, she followed me onto the train and rode one stop with me, holding my hand all the while, with tears streaming down her face. She must have had some foreboding that would be our last meeting.

I do not remember how my mother looked when she was young, but when we last parted, she was forty-three and looked much older. Thirty years later, whenever I met a woman in her forties still looking young and vigorous, I would think of my poor mother. She had aged so quickly.

After the Japanese surrender, the Sanqing Youth Organization, under Kuomintang control, infiltrated the school I was teaching in. My windows were broken several times, and on other occasions, students from this organization would start cleaning their guns in my classroom or follow me, clubs in hand. Still, I was not afraid, because more and more of the students were siding with the Communist Party.

Some of the students reported on me daily to the municipal garrison headquarters. Finally one day in July 1946, I received the Party's orders to leave immediately, as a large-scale arrest of Communists was imminent, and I was one of the main targets. I left all my belongings at the school, taking with me only two Tolstoy novels in English translation. According to Party orders, I was to return to Tianjin in two months.

At the time, the Communist underground in North China was placing hopes in the peace talks with the Kuomintang. The Party had even planned to nominate political candidates to campaign for offices against Kuomintang candidates in future municipal elections. It is hard to imagine what China would be like now, or what the Party would be like, if the Communists and the Kuomintang had had to coexist somehow from that time on. Coexistence and mutual supervision might have prevented or delayed the progress of corruption within the Communist Party, and much of the brutality and upheaval of later years.

I decided to spend this unexpected holiday in Harbin with my father and sister, whom I had not seen for a long time.

By then Harbin was part of the liberated area, under Communist military control. The whole city looked bleak. All the doors and windows seemed to be tightly closed, as if the residents were shutting out the Communists. I passed myself off as a college student from Beijing on a visit home, and claimed that my task was to work with the local Party and win over the local youth: I was to expose Kuomintang corruption and praise the Communist Party as the only force capable of saving China.

Back in Harbin, news of the Soviet Red Army's looting and raping during its march into Manchuria came as a great shock. At first, I refused to believe it. It was impossible, I told myself; the Soviet army was a socialist army, helping to free us from Japanese occupation. But rumors of the acts of the Soviet troops were everywhere, and after learning eyewitness accounts, I was obliged to believe the stories.

This evil news had caused much of the hostility of the citizens of Harbin toward the Communist Party. All of us young Party members in Harbin were embarrassed by the situation. The army led by the Chinese Communist Party had been a model of discipline. How then could the Soviet army act in such a disgraceful manner, without any consideration for the disastrous political consequences? One explanation was that the regular Soviet army had been decimated by the war, and these men were criminals conscripted from prison. Another explanation was that the marauding soldiers took their victims to be Japanese. But neither argument was convincing.

The Kuomintang had never controlled Heilongjiang Province, whereas the anti-Japanese armed forces and the underground led by the Communist Party had been active there for many years under the Japanese occupation. But even so, the local residents and the students still considered the Kuomintang as the national party and worshipped Chiang Kai-shek as the country's leader.

Here in Harbin, I put my public-speaking abilities to good use once again. At the founding ceremonies of the Northeast Democratic Youth Organization, my speech won me the greatest number of votes in the election for officers. My Party membership, however, had not yet been transferred from Tianjin to Harbin, so I could only become a vice-president.

The success of my public speaking grew out of the strength of my convictions. I sincerely believed that the Kuomintang was thoroughly corrupt. The fact that I and two other members of the underground at Yaohua Middle School could win over hundreds of students to the Communist side—students largely from wealthy, anti-Communist families—

convinced me that the Communist Party was certain to win over the entire country.

But during my public speeches in Harbin in 1946, I had to overcome one obstacle: how to account for the atrocities of the Soviet army during the previous year? I had to sing the praises of the first Communist state even though its army had pillaged our towns and violated our women! I tried to find a way around this, but the best I could do was contend that the atrocities had been committed by an army of convicts, and not the real Soviet Red Army! At the time, I did not know what the real Soviet Red Army was doing in Germany and Eastern Europe.

I was barely ten days in Harbin when the civil war broke out between the Communists and the Kuomintang. I could not return to Tianjin. The local Party organization decided that I would stay on in Harbin and work, as dean of the middle school, in the training center for young cadres, and later in the Youth League and its predecessor, the Northeast Democratic Youth Organization.

In 1946, my compassion and naïveté got me into serious trouble. While I was walking along the street one day, a man stopped me, introduced himself as Tian, and claimed he was a classmate of mine from middle school, but I could not remember him at all. He said he was out of a job and asked me to help him get in touch with the Party. I helped him register for the extension courses given during the winter holidays for college and middle-school students, and then got him a job at the Xinhua News Agency. Then the situation at the front turned against us, and our troops were at the point of withdrawing from Harbin. To play it safe, Tian had had a foot in each camp; after contacting me, he had also gotten in touch with the Kuomintang, while I, unsuspecting of all this, was still giving him reading materials about how to join the Party. Luckily, my only punishment for such carelessness was a reprimand from my superiors.

I have always been credulous and given my confidence easily—and probably I will never change. But looking back at my life, I can't say that I have suffered for giving my confidence to individuals; it has always been my implicit faith in the Party that has cost me much more.

In 1947, I joined the land-reform team on the outskirts of Harbin. The leader of our team gave orders to tie up a landlord and beat him. They tried to force him to confess that he had ties to local bandits, and had hidden arms and ammunition. The man denied everything and was beaten to a pulp. It was the first time I had witnessed such a scene. I could not interfere; I could only look the other way. As he would not confess, our team conducted a search, but we found nothing—no arms, no ammunition, no hidden valuables; all we found was a heap of ragged clothes and a few personal items. The landlord was just a miserable wretch who owned about an acre of land. But every village had to have its target of class struggle to arouse class consciousness, and that landlord served the purpose.

The leaders supervising land reform, among them Jiang Nanxiang, had repeatedly warned against physically abusing landlords. And yet, the leader of our team was never punished for the beating he ordered. In fact, had he not chosen a target of class struggle and put on a spectacular show, he would have been accused of rightist tendencies.

When I went to work as a member of a land-reform team, I helped distribute the possessions of landlords. The distribution looked like an American garage sale. Clothes, household goods, and other objects from several landlord families were arranged on tables. The most valuable items were fur-lined jackets, clocks, and the like. The distribution plan had been completed beforehand; we simply had to hand out the items. There was no air of festivity at these affairs. In fact, I felt quite ashamed, and once again I felt that my class consciousness was not quite up to par.

I thought that it was important to divide the land among the peasants—but not the family possessions, and especially the everyday household goods. Taking them could strip a family of part of its very intimate being. I felt that if Marx had been there, he would not have approved.

Again I had nagging doubts about the Party. In theory, landless peasants surely had a right to land. But there were also landowners who had, through a lifetime of hard work, scrimped and saved to buy up small plots of land. There were, of course, also loafers among the landless peasants. As everywhere in China, the peasants in the area where I worked needed a lot of persuasion before they dared to accuse the landlords of injustice and demand their share of land at mass meetings. This reluctance was attributed to fear of reprisals from the Kuomintang if they returned, which had indeed happened in places. But might there not have been another reason for their reluctance? Might not the reluctant accusers have had an uneasy conscience for depriving their neighbors of their hard-earned land?

The Youth Activities Center, set up in July 1946 on the banks of the Songhua River in Harbin, was the earliest Communist-sponsored youth center in an urban liberated area. A month later, the Northeast Demo-

cratic Youth Organiztion was founded, and the Youth League was established a year after that. At first, Communist control over the city had not
been consolidated, and young people in Harbin avoided the Party. To
attract them to the youth center, we had to cater to their special tastes,
by organizing singing and reading groups, showing films, and holding
sports events. Dealing with political issues, we relied on persuasion and
discussions. Gradually, with the consolidation of state power, the activities
of the Youth League became more and more politicized. Democracy
within the league's ranks decreased as it gradually became an official
institution. Following the liberation of the entire mainland, the Youth
League became an outright tool of the Party, and its activities could hardly
be distinguished from those of the Party. To be a member of the Youth
League was a coveted honor. The league was now in a position to pick and
choose its members. At the same time, however, it began to lose its vitality.

The Communist leaders from Yanan who were transferred to Harbin
brought with them the traditions of the liberated area. Their plain living
and hard work were, of course, very admirable, but their standards of
conduct, which had been shaped by the war years, were not to my taste.
The imposed uniformity of thought and conduct was very constricting.

The newcomers from Yanan did not trust the educated young people.
They were very aware of their status, and while they expressed a strong
commitment to a more egalitarian China, they were obsessed by a sense
of their own importance, determined by the date they had joined the
revolution and whether they had been in Yanan. I remember once in
Shenyang, after I had already advanced somewhat in the Party, going to
see a film. A VIP had come to watch, so security men were guarding the
door to the theater, trying to keep others out. The younger people were
being turned away; cadres of lesser rank were not admitted to the theater.
I argued with the guard, and the argument ended in a fight. I won, but
the fellow promptly arrested me.

I was quickly released, but the incident fueled an awareness of the
status-consciousness that pervaded the Communist Party. In the dining
room of the Party offices, there were three areas—a small one for the top
cadres, where the food was specially cooked, a middle one, and a lower one.
Such rankings always made me uneasy.

Perhaps growing up in Harbin had shaped this vision of equality. For
I sensed behind these distinctions in the Party something similar to the
status and privileges the Japanese enjoyed in the occupation—in all their
blatant and subtle forms.

Since I had joined the revolution during the Anti-Japanese War, I had a high status, though I was young. But I was also an educated youth, and therefore not looked upon by the younger comrades as one of their own kind. I personally resented that treatment—but resented more that the Party was treating people in such a way. Seniority meant too much—and still does, to the present day. I felt then that some cadres should live better; that this was justified by their ability to work better. But should this have implied a difference in human value—if someone was of lower status, was he or she somehow not as good a person, or suspect? Or if a cadre was idiosyncratic in that he loved to dance, for example, should he be looked down on as less moral? That I could not stand.

I had never played the dandy and never tried to attract girls with fine clothes, but from 1946 to 1956—which were the last ten years of my youth—I often had the desire to wear a red shirt. Was it a subconscious reaction against conformity? The fact that everybody was expected to wear clothes of the same style and color was not, I think, merely a relic of the war years; it was an expression of the uniformity that was imposed on our lives, both physical and spiritual, by the Party. Instinctively, I rebelled. While working at the training center for young cadres, I sometimes went around in a Western-style suit of my father's, in sharp contrast to everybody else around me. Fortunately, nobody interfered with me, but I still resented the criticism that others had to bear. Since summers were hot in Harbin, the girls wore skirts and blouses; to conform with revolutionary practices, they would wear a Mao jacket over their blouses and roll up the sleeves, baring their arms. This was not to the liking of the old cadres from Yanan, and they raised objections, which I thought was really going too far.

Predictably, my behavior did not find favor in the eyes of the older cadres. At a meeting, they raised objections to my singing—I often sang as I walked, or as I went up and down the stairs. They labeled it a "petit-bourgeois" affectation. But I just kept on singing, throughout the rest of my life. Singing cheered me when my spirits were low. When I was deprived of freedom, singing made me feel free.

chapter three

Seeking and Not Finding

I was not as exhilarated by the overthrow of Chiang Kai-shek and the founding of the People's Republic, on October 1, 1949, as I was by the victory against the Japanese. I am not sure why. In part, it was because I had already been living in the liberated area since 1946, and in part because this final victory was so long anticipated.

But maybe the more important reason was that in my own life I had already experienced the changes that were bound to come to everyone's lives after liberation. We would soon drive away the imperialists and the Kuomintang dictatorship; in this respect the Chinese people would be liberated. But after this liberation, it seemed to me, there would be something lacking: freedom—individual freedom. Considering this, I could not be overexcited about the emergence of the New China.

At that time, the Chinese Communist Party was full of self-confidence; it saw itself as bringing unity to a great and complex nation, a rare feat in Chinese history. It commanded the faith and following of almost every stratum of the population; even its bitterest enemies had to acknowledge defeat and bow down in submission. As a member of the Communist Party, I took for granted that such a relationship between the Party and the population would be permanent.

For several years, cadres of the Youth League spent their time determining what the young people in the big cities were thinking about. The purpose of this was certainly not to adjust the Party's policy to people's sentiments, but rather to rectify the ideology of the masses and to make them respond more readily to the rallying call of the Party. It was, unequivocally, a relation between the educator and those to be educated. Dissenting views were out of the question, and participation in the decision-making process unimaginable. As for the masses, the only distinction to be made among people was in how avidly they followed the Party. The latter's infallibility was never questioned.

The Party maintained that all the scars, all the blight on China's soil had been left by the Kuomintang, whereas the Communist Party was immaculate.

Thus a one-way relationship developed between the Party and the people: the Party handed down one decision after another, raised one rallying cry after another, and unleashed one campaign after another, while the people simply listened, submitted, and acted on orders. The Party became lost in a maze of its own making; it never stopped to rethink whether tactics that had been effective in individual struggles in the countryside could also be applied to the infinitely more complex job of running an entire nation. What's more, the Party proposed to undertake this job by disregarding all known theories and systems of management, except those of the Soviet Union, and starting from scratch.

For me, these thoughts, these doubts, were barely conscious. I felt uneasy, nonetheless, a feeling that was to increase with my first trips to Russia and Eastern Europe. In July 1949, I joined a hundred other young people on a visit to our long-cherished socialist motherland, the Soviet Union.

We were on our way to the biennial World Youth Festival with a performing troupe and a delegation to attend the Congress of the World League of Democratic Youth, which was founded in 1947. Previously, China had been able to send only two delegates from the liberated area, but now on the eve of the founding of the People's Republic, we were attending in the capacity of a national delegation.

The first stop in Soviet territory was a town called Otpor (now Zabay-kalsk), which meant *counterattack* in Russian, probably alluding to China's anti-Soviet policies of the twenties and the later Japanese threat. At the railway station of Otpor, we were served a sumptuous dinner. We thought it was a treat from the Soviet government, but to our surprise, we were given the bill after the feast was over, and it left a big hole in our allowance. Following this came a customs inspection. Grim-faced officers went through all our belongings. We were shocked. Since we were from a Communist state, we wondered why they should be on guard against us. But they took all our notebooks and film, which were to be returned on our way back. It left a bad taste in our mouths, but we soon dismissed it as an isolated incident, not to be confused with the attitude of the Soviets as a whole.

Our train crossed Siberia in eleven days. Whenever we had our meals, the glass doors at both ends of the restaurant cars would be closed tightly, with all the Soviet passengers jammed against the glass. At first we thought this was to give us more privacy during our meals, but later we learned that the Soviet passengers were not eligible for the same kind of food as we. Three poached eggs and a dish of butter were a great luxury for them.

Throughout our train ride we could see signs of poverty wherever we looked. Marks left by the war, we thought, which had nothing to do with the system.

Sometimes I would join the Soviet passengers in their cars and chat with them. A middle-aged woman asked me whether Mao Zedong would follow Tito's example and break with the Soviet Union. I was surprised and asked her how such an idea could enter her head. When she said the Chinese Communist Party had always been very nationalistic, I realized that this ordinary Soviet woman's question was simply a reflection of Stalin's long-standing distrust of the Chinese Communist Party and Mao.

I knew about Soviet chauvinism from personal experience. In the winter of 1948, following the liberation of Shenyang, the Communists took over the former headquarters of the Sanqing Youth Organization, a tall down-town building dating from the Japanese occupation. There we set up the municipal Youth League headquarters and a youth club. A movie theater, which was Soviet property, stood next to us. At the end of the year, the Soviet film-export company rudely demanded our building for its use. Of course we refused. It brought its demands to the highest authority in northeast China, the northeast bureau of the Chinese Communist Party, and made a personal appeal to the secretary of the northeast bureau, Gao Gang. He sent the Youth League secretary of the northeast bureau to negotiate with the Soviets, and he finally succeeded in persuading them to accept another building. What right did these people have to lord it over us in that way? Evidently they thought of themselves as our conquerors.

On our stop in Moscow, we stayed at the Metropole Hotel and met with another big surprise: the Kuomintang's embassy to the Soviet Union had only recently left, while their news agency, which had been in the same hotel as ours, had left only two days before we arrived. This despite the fact that the People's Republic of China was due to be officially established in two months.

Perhaps there were as yet no formal diplomatic relations, for no official Soviet representative came to greet us. We were met only by two young interpreters: L. Deliusin, who became a friend, and Sorokin. Both later became famous Sinologists.

In contrast to our stay in the Soviet Union, we were surrounded by an air of gaiety as soon as we entered Hungary. At every stop we were met by beautifully dressed girls who welcomed us with singing and dancing.

Emerging as we were from years of war and poverty, Budapest seemed like a fairyland to us: songs, dances, and flowers abounded, while friendly young faces greeted us on all sides. The black-eyed, black-haired, but white-skinned Hungarian girls treated us with special favor for they said that our ancestors had been neighbors.

Budapest still seems to me one of the most beautiful of all cities— certainly it was the most beautiful city I had visited by then. Perhaps it holds a special place in my memory because it was there I first came into contact with European culture. The architecture and streets of Budapest, the scenery on either side of the Danube, the beauty and gentleness of the people—even the soldiers seemed kind and gentle—all deeply impressed me.

The Soviet Union had also sent a big delegation and a performing-arts troupe to Hungary. But the minute their performance was over, they would all climb into their bus and retire for the night. The building that housed them was forbidding; its iron gates were always closed. One never saw people going in or coming out. The Chinese delegation had much more freedom to move about—apart from scheduled activities, we were on our own. It was still a transitional period for our country. The civil war was practically over, but the People's Republic had not yet been founded, so the regulations that governed later delegations abroad had not yet been formulated. The novelty of visiting a foreign country and experiencing a general atmosphere of gaiety gave us a moment of respite from traditional conventions and political restraint.

On our return from Hungary, we stopped again in Moscow, where we spent October 1, the day the People's Republic of China was founded.

Since I had grown up in Harbin, a city with marked Russian influence, Moscow seemed merely an extension of Harbin to me. But there were nearly a hundred actors from Yanan in our delegation, some of whom had never been to a big city before. Moscow was a wonder to them, a New York or London in their eyes.

In the following thirty years, Moscow had a double significance in Chinese eyes; it was the socialist elder brother, and at the same time, it represented Western culture. Ironically, the conflict between traditional Chinese culture (and its in exemplification of the Chinese Communist Party) and Western culture was reflected in the relations between the two Communist countries.

For several nights running, we were treated to ballet and opera perform-ances at the Bolshoi Theater. *Swan Lake* shocked some of the people in our delegation. "How could such things be permitted in a socialist coun-try?" they murmured, back in the hotel. "It's downright bourgeois stuff!" a veteran Party member said. "The plot is totally without political signifi-cance. What can it do for the people? Nothing!" Many people agreed. Then he exclaimed that the female dancers had actually shown their legs. Disgust was written all over his face. I did not reply to this, but was nonetheless amazed by this kind of reaction to the ballet.

A year later, I was in Moscow once again as interpreter for a Chinese Youth League delegation. At a dinner hosted by the local Comsomol, I heard a municipal Party secretary tell an obscene joke that I found outra-geous. Countless jokes such as this were circulated between close male friends in China, so on this occasion, the Chinese guests did not take offense. They simply laughed it off as an example of differences in national behavior, but we all agreed that we were certainly not going to emulate our Soviet big brother in this respect.

I noticed that there were love scenes between an officer and a nurse in the war novel *Days and Nights,* by Simonov, in China one of the most popular Soviet writers. In another prize-winning Soviet war novel, *The Ordeal,* the director of a factory and his secretary slept together while they were evacuating the plant and workers to the Urals. Such actions were strictly forbidden in China, and of course never written about in novels.

In 1950, Simonov traveled to China (he later based a documentary film script on his trip), and someone said to me, "That secretary he travels with is his mistress!" I thought that it might be possible, but I answered, "Why bring it up? Did you see anything?"

I was in many ways startled by what I saw on those two trips to the Soviet Union—particularly by a sense of openness. My friends and I did not know about the terror under Stalin or the general hunger in the Russian countryside. What impressed me was how easily people could move about, and that they could choose their own professions. The mili-tary and the police did not seem omnipresent; lifestyles seemed more relaxed. At parties you could hear people using profanity; life was less puritanical. And art often seemed free of direct political influence. There was no parallel in China to Stalin's role of protector of a writer and his work, of his protection of Sholokhov and *Quiet Flows the Don.* Writers were shot in Russia, but rarely for a specific piece of writing, and the writing seemed freer, and artists freer, than in China. The dictates Soviet writers followed seemed less strict.

Of course I did have a chance to see the other side of the coin. At the age of fifteen I had read a Japanese translation of André Gide's account of his trip to the Soviet Union. Gide had lashed out at censorship in the Soviet press, and I completely agreed with him on this point, especially since the Japanese were also censoring the press at the time. On the other hand, I felt Gide was playing into the hands of the imperialists, who were slandering the Soviet Union. In any event, I thought that any defects in the Soviet Union must be seen against a broader background.

Actually, I certainly couldn't say that I had not seen real defects in Soviet society. For instance, neither the young interpreters who worked with us day after day, nor the people who had been so friendly at the railway stations, wanted to give us their addresses when we said goodbye. Was it because they were afraid to be involved with foreigners? And the Soviet electoral system, with its single candidate, seemed ludicrous. In the winter of 1950 in Novosibirsk, an account of Stalin's 1938 massacre was more or less forced upon me. One morning, an old woman who was staying in the same building as our delegation insisted that I have a chat with her in her room. She took out a photo album with several faded pictures of men in army uniforms. She pointed out one of them, who had been a friend of her husband's and told me what a gifted commander he had been and what an impressive war record he had achieved—but nonetheless he had later been killed, a completely innocent victim of Stalin's purges. Later, when I read Khrushchev's secret report on Stalin in 1956, I realized that the man she was talking about was none other than General Tukhachevsky. The old woman had struck me as a bit garrulous, but I had not questioned her story, though I was surprised by her audacity in telling it to a foreigner. Even so, I took her account to be an exceptional case, and never imagined the mass murders that had taken place in a socialist society.

With the founding of the People's Republic of China in 1949, I was faced with a new choice. I had always regarded my political involvement as a part of the struggle for national liberation, but in terms of my personal career, I regarded these activities as an interim stage. Now that liberation had been achieved, I wanted to choose my own job. I decided to be a reporter, a dream I had cherished since my teens.

My second trip to Russia, in the winter of 1950, had been with the

Youth League delegation. The papers *China Youth News* and *Young Vanguard* were being planned, and the editors needed to learn from their Soviet counterparts. I worked with Zhang Liqun, the editor-in-chief of the twice-weekly *China Youth News,* and Zhu Hong, my future wife, a founder of *Young Vanguard,* a weekly for students from nine to fourteen. I also interpreted for the editors of *Komsomolskaya Pravda* and other papers as they presented their experiences to us. This interpreting job gave me the chance to seek work at *China Youth News.*

My work at *China Youth News* drew me into the familiar world of young intellectuals—recent college graduates, most of them single, who had worked in the underground. I was the oldest among them. We soon became an intimate group, working closely together, and without any conflict of interest or any need to be on guard against each other. At the endless meetings during the various campaigns of those early days, virtually no one expressed an opinion differing from the Party line. This was not due to fear, but rather to implicit trust in the Party.

China, barely recovered from the ravages of war, was confronted with one political campaign after the other. The campaign to resist the United States and aid Korea and the campaign to suppress counterrevolutionary activities progressed side by side. Thus, on the one hand, you saw thousands of youngsters flocking to join the army, while on the other hand, former officers and agents of the Kuomintang were giving themselves up to the government. The masses in the towns and in the country rushed to donate money and supplies toward the war effort on one side, while exposing reactionary elements, including their own parents, on the other. Festive farewell gatherings held for new soldiers and ruthless denunciations of enemies took place side by side. The people threw themselves into these movements and reveled in the arrival of a new era, marked by an end to inflation, the restoration of public order, and an improvement in the standard of living, all of which were of course attributed to the Communist Party.

The staff of *China Youth News* worked night and day editing the paper and attending endless political meetings, while at the same time conducting investigations into the pasts of certain colleagues. While the campaign to suppress counterrevolutionary activities was occurring within the society as a whole, another campaign was taking place within each work unit—the so-called "make a clean breast of it" campaign, wherein every person confessed his or her own wrongdoings and wrong thought to the Party. In the early 1950s, people were not made to confess through the threat of violence or the use of force. But something did happen that shocked me. A man who worked under me and sat across from my desk—Ding Fuoen—did not report to work one morning, and as far as we were concerned that was the end of him. There was no notice, no explanation. Rumor had it, however, that he was a Trotskyite. The man had come from Anhui Province, and had been a leftist since middle school. He had planned to travel to the revolutionary base in Yanan to join the Party. A friend introduced him to a Party group, which turned out to be the Trotskyite clique and not the Communist Party. And so the man became a Trotskyite.

Ding had struck me as a man of few words, who worked very hard and was good at his job. If he had joined the Trotskyites unintentionally and had no criminal record, why should he be punished? In the strident political atmosphere of the times, however, there was no room for second thoughts about the Party's decision. Aren't you being too lenient? Isn't the man's silence the sign of a guilty conscience? No one questioned the secret arrest. It was accepted as a necessary part of the revolution.

In March of 1951, a luxurious sedan—a rare sight in those days—glided into the courtyard that housed the Youth League Central, to which we were affiliated. It was whispered that Mao's wife Jiang Qing was in the car, and we all rushed to have a look. At the time, she was still young, quite slim, and graceful. She had come as an envoy of Mao to see Xu Liqun, the deputy head of the propaganda department of the Youth League Central. Xu was a noted intellectual of the time, well versed in philosophy and Chinese history. Soon, we discovered the reason for this visit, which was to launch a national campaign to attack the film *The Life of Wu Xun.* The *People's Daily* editorial that began the attack was written by Xu Liqun on Mao's personal orders, which had been relayed by Jiang.

The Life of Wu Xun had been filmed on the eve of the liberation by leftist writers, directors, and actors; it praised an individual's spirit of self-sacrifice in service of the people. The film was based on the true story of the peasant Wu Xun, who spent his whole life begging and who used all his savings to set up schools for village children. The film had been well received at its premiere; it had even been praised by some high-ranking Party leaders in art circles. Nobody could have imagined that Mao would decide to attack it on such a national scale.

When we saw the film, it had already been denounced as "negative" and targeted for attack. Even so, Wu Xun's spirit of self-sacrifice touched us deeply. Mao and his handpicked critics claimed the film "denigrated the peasant revolution," and "put education above the revolutionary struggle." This sounded far-fetched to me, but in such cases I always looked inward to strengthen my own concept of class struggle. Mao, it went without saying, was always right; in the film he had seized on an issue of strategic importance as revealed in the life of the main character.

I was not against criticizing *The Life of Wu Xun,* but after seeing the film, I felt that launching a campaign against it was making a mountain out of a molehill. As for the short story *Between Husband and Wife,* which was also under attack, I had not read the work. I worked in the same courtyard as its author, Xiao Yemu. He was a nice man, and I thought to myself, even if the work has its faults, is this national barrage of criticism really necessary? I had my doubts. At the time, who could have foreseen the fate of Xiao Yemu—a target of the "three-anti" campaign in the early fifties (anticorruption, antiwaste, and antibureaucratism), labeled a rightist in 1957, hounded to death during the Great Proletarian Cultural Revolution? And who could have foreseen the pernicious repurcussions of all these literary attacks, not only on literature itself, but on the development of the ideology as a whole?

Perhaps because I had fallen in love at the time, my interest in politics was cool. The campaign against the United States in Korea was sweeping across the country; meetings of the campaign to suppress the counterrevolution continued night after night. I was certainly not opposed to them, but I lacked enthusiasm. I was more interested in the fate of our soldiers in the United States POW camps, as well as the struggle of Iran's prime minister for national independence.

In July 1951, a huge meeting was held in the Xiannongtan Stadium to commemorate the thirtieth anniversary of the founding of the Chinese Communist Party. In a drizzle, a huge red banner spanning the width of the stadium was unfurled, reading, "Long Live the Glorious, Great, and Correct Chinese Communist Party of China!" It suddenly occurred to me that it was perhaps too early to make such a statement. Shouldn't such statements be left to others? I realized that my thoughts bordered on the seditious, but I couldn't bring myself to accept that slogan.

I lost interest in politics at the same time that I lost interest in political theory. I had been interested in theory ever since my youth and had bought books on political theory during my visits to the Soviet Union. But I discovered that once the Communist Party had seized power, the role of theory was limited to expounding the leaders' views in books or articles; new issues or independent views were never put forward. The dearth of subject-matter and the monotonous literary style in the works that were available were equally unbearable. I had no ambition to be a political theorist, but I certainly was not interested in repeating and memorizing what the leaders had to say. In our everyday lives, there were no opportunities to participate in the process of decision-making. There were not even any discussions. Our role was to listen to orders, remember them, and act accordingly. It was a very lonely feeling. There were no truly independent groups or organizations; every single aspect of one's social life was supervised by the Party. There was little room in which the individual could move.

My new wife, Zhu Hong, was a political activist. I remember once during the "three-anti" campaign, we were all gathered in the great meeting-hall—the entire staff of the Youth League Central, several hundred people. The object of denunciation was again the writer Xiao Yemu, not for his writing this time, but for a case of embezzlement. Zhu Hong kept shouting with the crowd: "Confess! Confess!" But later on, I asked her, "How much evidence did you have of his guilt?" As it turned out, her only source was some "internal information" that had been disclosed from above—some vague, unsubstantiated suspicions. On the basis of these suspicions, the leaders had called a mass meeting in hopes of making the man confess, and of scoring a major victory for the Party.

I had first met Zhu Hong on the 1950 trip to the Soviet Union to study publishing methods for the Youth League, on whose publications we had both worked since. She was born in 1929 in Tianjin, and had moved to Shanghai, the city of my youthful dreams, when she was eight. Her father, a banker, had been able to send her to an expensive missionary school, and later to Yenching University.

We were married in 1951, the model revolutionary couple. That meant there were no special arrangements for the wedding; we were merely made honored guests—along with another couple—at a regular Saturday-night dance. That was all. When we returned to our room, it was very quiet—no songs, no celebration, no wine, no one to have fun with. And the only gifts were a pair of pillowcases and a book, *The History of the Soviet Bolshevik*

Party. We did not even take the three-day holiday that was officially allowed. Such things as honeymoons were disdained by true revolutionaries.

At first we lived in one room in the dormitory, with our two chairs, one desk, one bookshelf, and a small shelf for the wash basin. Later we moved into an even smaller room, with hardly space for the chair.

At that time our private lives were undergoing a test that was closely linked to the fate of the nation. Neither of us wanted to have a baby yet, but contraception was discouraged and abortion forbidden by government policy. By 1952, contraceptive devices had disappeared from the market. I remember a man who worked at the Youth League Central and whose wife kept on having children until she was completely exhausted. She had eleven, and for every new birth she received a stipend. Mao Zedong had said that socialism was not threatened by population growth, and so women having large families were rewarded.

I had given little thought to the population problem, but once we were married, my wife and I lived under the perpetual fear of her possible pregnancy, and there were many others who shared our problem. Why wasn't the Party aware of the real situation? My wife had to have several abortions, and since they were illegal, she could not take sick leave afterwards. Then, of course, there was also the recurring tragedy of working women in Beijing and Shanghai who tried to abort themselves.

How far, I asked myself, could the individual go to protect his or her own rights? Politics had seeped into every aspect of our lives; there was virtually nothing left for the self. Political interests took on the form of lofty ideals that were to be submitted to without question. A term that was hammered into our heads all the time, at meetings, in the office, even in the home, was *bourgeois individualism.* For Communist Party members and nonmembers alike, withholding anything from the Party—one's private history, family connections, or misguided thoughts—was the most dangerous form of individualism. Not to attempt to join the Party was also an expression of individualism; to attempt to join and be rejected and then feel downcast was yet another. Individualism was also exhibited in one's work, mistakes, carelessness, indifference, or insistence on one's own opinion. To express a desire for more education, to ask for a change in job assignment for any reason, or to request a change of workplace so that one could be reunited with one's family—all of these were viewed as displays of individualism.

To fight individualism was the basic political strategy that Mao personally established on the eve of the liberation of the mainland. Since we all carried the stigma of individualism, we all had to hope for absolution through "thought reform." *Individualism,* as it was defined, however, encompassed everything pertaining to the individual and all of his rational interests; thought reform was a never-ending process, leaving no hope for eventual absolution.

Just how far would this thought reform be carried? I remember a standing joke we had about a woman cadre who worked at the kindergarten of the Youth League Central and only saw her husband on the weekend. The first thing she always did when they met was to have him report all his thoughts of the week before they would go on to anything else. It was a standing joke among us, but then, it occurred to me, wasn't it a case of the pot calling the kettle black?

"Give yourself to the Party!"—"Give all to the Party!"—"Follow Party orders in everything!"—these are the slogans that have governed people's lives for the last forty-odd years. And nobody realized how much these slogans damaged the Party itself. Although the Party enjoys supreme authority, this authority can be exercised only by its members—who are, of course, individuals. And yet, these members of the elect were not expected to practice thought reform, while they required it of others. And it was precisely this privileged position that bred the most destructive kind of individualism. Under the leadership of the Communist Party, it took only a few years for this disease to spread, and no efforts of the last forty years have been able to stop it.

Within the Party itself, iron discipline was the rule. As a result of the long years of war and underground struggle, the Party operated on the principle that orders were to be obeyed. But since the leaders were only human themselves, I often had my doubts about the infallibility of their orders. Shouldn't some limits be put on the degree of obedience demanded by the Party? My doubts did not grow from idle speculation. One day in about 1953, at a meeting of the editorial board of *China Youth News,* we somehow began to discuss this problem. Somebody took the issue to the extreme and finally asked, "Suppose the Party asks you to commit a murder. Do you have to do it?" To my surprise, an old friend, a senior cadre from Yanan, actually replied, "Yes, you must!"

This type of mentality frightened me, but it did not surprise me. It was the idea of "iron discipline" pushed to its logical extreme. At the time, I could not have foreseen that during the antirightist campaign in 1957, a

million people would become social and political outcasts on the orders of
the Party leaders. Much less could I have foreseen that a dozen years later,
actual murders would be committed on a large scale. At the time, I was
mainly concerned with the fact that people unquestionably accepted the
will of the Party, even when it destroyed their own lives.

A young woman on our editorial staff, full of promise as a reporter, had
an affair with a married man and became pregnant. She was summarily
removed from our staff and expelled from the Youth League. No one raised
any objections to her punishment, least of all the girl herself. She left
without a sound, afraid to look anyone in the face, as if she had committed
a despicable crime. We all knew that her whole future was ruined. Although I silently sympathized with her, even I could not avoid regarding
her as guilty. The tyranny of traditional sexual ethics and the merciless
verdict of the Party went hand in hand.

The "three-anti" and the "five-anti" campaigns (against bribery, tax evasion, and other related economic offenses) finally ended, and in 1953, the
First Five-Year Plan was launched. I was the member of the editorial staff
in charge of reporting about young workers; since the national emphasis
was on industrial development, my job kept me busy.

Modeling my reports on those in the Soviet newspapers, I wrote many
articles on the achievements of young workers and technicians, spurring
on socialist competition. These reports were often full of figures and
technical terms, which did not particularly interest me.

The pages of *China Youth News,* as well as other publications, were full
of good news: the progress of the political movements, the achievements
of economic development, the heroic accomplishments of model workers.
In addition to these, there were didactic articles, exhorting the youth to
overcome various wrong notions and answer the call of the Party by
throwing themselves wholeheartedly into the current campaign, whatever
it may have been at that particular moment. These articles were written
in a style of their own, which dominated the press of the fifties. There were
no differences of opinion. Apart from references to "faulty ideology" on
the part of the masses, there was never any mention of the dark side of
our society. The Party acted as if people would lose faith in socialism if
they were given a glimpse of the negative side of things. It acted as if the
morals of the people would deteriorate if they were shown anything other
than images of revolutionary heroes. The Party expected the people to shut

their eyes to the world around them and leave everything to be "ordered by the Party." Of course, there was a measure of truth in the dry monotony of our papers—it was a reflection of our lives.

I was dissatisfied with the state of our paper. I tried to publish some criticisms of bureaucratism and waste in the factories but was given the red light. If China was modeling itself on the Soviet Union, I asked, why shouldn't we follow the Soviet example in publicly criticizing bureaucracy? This question dogged me for thirty years, and twice I nearly paid with my life for my convictions on this issue.

To borrow the terms that were later used to attack me, I was suffering from "self-inflation," while at the same time unscrupulously seeking "self-expression" and "attempting to recast the Party in my own image." I was blissfully unaware of the future and pursued my own interests. I figured that since the workers were "masters of the country," they shouldn't merely be used as tools for production. They should, as I believe, "cast their penetrating glance right and left, and interfere in everything pertaining to the interests of the country." I decided to seek out this kind of worker and write about him.

I asked the reporters working under me to help me find this kind of worker. I combed the articles submitted to our paper for clues. I traveled personally to Tianjin to interview workers in factories and department stores. However, I was not satisfied with the results of my search. I met one or two interesting workers, but somehow they did not live up to my ideal.

Finally, in 1954, I met my man in Shenyang. As was the case everywhere else, the members of the Shenyang Municipal Youth League Committee gave me a lot of information about model workers, their innovations, and the resulting increases in efficiency. But our paper was already full of such articles. Perhaps my host noticed that I had lost interest in such repetitive stories, and as an afterthought, he added, "We do have an eccentric worker here, Yang Youde. He used to be a model worker, but he isn't anymore. Do you want to hear about him?" I sat up at once, and he continued, "The man is a lathe operator—very smart; he often thinks of technical innovations and receives honors and rewards. The main problem is the fellow doesn't know his place. He noses around other workshops and offers unsolicited advice. Take the Number Seven Workshop, for example, which was making mining carts. He looked at their work and said there was a problem with the wheels. Nobody listened to him, of course,

but later on, the carts were returned by the mine operators because the
wheels had malfunctioned. Then there were the electric fans. He said the
blades were at the wrong angle, and as it turned out, he was right again.
And so you see, he managed to offend a lot of people. Now people avoid
him like the plague."

I decided to look up Yang Youde. We met in the factory offices. He
was a neatly dressed young man in his middle twenties. Why doesn't he
see me in his workshop? I thought to myself. His manners were quite
refined, but his appearance surprised me. He was so pale and seemed so
melancholy, and he looked around nervously. As it turned out, he had been
reassigned to desk work. It was a promotion for him, but he was not happy.
He said, "Now I am chained to this desk, and I can't go around looking
for problems in the workshops. Now the leaders can rest at ease." Yang
Youde took me home with him. He had a very small room, but it was
overflowing with books, including some in Japanese. I was puzzled when
I saw a padded blanket on his bed and a basin of water standing nearby.
He explained that because the noise in some of the workshops was intolerable, he was experimenting with soundproofing devices in his spare time.
He would crouch under the blanket and beat a drum, while observing the
vibrations in the water. All of this, of course, greatly annoyed his wife.
Although this was not his assigned work, he devoted all his spare time to
it, and his experiment would probably fail. But that didn't seem to matter.
Searching, discovering, and creating were in themselves joys to this man,
even though he was by no means a professional scientist.

I became immediately interested in this young worker. He was not in
charge of the workshop, but he was more concerned than the actual head
was about everything that went on in the workshop. He was not the
manager of the factory, but he was more concerned than the manager
himself about the number of substandard goods the workers were producing. In order to improve the quality of the factory's products, he began to
design in his spare time; most of the time, his designs were lost by the
leaders to whom he submitted them, but he kept on trying until the quality
of the factory's products was eventually improved. He often stopped the
factory manager at the gates and drew his attention to defects in his work
or possible inaccuracies in a speech he had just given. To the cadres, Yang
Youde was a pain in the neck. They reassigned him to some routine desk
work to keep him out of the way. What they found most intolerable about
this fellow, however, was that he often sent his criticism to the papers.

I wrote a feature story on him, in hopes that his qualities would be held up for emulation. It was only after several years that I realized this was impossible. In the early fifties, urban factories were filled with young peasants from the countryside who, for the first time, received a fixed salary in cash and had full stomachs. They were very satisfied and eager to keep their jobs. It was futile to expect them, uneducated and rather narrow in their vision, to act like Yang. The prevailing political climate rather repressed than encouraged such behavior as Yang's. Yang Youde was, in fact, an intellectualized worker.

chapter four

A Foretaste
of Things
to Come

The summer of 1955 in Beijing was the hottest in memory. At night, people living in the narrow alleys of the city would put up makeshift shacks and sleep in the open. There were many reports of people dying of sunstroke while walking outside in the heat of the day.

That summer I passed through a dangerous crisis, for I was suspected of being a counterrevolutionary. The inquiry into my case came to a head in the stifling heat of that summer.

It all started because of my own lack of vigilance. There was a young graduate of Shanghai's Fudan University named Zhu Zhiyan in the section on industrial youth that I was heading. His father had been a general in the Kuomintang army, and he himself was stout, just like the stereotype of a reactionary army officer in Chinese films of the period. But he was actually a likable fellow, very efficient in his work, full of new ideas, and I treated him as a comrade just like anyone else. Earlier that year, I had been warned by the Party Committee that Zhu was politically suspect and that I was to be on my guard in dealing with him. I didn't pay much attention to these warnings, however, and things went on as usual. The Ministry of Engineering was planning to hold a meeting of some sort, and notified us to pick up our press passes. I sent Zhu to pick them up. He should have returned that same morning, but he didn't come back until the day was almost over. As it turned out, the ministry had issued a stack of documents, along with the passes, and Zhu had taken these documents and gone through them in his dorm before delivering them to us. Certain members of my department had come across the red pencil marks left by Zhu on the documents. Of course I was responsible, but I excused myself on the grounds that I had only sent Zhu to pick up our passes. How could I have known that other documents were being issued at the same time? Still, I could not believe that Zhu was an enemy: if he were out to steal sensitive information, would he leave pencil marks all over the papers?

The campaign to purge counterrevolutionaries was just beginning, and

Zhu was held for interrogation. He was locked up in a room in the same building where I lived. Every day on my way to and from work, I had to walk past that door, knowing that a secret trial was taking place. I had heard about these nonstop interrogations; detainees were questioned for days without a break. Such interrogations had begun in Yanan during the early days of the Party. I had personally met an old cadre who had become mentally deranged as a result of such interrogations. I had mixed feelings about Zhu's case. Could he be a counterrevolutionary? I doubted it. But I had no reason to doubt the special team in charge, who claimed to have evidence. But I did doubt the prevailing logic that if he was an enemy element, any means would be justified in extorting his confession.

At the time, there were eight people in my section. Three of us were Communist Party members. Of the five nonmembers, Zhu was different in that he did not "keep close to the Party" and never expressed a wish to join it. But this wasn't surprising, since he was not eligible to join the Party anyway because of his family background. He was talented, knew his own mind, and simply did not conform. This was enough to make him an alien element. The other nonmembers regulated their behavior according to Party requirements, professed implicit faith in the Party, and maintained their revolutionary stance at all times. Hence, they were ready to pounce on Zhu. In my section, the campaign against counterrevolutionaries was headed by a woman named Jin. The other Communist Party member and I were not involved. She was part of a special team, and we were not informed of its progress.

Still, we all attended the meetings to expose Zhu, and discuss anything that was suspicious about him. Zhu was careless in ordinary conversation, often off guard, and so a great deal of evidence could be assembled against him, particularly if every detail was put under a magnifying glass. In the previous year, 1954, many places in China had been flooded. It had also rained incessantly in Beijing. Zhu was heard to have said, "The more rain the better." Wasn't that a sign of hostility? Nobody asked in what context those words were spoken, or whether Zhu had in fact spoken them. And of course no one stopped to think whether a true counterrevolutionary would be so obviously hostile. The strongest evidence of Zhu's counterrevolutionary activity was the fact that whenever Hu Yaobang, then general secretary of the Youth League, made an appearance, Zhu would go and chat with his chauffeur until they came to be quite friendly; sometimes Zhu would even sit in Hu Yaobang's car while they chatted. Now why would he do this, unless he wanted to steal secret information, or assassinate Hu Yaobang?

These meetings and discussions were also being held to test the participants' loyalty, but at the time, I was completely unaware of this.

Soon afterward, I found that I too was an object of suspicion and investigation. I was excluded from certain meetings, and certain internal documents were not shown to me. I assumed it was because of my involvement in Zhu's case. That was one reason, of course, but it was not the only reason, and certainly not the main reason, as I soon discovered.

Suddenly one day, on the wall facing the spiral stairs outside my office, I was confronted by proofs of two articles of mine that were temporarily being withheld from publication, as well as the draft of another article that I had just finished. They had been pasted up on the walls under the large heading: "Samples of Liu Binyan's Anti-Party Stance." This was the first time that my name had been linked with the term *anti-Party*. I was surprised by this, but I did not panic.

One of the pieces, "Coldness" (which was eventually published), was directed against unsympathetic doctors and cadres who were wasteful of state funds. At the end of the article I wrote: "In one of Gogol's short stories, a man goes to his office one morning and discovers that he has forgotten his nose. Likewise in our society, there are those who only remember to carry their work certificates, their identification badges, but leave their hearts behind."

I had been deeply struck by the callousness of doctors. Of all professionals, I felt, doctors should stand out as the most humanitarian. Therefore, I found their insensitivity especially galling. I had once planned to write on the subject, to suggest that courses on humanism be included in the curricula for students of medicine and that people without a sense of humanitarianism should be excluded from the profession. Long before my article ever materialized, however, the Party's attack on humanism and humanitarianism as counterrevolutionary ideology was in full swing. Since every individual was thought to harbor certain residual feelings of class sentiment, an all-inclusive love for human beings could not exist.

According to later denunciations, my offense in this article had been to smear socialist society. Since we were a socialist society, it went without saying that people's relations with each other were close and warm. My accusation of "coldness" was therefore totally unfounded.

The offense in the other piece, "A New Voice," was even more serious. It included the following passage:

The man's eyes are continually before me: I see him lift up his head, his face shining with ardor, his eyes expressing his thoughts. Then he looks around him, his eyes cloud over as he lowers his gaze. . . . At that moment, I hear a voice: "Don't stick your neck out. Can't you see that everybody else is holding back? Why risk your neck?" It is this voice that snuffs out the light in his eyes.

This article was the result of my search for the man "who is not afraid to differ." My motive was clearly explained in the article itself. I wrote: "With the task of construction before us, there is a crying need for people who have something to say, something new, something useful, something different. Where are those people, why are their voices so weak? I want to know." In the same article, I also opposed just reciting the directives of the Party; instead, I wrote, "get down to brass tacks, pin down new problems, and deliver up your own solution. That's the way to tackle the task set before us by the Party. One suggestion with a spark of truth is worth a hundred repetitions of sound platitudes." Now this bordered on the irreverent.

In the same article, I also had something to say about another type of person: "a face with a fixed, deferential smile, with eyes alert to every change of expression on the face of the leader, a pair of lips always ready to say 'yes' . . . 'how right.' . . . These are the pets and favorites of the Party, perfect companions for Party leaders 'who only speak and do not hear.' They are," I added, "and will continue to be, a force to be reckoned with in China."

The posting of these particular articles convinced me that, apart from my involvement in Zhu Zhiyan's case, I was suspected of being a counterrevolutionary primarily because my ideas seemed subversive in a time of rampant political conformism. Immediately I began to be attacked at meetings of the editorial board. Everything I had said over the last few years, whether at meetings or in private conversations, everything I had written, whether published or not, was scrutinized. My views on social issues, as well as on problems of literature and journalism, were all cited as evidence of my guilt. Finally, the inquiry focused on one basic issue: Why are you always calling for public exposure and criticism of the Party? Why are you always making insinuations about the dark side of our society to the other reporters and encouraging them to write exposés? If you are not acting out of hatred for socialism and the Party, what then is your motive for this behavior?

One morning a few days later, the general secretary of *China Youth News*—the person in charge of the financial and administrative end of the paper—asked to see me. As usual he smiled affably, and said that the division of labor within the staff required that I be moved to the managing editor's office. I had been prepared for worse, for interrogation behind locked doors, as they had done with Zhu Zhiyan. Anyway, the new assignment was quite a favor, considering that I was under a political cloud. My previous work had given me access to sensitive data and figures, as well as contact with top-level government administration. Work in the managing editor's office, by contrast, was the last step in the process of producing the paper—all decisions had been made.

In my new job, all I had to do was send out edited copy to be typeset. I was put out of touch with reality, which made subversion impossible. I continued working while at the same time submitting to an investigation.

I have never considered myself exceptionally brave or above personal self-interest, nor am I very tough. Looking back over this period, however, I am surprised how I could have remained so calm. My life continued as if nothing had happened. I ate well, slept soundly without nightmares, and enjoyed an untroubled married life. I did not lose a single one of my 140 pounds.

At first the investigation into my case had been conducted secretly. Most people did not know what was happening and treated me like everybody else. But once the articles were posted, their attitude toward me cooled. I felt myself being pulled closer and closer to the edge of the "counterrevolutionary" abyss. Standing in front of this display, I felt the full sting of the insult and the gravity of the threat. Yet I was surprised by my own calmness. Of course, I was confident that my articles and everyday conversation could withstand any amount of scrutiny. As for my relations with Zhu Zhiyan, I felt it was only a matter of time before everything would be cleared up. I was not overly confident as a rule, but this affair seemed too preposterous. How could I, who had never suffered from the revolution, who had nothing to hide, be politically suspect? It was simply a misunderstanding that would soon be resolved. So that my wife wouldn't worry, I kept the whole affair from her and succeeded so well that she did not notice any change in me.

One hot night in August of 1955, the head of the organization department of the Youth League Central, a leading cadre in charge of personnel and organizational matters, attended the meeting on my case, and the situation looked very serious; nevertheless, I remained unshaken. At the end of the meeting, the department head summed up my situation as follows: "On the basis of findings after several months of investigation, we must reassess our previous evaluation of Liu Binyan's character. We must take a second hard look." I could not tell whether this was an empty threat or not. That night, I lay in bed thinking over his words. It seemed that they were going to label me a counterrevolutionary.

Things went from bad to worse. I soon discovered that I was being suspected on even more serious grounds.

Before that last meeting, I had already been shown photostats of a letter with my signature. When the photostats were passed around the office, everyone was sure it was my handwriting, but I saw at a glance that it was a forgery. Later I learned that several letters abusing Premier Zhou Enlai and Hu Yaobang had been written in my handwriting and signed in my name, and that another letter, in the same hand, had accused the then editor-in-chief of complicity with a counterrevolutionary clique and had requested that Liu Binyan replace him.

At the same time, public security was investigating another person as the source of these suspicious letters. But they were working independently, and our leaders continued to interrogate me about the same case. The months dragged on.

One night, another meeting was held on my case. It seemed to be the final showdown: they put copies of all the "counterrevolutionary" letters on the table, everyone inspected them, and again they asked me to confess. The general secretary, a well-meaning comrade, scoffed: "All the proof is here; how can you deny it? Why not make a clean breast of it?" But I stuck to my word and the truth. At about nine o'clock, after the meeting had already been dragging on for two hours, the dramatic moment finally came. The door suddenly burst open, and a woman was pushed into the room by two public-security officers. After I recovered from the initial shock, I recognized the woman as Comrade Jin, the wife of the editor-in-chief, she who had formerly worked under me in the section responsible for reporting on industry and was currently in charge of the campaign to purge counterrevolutionaries there! She was the writer of the letters!

Comrade Jin, the daughter of a capitalist in Shanghai, had joined the Communist Party as a college student before liberation. She was a seemingly artless woman, and with her hoarse voice and careless style of dress, she was the last person one would suspect of calculated malice. But in fact, she was a habitual liar. A few years earlier, she had lied about her ancestry, saying she had French blood. And during the current campaign, she had tried to plant evidence against more than a dozen people, causing a great deal of confusion and leading the other cadres on a wild-goose chase. She was also clever at imitating handwriting, and had written the letters implicating me and others implicating Zhu Zhiyan.

Soviet experts who were with public security at the time immediately identified the letters as forgeries. How they ever traced them to Jin has remained a mystery to me. She had asked her maid to mail these letters from a mailbox on a busy street far away from our office and her home. Then, while on a business trip to Shanghai, she had mailed letters from Shanghai and was arrested on the spot.

Why had she done this? Many said it was out of class hatred, as revenge against the Communists on behalf of her family. I never believed that. A more likely explanation might have been resentment for the unjust treatment of her husband, who had been suspended from his job for his involvement with the "counterrevolutionary" Hu Feng.* But there had been no final decision on his case. What's more, she confessed that she had been forging letters since 1952, long before her husband's problems had begun. Her motive remains a mystery to this day.

Zhu Zhiyan, a fellow victim of her forgeries, was also cleared, after undergoing more than six months of investigation. All the others who had been victimized by her schemes were cleared as well. Comrade Jin was tried and sentenced to several years in prison for counterrevolutionary activities.

Thus the curtain was drawn on the campaign to purge counterrevolutionaries, with one of its chief activists becoming one of the main casualties of the campaign. The irony was that had she not been in charge, she would not have been able to implicate so many people.

Did anyone draw any lessons from this fiasco? It was generally acknowledged that the campaign had unjustly implicated too many people, but

---

*Hu Feng, a poet and Marxist literary critic, wrote a long letter to the Party protesting its restrictions on writers and artists; that and his letters to his friends led Mao to accuse him of leading a counterrevolutionary clique. He and many of his friends went to jail in 1955, and were not rehabilitated until the 1980s.

why then were similar campaigns lauched again and again? Shouldn't there have been laws to prevent it from recurring? It seemed that nobody ever raised the issue—not even the victims.

I felt that since the Party Committee had wrongly accused me, they at least owed me a public apology. But nothing was further from their minds. They did not even express any remorse in private conversations. I was bitterly disappointed by their attitude.

Now that I look back, I realize that I had never thought of my constitutional rights either.

In 1954, the first constitution of the People's Republic had been ushered in with great fanfare. Many children born in that year had been named Xian in honor of the constitution (*xian fa*). Later on, however, when the constitution was violated, no one thought of protesting. Nobody ever openly proclaimed that the constitution was just a hoax, but as a twenty-nine-year-old Party member, I too knew even then that the constitution was just for show, something to be displayed to foreigners. But I sincerely believed that all that really mattered was the leadership of the Party; so long as it was correct, we didn't need a constitution. Besides, the logic of the day went, if we started to take the constitution seriously, it would protect all the unexposed class enemies, and the class struggle could not proceed.

In late 1954 and early 1955, during the campaign against the Hu Feng counterrevolutionary clique, Mao Zedong had personally inspected and written comments on the private letters of those who were implicated. These letters were published as evidence of the counterrevolutionary guilt of the accused. At the time, nobody viewed this as a violation of their basic human rights. The prevailing view was that constitutional rights did not apply to class enemies.

It wasn't until 1966, eleven years later, when millions of Red Guards took over and those in power were toppled, that many of these leaders suddenly remembered their constitutional rights. The deaths of Liu Shaoqi, Peng Dehuai, and others, founders of the republic, were strong reminders. During the Cultural Revolution, tens of thousands of Party leaders were victimized, some sent to their deaths. During those moments of humiliation and torture, maybe they remembered their constitutional rights, and their basic human rights. But most of them did survive, and when the nightmare was over, they quickly forgot such "legal niceties."

When I regained my freedom to work in 1955, my first assignment took me to the Sanmenxia Dam, then under construction. My heart was lighter than ever. The nightmare was over, and would never be repeated. Why? What were the grounds for my optimism? I never stopped to think. Now that the case against me had been thrown out, I felt confident, as if the Party were really more reliable than ever.

I did not draw any lessons from the false accusations made against me and the Party's methods of determining guilt. It had just been a false alarm, and it was over. I could no longer be accused of being a counterrevolutionary. I assumed that the attacks on my writings had also become null and void. I did not realize that these were separate issues and that one day, the same kind of posters would be put up again to attack me.

And so with a light heart and all of my belief intact, I went to Henan and Gansu to resume reporting for the paper. Since joining the underground at age eighteen, I had postponed my plans to do literary writing again and again. But now I was seized by the impulse to write something more challenging than the news stories and commentaries I had been doing. I felt as if I could say what had never been said before, as if China were waiting for my words. I wanted to use my pen to slash the pall hanging over China, to dispel the gloom and open up the mental horizons of the people. In Gansu, at the construction site of the first railway bridge across the Yellow River, I heard of an accident that seemed to provide me an opportunity to express my own long-harbored thoughts.

It had just snowed when I arrived at the site, outside the city of Lanzhou. The deputy secretary of the Youth League at the construction site, a young man named Kang, welcomed us warmly. We were taken to a shack that served as his living quarters and office, and we talked late into the night. This young man was bubbling with ideas and information. During our conversation, he told a fascinating story about several members of the construction team and a dramatic event that had taken place during the construction of this bridge. I encouraged him to continue talking. As he spoke, I realized that these people and their story was just the material I was looking for to send out my message.

The captain of the construction brigade, Luo, was an experienced bridge-builder, but he was also a cautious man who tended to shield himself behind his achievements. If there was any loss or injury, he would hide behind such slogans as "achievements outweigh mistakes," "we must always hold steady to the guidelines of the Party Central," "to avoid mistakes is in itself a victory," "say what you will, the bridge will be built," and so on. Zeng Gang, a young engineer who was leader of the No. 3 Construction Team, was his complete opposite. He was a new-style leader, who knew and cared for the workers and wanted to inspire their creativity. He worked hard to increase efficiency and cut costs, sometimes taking risks to achieve these goals. Predictably, he came into conflict with Luo, his boss. When Zeng Gang wrote to their superiors outlining their differences, relations between the two were further strained.

In the autumn of 1954, the annual flood arrived earlier than usual. Luo was totally unprepared, and instead of taking emergency measures, he waited for orders from above, and one of the bridge supports was washed away. Zeng Gang, by contrast, who was working at another construction site, had wasted no time waiting for orders and had taken preventive measures on his own. The bridge support at his site was saved. In the end, however, Zeng Gang was demoted for breach of Party discipline and was reassigned to a cement factory, whereas Luo was rewarded for "following the leadership," and continued climbing the official ladder.

I spent the Spring Festival holidays writing this piece of literary reportage and sent it to *People's Literature* before I left for Poland. What I wrote presented the facts, with only slight changes to the names of some characters, in a narrative style rather like a short story. This was the first time I had written a literary piece in sixteen years, since 1939. I was not sure what the response of readers would be; I wasn't even sure whether it would be accepted for publication.

chapter five

The

Gathering

Storm

In March 1956, I accompanied
Deng Tuo abroad for the second
time. He was the head of the *People's Daily,* and was on his way to
Warsaw to attend a meeting of
the Council of the International
League of Journalists. It was the
third spring since the death of Stalin. During our stopover in Moscow, I took a walk in Gorki Park.
Spring had come early that year. In the streets, girls were out in colorful
spring outfits. As they walked along, their light-colored coats swaying in
the breeze, they seemed heralds of a new political order. The atmosphere
in Moscow was very relaxed. What I didn't realize was that at that very
moment the Twentieth Party Congress of the Soviet Communist Party
was convening secretly.

The mood in Warsaw was darker, perhaps because of the recent death
of Party leader Bierut. His photograph hung in shop windows, flanked by
red and black silk ribbons. In the city, all ravages of the war had been
removed. The Warsaw Cultural Palace, designed and built with Soviet aid,
closely resembled Moscow University in architectural style, but was not at
all in keeping with the rest of the city.

Deng Tuo was well known as a highly cultured man from a scholarly
family in Fujian Province. During the Anti-Japanese War, he had edited
the paper of the Jinchaji Communist base. I first met him in 1954, and that
spring, when Dmitri Shepilov, the editor-in-chief of *Pravda,* invited a
delegation of journalists from the *People's Daily* to visit the Soviet Union,
Deng Tuo, as head of the delegation, asked me to be the interpreter.

Despite Deng Tuo's seniority rank in the Party and his many talents,
he was a remarkably modest and unassuming man. I never hesitated to
raise questions with him that I would not have brought up with other
leaders. Once, when we were staying at a hotel in Moscow, I asked him
who had started the Korean War anyway, North or South Korea? To my
surprise, he gave me a straight answer right away, without a thought of
possible adverse consequences for himself, that the North Koreans had
fired the first shot.

He also opened up to me quite unreservedly on other occasions. Once

I said that I was dissatisfied with the way the *People's Daily* was run; so many official documents filled its pages, while so few reports on the true state of things at the grass-roots level ever appeared. I felt the voice of the people was left unheard, and criticism directed at leading bodies was virtually nonexistent. He agreed with me; he said he didn't like the paper either. Then why not improve it? I asked. Deng Tuo poured out his heart to me. "The editor-in-chief of *Pravda*—first Bukharin, now Shepilov—has always been a member of the Politburo. As for me, I am not even a member of the Central Committee. Many ministers of the government, on the other hand, are members of the Central Committee and can sign orders for the *People's Daily* to publish their speeches, articles, or reports of meetings. I know better than anybody else that readers don't even look at that stuff, but even so, I can't refuse to publish it."

Only years later did I realize it was not only a question of Deng Tuo not having free rein to run a paper but also a matter of his being an intellectual within the Party. Two years later, at the Eighth Party Congress of the Chinese Communist Party, Deng Tuo had still not been elected to the Central Committee, but he was not the only intellectual to suffer discrimination.

In addition to members of the editorial board of the *People's Daily*, editors of several provincial and city papers were also in the delegation, among them Zhang Chunqiao, then editor-in-chief of the Shanghai *Liberation Daily* and later one of the Gang of Four. Our main purpose on this visit was to learn from the Soviet press. Our schedule was packed, with one seminar in the morning and one in the afternoon, during which the various heads of departments at *Pravda* told us about their experiences and work while I translated.

Most of the members of our delegation took the visit seriously, taking copious notes, ready to apply the Soviet methods and ideas to their own papers. But Deng Tuo was not satisfied. Based on his own experience of many years, he felt that the Soviet experience was not everything. He went a step further and asked himself, What exactly was the function of a newspaper? What was its position within society? Deng looked elsewhere for answers. He asked for theoretical writings on journalism from the West, but no such material was available in the Soviet Union.

Two years later, in 1956 in Poland, Deng Tuo again gave me the same task, to search for books on Western journalism. I had expected to have better luck in Poland, since the climate was much more liberal and relaxed. But after much searching, I was equally disappointed.

Still, the press was undergoing a drastic change. During our 1956 meetings, we visited the editorial staff of the *Workers' Tribune* and *Life in Warsaw*, and what we heard from journalists at these two papers was very encouraging. Gomulka, the new Polish leader, had loosened the reins on freedom of the press, and the papers had broken away from the hitherto Soviet-style censorship, which had been in force for years. Criticism of mistakes and defects in the work of the Party and the government became more outspoken. News was not limited to political and economic issues; reports on all aspects of life and many unorthodox views were now freely aired. Reports from the West were no longer limited to "unemployment, strikes, and crime"; the *Workers' Tribune* started publishing regular coverage of new achievements in the West in the fields of science and technology. At the time, such things were still unthinkable in the Chinese papers.

Once I walked into the public reading room of a library in Warsaw; it was clean and bright, and the stacks were filled with many foreign papers, all available to the public. Not only were the Communist papers like *L'Humanité* and *L'Unità* there, but also the *New York Times* and the *Herald Tribune;* in other words, newspapers that were always considered reactionary in China. The open-mindedness of the Polish people and even of the ideology of the Polish Communist Party far exceeded my expectations. At the time, I never imagined that China would still not have come that far a full thirty years later.

After the meeting in Warsaw, we visited several cities. One evening at the Sailors Club in Gdańsk, we saw a not-too-young woman sitting alone over a cup of coffee, evidently waiting for foreign customers. At the time, China was also opening her ports to foreign ships, and once on land, sailors would look for fun. But the Chinese are strict about sexual relations outside of marriage; neither the government nor the public would tolerate legal prostitution. I suppose foreign sailors in China had to live puritan lives on Chinese shores. The Soviet Union was also strict in this respect. I still remember a poem published in *Literaturnaia Gazeta* about Polish girls who sold themselves for a stick of lipstick or a pair of silk stockings. But a few years later, in the early sixties, the Soviet papers reported that streetwalkers had appeared in the Soviet Union. At the time, I firmly believed that prostitution should never exist in a socialist country. In China, one of the first things we did after the Communist Party took over the cities was to abolish prostitution.

On our way back from Poland, we stopped over in Moscow. *Pravda* invited Deng Tuo to spend a vacation in the Moscow suburbs, while I accepted the writer Valentine Ovechkin's invitation to stay with him at his home in Kursk.

During my stay, Ovechkin would spend the days working in his study, while I sat in his parlor and read his letters. Many letters were from victims of Stalin's purges, telling him what they had gone through. Other letters exposed corruption in towns and in the country, asking Ovechkin to come and write about it. Readers wrote thanking him, praising his courage, hoping that he would go on writing. I was very touched by these close ties between reader and writer, and impressed by the number of letters.

In the evenings, I would talk with the writers invited over by Ovechkin, or he and I would talk. He had a deep affection for China and was very interested in what was happening at the moment.

In the autumn of 1954, I had acted as interpreter for Ovechkin and a group of Soviet writers on a tour of China. Before I met Ovechkin, I read everything he had published since 1930. He had exposed the problems on the collective farms soon after they were organized. In one of his novellas published during the war, *Salute to the Front*—which was written as a series of letters from a soldier wounded at the front and now recuperating on a farm—Ovechkin wrote a scathing exposé of the privileged leaders and their excesses, and the hard life of the women who did all the work while their husbands were at war. After the death of Stalin, Ovechkin became a leader of the new wave in literature, under the banner of sincerity, seeking to portray life unvarnished. His first piece of reportage, *Everyday Life in the District,* exposed how the policies of the Soviet Communist Party in the countryside had damaged the development of agriculture; it also satirized a district Party secretary whose name subsequently became a household word for bureaucratism.

This piece of reportage created a sensation, and after that, some of his articles appeared on the front pages of *Pravda.* It was said that in 1953 when the Central Committee of the Soviet Communist Party held its September meeting to pass important resolutions on agricultural reform, Khrushchev read from Ovechkin's work and exclaimed, "Why, it seems this man was present at our meeting. He is writing about all the problems that we have been discussing."

Only three years had passed since Stalin's death, but changes were clearly discernible in the Soviet Union. In literary circles, it became the vogue to write about the negative aspects of Soviet life. At the forefront of this trend was Ovechkin. He had started publishing in the early fifties without attracting much attention. But with the publication of *Everyday Life in the District,* he became the most talked-about writer in the Soviet Union.

Ovechkin looked and behaved like a peasant. He had spent most of his life among peasants and was also deeply concerned about Chinese peasants. When I took him to visit a rural cooperative in Sichuan in 1954, he was very impressed by our work-point system and thought that Russian farmers could learn from this.*

During this visit in 1956, I accidentally heard of Khrushchev's coldness toward Ovechkin. He told me that he had written several long letters to Khrushchev, putting forth suggestions for social reform, such as that the salaries of Party leaders in the countryside should be linked with agricultural output. But Khrushchev had never responded. I was shocked by Khrushchev's arrogance toward such an influential writer, particularly since he was a reformer himself. I asked myself, Don't Party leaders in socialist countries need to listen to the voice of writers?

At the end of my visit, he saw me off at the Kursk station. We embraced, and there were tears in his eyes. Did he foresee that we would never meet again?

At the Beijing airport, I was met by two members of my staff. Zhu Zhiyan was his same old self, not a sign of resentment for the six months of unjust treatment. They gave me good news: "On the Bridge Construction Site" had been published in *People's Literature* to rave reviews. Qin Zhaoyang, the editor-in-chief of the magazine, had written an editorial note, recommending it to readers. I had not expected such a warm response. Of course I was pleased, but I did not lose my head. Later, when I heard more praise, I actually felt somewhat uneasy, because I knew there were weaknesses in the work, especially in the control of the language.

The first thing I did when things quieted down was to look up Khrushchev's secret report on Stalin among the classified documents. According to regulations, only "higher cadres"—the thirteenth category of Party membership and above—had access to them. Luckily for me, I had just

*Chinese peasants were credited with work points according to the amount and quality of their work. At the end of the year, they would get money and grain based on the number of points accumulated.

gotten a promotion, which qualified me as one of the higher cadres.

I have never been as shocked as I was when reading that secret report. I trembled as I read about the mass murders committed twenty years earlier. I cried as I read of the fate of those earliest members of the revolution. I read the report twice; my outlook on many thing was forever changed.

Now I knew why after my visits to the Soviet Union I always felt a strange sense of depression. It was not the climate; no, it was because the Soviet people lived in fear. Now I understood why the Soviet people who met with us, or worked with us, or interpreted for us, never gave us their addresses. They had drawn lessons from what had happened, and did not want to be involved with foreigners. Now I knew that the losses the Soviet Union suffered during the early years of war could have been averted. I was quite familiar with the history of the Russian Revolution, the price that the early pioneers paid to overthrow the czar; and so the bloody excesses of Stalin seemed absolutely abominable to me. And this bloody despot had been elevated to a position of absolute power to be worshipped by all the Communists of the world!

Soon afterward, the Central Committee of the CCP issued the document "On the Historical Experiences of the Dictatorship of the Proletariat" and then a second document on the same theme. Still I was not satisfied. They did not condemn Stalin sufficiently. I also could never accept Mao's later dictum that Stalin should be assessed according to the "three-seven" principle; that is, three parts of his rule were negative, and seven parts were positive. I also could not understand why a report of Stalin's crimes was not made public in China. Khrushchev's report had already been made public in the greater part of the world, while in China, the Soviet Union, and other socialist countries, it was still a classified document. Ironically, therefore, most Party members in these countries knew next to nothing about what affected them the most. One year later, it was still a criminal offense for Chinese college students to try to translate the document into Chinese—from the *New York Times* version of the text.

Why this secretive attitude? What political need did it serve? At the time I did not understand, but the effects of such a policy are now apparent to me. Many Party members, including intellectuals, did not know what Khrushchev had accused Stalin of, and since the Chinese Communist Party did not follow in Khrushchev's footsteps, they automatically regarded him as a heretic. In the summer of 1957, when the news of Molotov's and Kaganovitch's fall from power was broadcast, many on the staff of *China Youth News* sympathized with Malenkov and opposed Khrushchev. I was shocked by the unanimity of this response; clearly they knew next to nothing about the inner Party struggles of the Soviet Communist Party. I was on Khrushchev's side, perhaps because I had read his secret report. Soon after, many people in the West withdrew from the Party. This and Khrushchev's domestic and foreign policies were all denounced by the Chinese Communist Party as "revisionism," since it still regarded Stalin as a revolutionary leader and a representative of orthodox Marxism. As late as the mid-1980s, Stalin's huge portrait still appeared on special occasions towering over Tiananmen Square.

All of this seems to have run counter to Mao's own dislike of Stalin. Stalin had repeatedly interfered in the affairs of the Chinese Communist Party; he had always suspected Mao of being a rabid nationalist. When Mao visited the Soviet Union, Stalin purposely gave him the cold shoulder, and there was a marked strain of chauvinism in all of his policies toward China following the founding of the People's Republic. In addition, Mao aspired to a position of leadership in the world Communist movement after Stalin's death; deprecating Stalin would have been to his own advantage. Why, then, did he pursue a contrary line of action?

I had admired the Soviet Union since my youth, and regarded it as an upholder of orthodox Marxism. Khrushchev's secret report, however, shattered my illusions. During that summer, Mao's report on "The Ten Great Relations" was relayed to us; slightly earlier, he had also announced the launching of the "hundred flowers" campaign. Both made me admire him. I thought China had found its own way to socialism and that Mao represented a new development in Marxism.

But at the same time, I was following what was happening in the Soviet Union. They were actually ahead of us in freeing literature from ideological restraints. I subscribed to a few Soviet magazines and papers and was paying close attention to changes in the literary scene. I hailed Dudintsev's novel *Not by Bread Alone,* published in *New World,* and recommended it to Chinese readers. Interestingly, it was banned in the Soviet Union when it was being translated into Chinese. When it was finally ready for publication in China, the antirightist campaign had begun, and only a thousand copies were printed. It was sent to a few libraries, where it lay unread among other "internal publications" designed to reach only officially approved readers.

Twenty years later, looking back on the turmoil of the Cultural Revolution, most people felt nostalgic for 1956 and regarded it as the best period in the history of the People's Republic, calling it "the golden year." Some thought if it had not been for the antirightist campaign of the following year, Chinese society would have developed in a far more humane way. The year 1956 was indeed a prosperous one for China. The Party was full of self-confidence; the socialist transformation of private enterprise went off without a hitch, with no resistance from the capitalists. The previous year, the farm cooperatives had been taken a step further to become "advanced farm cooperatives": farmers gave up residual claims to the land, and they put their farm tools and animals into the collectives, thus giving up private ownership. Industry enjoyed a high rate of development. All this seemed to show that we would enter socialism earlier than expected.

Thus the year seemed to begin with great promise. It could have been the start of a new era, but it ended on a note of crisis that precipitated the tragedy of the following year. The year had begun in jubilation as festivities heralded the socialization of all industry and commerce across the land. My article on the front pages of *China Youth News* on January 14 began, "This morning, a shop owner in Qianmen Street climbed a ladder and took down his shop sign, the same sign he had personally hung up thirty years ago." At the end of my article, I quoted some verses written by shop owners celebrating their break with capitalism. At the time, I felt it was a great innovation, this peaceful transition from capitalism to socialism. I even contemplated writing a book, on the decline of capitalism in China.

But by the summer of that same year, the price of pork went up in Beijing, and eggs became scarce. Many consumer products disappeared from the shelves. For the first time in the seven years since liberation, beggars were seen on the streets. I came across a beggar in Changchun while on my way to Harbin. As I entered a restaurant, I noticed a young man hiding behind a screen in the doorway, popping his head out now and again to keep an eye on the movements of the customers. After I had eaten and paid the bill, the young man came out from behind the screen and moved toward my table. Only then did I realize that he was a beggar. Hadn't it been announced that China was a beggar-free country after liberation? After watching him finish my leftovers, I walked up to talk to him. He said he was from the Anhui countryside. The year before, the state conscription of grain had been excessive and had left the people without enough to eat. In the general lethargy resulting from forced collectivization of farms, they had no desire to work and no choice but to go begging. He was planning to make his way to northeast China.

It was June when I reached Harbin—the time of year when Harbin is most beautiful. But after several years' absence, I felt Harbin had lost its most endearing features. On Main Street, which had once been the most Russian part of the city, the signs of all of the formerly Russian-owned shops had been painted in red, as if the color alone made them genuinely socialist. Under the June sun, the red signs glared.

There were very few foreigners in the streets. Khrushchev had canceled Stalin's edict against Russians living abroad, and many who had taken out Soviet citizenship after 1945 were permitted to return to Russia or go to any other country ready to accept them. Many Russian expatriates left to settle in America or Australia, where they had relatives; only a very few of the old ones did not want to move, and stayed on.

Harbin had grown from a modest commercial city of eight hundred thousand people into a large industrial center of 1.6 million. But the ranks of government cadres and Party functionaries grew much faster than either industry or population. When I left Harbin ten years earlier, the municipal government had occupied a modest two-story building, and there could not have been more than two hundred cadres. But now the city population had doubled, and the number of government cadres had increased to thirty-seven hundred. If you added to that the number of Party, Youth League, and labor union functionaries, you had five thousand. And if you added to that all the Party functionaries in all the various units at the grass-roots level, you would be astounded at the figure. And this does not include the four thousand or so security people and police.

People in the streets were better dressed than before. Harbin had been one of the first major cities to be liberated, and with the added influence of Russian culture, the girls in Harbin had evidently been the first to answer the 1956 drive to dress better. The material living conditions had decidedly improved in a decade. Restaurants and shops were filled with customers. But I still felt something was missing. Or, to put it another way, it seemed as though the tenseness of the 1946 period, when the city was under martial law, still lingered. It was just too quiet and too orderly. The red shop signs on Main Street were symbolic of the whole situation— politics, economy, culture, and thought, everything was under the uniform control of the Party. There were two papers in Harbin, but even the editors themselves were sick and tired of their repetitious style.

The Party had taken over every aspect of people's lives, leaving not a trace of privacy.

The problems arising from this bureaucracy had already become apparent. The greater the division of labor and the larger the staff, the less work that was done. With too many leaders giving conflicting orders, all initiative at the grass-roots level was stifled, while the leading organs, playing conflicting roles, assumed no responsibility. The state of affairs was described as "a cup of tea, a cigarette, and a copy of today's paper make up a day's work." Across the nation, the growth of industry—heavy industry in particular—had become the main concern, and the growth rate reached its highest level in 1956. Production was the primary preoccupation. At the time, the workers were still in high spirits, and worked hard. Working overtime to finish quotas was common, and then all the worker's spare time was taken up with meetings and political studies. Exhaustion was widespread and led to a rise in accidents.

In order to appreciate the workers' dedication, however, one had to consider their living conditions. A friend at the Youth League Municipal Organization told me that during those years, prices of consumer goods in Harbin were climbing at a rate of nearly 15 percent a year, while the workers' wages had not risen for several years. Some temporary workers had been on the job for seven years without getting a permanent position. In 1956, the taboo on colorful clothes had gradually faded. Once it had been assumed that the more plainly you dressed, the more revolutionary you were. Now this had changed. Colorful clothes appeared—but many girls in Harbin had had to save for months to buy a cotton print skirt or dress.

Everything—labor, raw materials, and wages—was controlled by the central government. Local enterprises were not authorized to raise the workers' pay, but if they wanted to lower the wages, they could. Since the work of a factory was evaluated according to the profits it turned over to the state, the directors of the factories, in order to cut costs, would cut the workers' wages, earning praise for themselves.

I was astounded by the news that my friend at the Youth League passed on to me. "We kept telling the workers that they were the owners of the country. But when we would visit the factories, we saw that the workers did not behave like masters at all. They stole public property all the time—understandably, because they were so hard up. They were full of resentment, but would not even speak to the investigation teams sent by the local or even the provincial authorities. Apparently those committees had come time and time again but had solved nothing. I had never expected the Party to lose the confidence of the workers after so few years in power."

I went to investigate at the Harbin Electric Engineering Factory, which had been built with Soviet aid. I put up a notice in the cafeteria: "Liu Binyan, reporter for *China Youth News*, is staying in room 221 of the factory guest house. Young workers are welcome to visit and talk."

This act of mine, of course, was highly irregular. According to standard procedure, everything was always done through "official organizations." Reporters seeking interviews met with people designated by the Party, the factory administration, or the Youth League. Putting up such a notice as mine could be considered a violation of discipline, a sign of my intention of instigating opposition to the above organizations. A year later, in fact, this act of mine was to be included on the list of my offenses.

The factory had ten thousand workers, but only twenty turned up to see me. Looking back after thirty years, their complaints seem minor: dissatisfaction with job assignments, no permanent job, low pay, unjust allotment of housing. At the time, the tensions between the leaders and the masses were not very great, but there were disquieting signs nevertheless. One worker told me: "When things used to go wrong, the class enemy was always blamed, but now the workers blame the leading cadres."

A young worker by the name of Liang sought me out, and spoke for many others. He spoke haltingly, evidently nervous and not used to speaking out in front of strangers. He said: "They seem to forget that we are human beings. Two whole years have passed since we left technical school. There are two hundred of us around the factory, but none of us has been assigned proper work. We are just given odd jobs, or ordered to do the cleaning. We talked to the cadres, and asked to be let go since we were obviously not wanted there. We want to go to Liaoning where the factories are short of hands. But they won't let us go. They'd rather keep us in storage. 'What if production expanded next year; what then? Where would we get hold of people?' they said. 'Yes, but what if production is not expanded; what's going to happen to us?' we asked them. We are human beings. We are being stored like goods in a warehouse. In the meantime, we have no permanent job, no chance of promotion; it's even hard to meet a woman in our position."

I found that people rarely had a chance to express their dissatisfaction.

Even foremen and department heads had no chance to voice their concerns, much less the ordinary worker. And yet, from the highest to the lowest, there were constant meetings—but no chance to speak out. As far as the workers were concerned, the meetings consisted of orders and quotas relayed from above, or of political indoctrination. But with the end of the Korean War and the decreased emphasis on class struggle, political agitation had lost its hold. Workers were preoccupied with the problems of their daily lives, such as housing, which was not available for young workers. Inevitably, there were cases of premarital sex and pregnancies, which were severely condemned. Any young worker's request to transfer to another place of work or to go to a university—in other words, anything suggestive of personal gain, even if it did not conflict with the collective interest—was condemned as a sign of bourgeois individualism, and harshly repressed.

That autumn, I went to Hunan, and found that the problems in Harbin applied to the whole country. In the provincial capital of Changsha, I was shocked as I walked into the headquarters of the Party Committee. What an imposing building! I thought, wondering whether it wasn't too extravagant in light of the level of economic development. And what were all these functionaries busying themselves with, anyway? I walked into the Department of Industry and asked a few questions, but I couldn't get an answer from anyone. As I walked out, the building seemed even more superfluous than before.

I also spent some time living with truckdrivers in the mountainous area of Enshi in Hubei Province, and what I saw and heard there was the same story: general exhaustion, low pay, no consideration for the workers. At the local level, the effects of the "Party leadership taking charge of everything in the country" were more disastrous than ever. It had led to alienation and antagonism between Party leaders and the masses. I was witnessing a frightful process—although at the time, I did not realize the gravity of the problem.

The wave of reform sweeping the Polish press strengthened my own belief in the need to reform the Chinese press. From Harbin in the north to Hubei's Enshi County in the south, I described the reform of the press in Poland to people wherever I went. I told my colleagues everywhere how reporters in Poland bravely investigated and exposed negative aspects of life, thereby promoting the democratization process as a whole. My talks were well received, particularly since my audience was also losing patience with the existing state of the press.

The editor-in-chief of *People's Literature*, Qin Zhaoyang, asked me to write something. I decided to do a piece on the state of the media in China and air my views on the subject. That same year, *People's Literature* published my second piece of literary reportage—"Inside Story." It is about a municipal newspaper run by a despotic and ignorant editor-in-chief and a prematurely aged managing editor interested only in saving his own skin. The young reporters' initiatives are stifled. The paper plods along, until one day the rules are changed. Newspapers are no longer subsidized by the government, but by readers, and suddenly the newspaper finds itself without a single subscriber. "Inside Story" was more to the point in its critique of the inadequacies of the leadership, and it also touched on the problem of freedom of the press. Thus readers' response was even more enthusiastic than to "On the Bridge Construction Site," and inevitably, opposition to it was also more heated.

"On the Bridge Construction Site" had been the first piece to criticize the Party itself since Mao Zedong had laid down the dictum in 1942 in his "Talks at the Yanan Forum" that writers should "extol the bright side of life" and "not expose" the darkness. Though the tone of "On the Bridge Construction Site" was mild, it had attracted nationwide attention. "Inside Story," however, went one step further. It raised the issue of reform of the press as a whole, and thus caused a greater shock. Today, thirty years later, that problem has still not been solved. Following my story, nevertheless, every paper and every broadcasting station was galvanized into doing some hard thinking on the state of the media.

Those two pieces pushed me to the forefront of the literary scene as a reformer. That same year, all government personnel were promoted one category up the administrative ladder. I was promoted to the thirteenth category, joining the ranks of the so-called "higher cadres." Following that, in the ranking of intellectuals, I was ranked a "higher intellectual," the only one at *China Youth News* so honored. I was showered with praise, and congratulations poured in. It was gratifying of course, but my lifestyle remained basically unchanged. I still ate at local restaurants on job assignments and drank the cheap house wine. The only difference was that I smoked a luxury brand of cigarettes, and was allowed to book a sleeper berth on trains when I went on business trips.

I sent half of my monthly salary to my elder sister. Her husband had committed suicide during the campaign to purge counterrevolutionaries in 1955, leaving her to support five children on a schoolteacher's meager salary. Her eldest daughter had been staying with me. Later, my younger brother, a surgeon in Beijing, and I helped bring her second daughter to Beijing for schooling. I felt I had never fulfilled my filial duty to my mother, who died early, and tried to make it up by helping my elder sister, who had sacrificed so much for our family.

Praise always made me feel unworthy. Although I was thirty-one years old, I felt I was not as widely read as I would have liked. In 1954, a Soviet friend gave me a book, which made me even more aware that there were books on the reading lists of Soviet middle-school students that I had yet to read. I had read many nineteenth-century Russian and French classics, but simply reading the story is not enough if you want to absorb something as a writer. Apart from literary works, I also needed to read books of philosophy, history, and other subjects. And then there were the books I used to bring home from the International Bookstore on weekends, all waiting to be read. Where was I to find the time? I was the most bookish member of the editorial staff, and even during editorial board meetings, I would read on the sly if a speaker bored me. I knew this was impolite, but time was too short and I couldn't be bothered by such scruples.

For a long time, Chinese literature had been restricted to "serving the workers, peasants, and soldiers" and "the political objective," as well as to singing the praises of the Communist Party—so much so that it was now on its last legs. Following publication of "On the Bridge Construction Site," the young writer Wang Meng published his novella, *A New Arrival at the Organization Department,* which caused a great stir as well. He created a portrait of Liu Shiwu, a character who will go down in Chinese literature as the epitome of the obsolete bureaucrat, sitting out his time. At this time, writers were finally beginning to write exposés of public situations as well as studies of private life. For the first time since the founding of the People's Republic, we enjoyed, to a certain extent, freedom of the press. Critiques and exposés began to appear in the papers; in addition to articles on politics and the economy, articles of general interest began to appear, and there was more news.

But all of this was short-lived. In the autumn of 1956, the protests in Poland and the Hungarian Uprising stirred a fateful reaction in China. The conservatives who had been waiting for their chance now came into the open. In January 1957, two events occurred: On the front pages of the *People's Daily*, the dramatist Chen Qitong and three others published an open letter deploring the state of literature and calling for a return to the old order. At the editorial office of *China Youth News*, a meeting was held to discuss Wang Meng's novella *A New Arrival at the Organization Department*. The purpose of the meeting soon became clear. Before we began, everyone was handed a copy of Wang Shiwei's *Wild Lilies*, for "internal reference." *Wild Lilies* had been damned as "counterrevolutionary poison" in 1942 in Yanan, and Wang Shiwei had been condemned as a Trotskyite and put to death for criticizing the privileges of the leading cadres.

I attended the meeting, waiting to hear what those notables who were present—the editor-in-chief, the head of the publishing house, the head of the propaganda department of the Youth League Central, and the deputy head of the Dongsi District Party Committee of Beijing (the basis for the time server in Wang's story)—had to say. "Untrue" was the general verdict: "An attack on the Party," "full of bitterness against the Party," "more harmful than Wang Shiwei," "in line with Chiang Kai-shek," "in tune with the Petöfi Club in Hungary," It was "an instigation to the masses to rise against the Party."

As the meeting was coming to an end, the head of the editor-in-chief's office made a suggestion: namely, that "Inside Story" should also be put to open discussion. I had written about the head of an editor-in-chief's office, a mass of inertia, and the man suspected that my caricature had been based on him. He also added: "One should not bear malice toward one's comrades."

As far as I remember, I did not speak. I had already written an article to be published in the March issue of *Literary Studies* defending Wang Meng. The title of my article was "Seemingly Cold, Yet Full of Love," and in it I had tried to prove that those who were criticizing social evils were not hostile to the Party or the society, but were motivated by a deep love of both.

These two events, the letter and the meeting, were very significant, for they showed that before Mao gave the signal to attack, a handful of people were already starting something similar to the antirightist campaign that was to come. Within this year, both Wang Meng and I had been labeled rightists. All this was to occur, however, after that brief moment of hope and apparent openness—the "hundred flowers" campaign.

chapter six

A Trap
Laid for
a Million

I do not remember a moment in my life more exhilarating than when Mao Zedong's February 1957 speech to the State Council was released. My estimation of him soared to sublime heights. At *China Youth News* the response was equally enthusiastic; it seemed as if we were at the beginning of a new era for China.

In his speech, Mao distinguished between two basically different sets of "contradictions"—antagonistic and nonantagonistic. In so doing, he appeared to be announcing that the era of class struggle was over, that "internal contradictions" (including those between the capitalists and the working class) were the main ones within our society, and that foremost among these were contradictions between the Party and the people. These were seen as nonantagonistic conflicts. This also meant that the Party must be placed under supervision of the people and that the fight against bureaucratism was a major task, requiring our full and constant attention. In that speech, Mao announced that dogmatism should not be mistaken for Marxism; he reiterated his policy of letting "a hundred flowers bloom and a hundred schools of thought contend"; he advocated open criticism and reiterated that senior party leaders should not be exempt from criticism. As for strikes by workers and students—unprecedented since the founding of the People's Republic, and now taken seriously for the first time—he said the right way of dealing with them was not by force or coercion, but by overcoming bureaucratism.

These issues were exactly the unspoken ones that had been weighing on me for the last few years—special privileges within Party ranks, bureaucratism, and dogmatic tendencies. Now my disquiet had been dispelled as if by magic. The political climate in Beijing cleared up; the mood of intellectuals brightened; everything seemed to take on a rosy hue. Mao was virtually advocating more democracy and liberalization in matters of ideology; as a journalist and writer, I now felt I had a free hand in pursuing my vocation.

In March I went to Harbin and Changchun, two big cities in northeast China, and I was shocked by the state of things I saw. The local Party

Committee's attitude to Mao's speech was diametrically opposed to that of the intellectuals; local officials just sat back, waiting for a change of wind. The Party Committee in Harbin was conducting its own criticism of "bourgeois ideology." The municipal Party secretary had decided that bureaucratism was a form of bourgeois ideology, so opposing bourgeois ideology covered everything.

Another thing that shocked me was the diametrically opposed interpretations of Mao's intentions. Mao's talk was filtering down to Party cadres in these two cities, and among those who had heard and studied the talk, some felt that Mao was attacking dogmatism and leftist tendencies, while others felt differently. It is true, the latter conceded, Mao had criticized Chen Qitong's January letter in the *People's Daily* attacking liberal tendencies in art and literature. But that criticism, they argued, was leveled at Chen's ineptitude in timing and presentation, not at his basic stand.

Thirty years later, I reread Mao's speech (the original version, not the one revised for publication) and realized that at the time, I had been too preoccupied with his main drift to detect hints of other tendencies hidden between the lines. For instance, he did not mince words over Stalin's dogmatism, but then insisted that Stalin must be assessed on the "three-seven" principle—that is, seven parts merit to three parts fault. Again Mao considered "democracy" as basically a tool to mobilize the people for the Party's own ends, and he wrote off any possibility of real freedom and democracy in capitalist society. He never acknowledged any defect in the work of the Party in the period from 1949 to 1955, such as in the witch hunts and the arrests carried out during the campaign against counterrevolutionary elements or the one against the Hu Feng clique, which had challenged Mao's ideological line on literature. On the contrary, he felt that the Chinese Communist Party was superior to other Communist parties in this respect—according to him, the Soviet Union was too "leftist," while Hungary was too far right; China, he said, had indeed committed "leftist" mistakes, but only in the distant past. In this speech, he twice attacked the famous critic Zhong Dianfei's article on the grave situation in the film industry, which had criticized its dogmatism. Mao said Zhong's article would be welcomed by Taiwan, because it "painted everything black." On this rereading, I found that Mao was not a whit less prejudiced against intellectuals than before: he acknowledged that most Party cadres were undereducated and liable to error, but then added that more education did not ensure against errors; in fact, he went on to say, the errors intellectuals made were even more serious. Later, he remarked that "problems always arise when intellectuals gather."

Young and naïve at the time, we never saw through Mao, never perceived that he didn't give up any of his deep-rooted prejudices. We did not realize that the problems he set out to deal with in that speech had been fostered by the very prejudices lurking beneath his speech. What had taken place was merely a change of tactics and strategy. Attacking dogmatism did not hurt Mao one whit—Stalin was blamed for everything, while Mao himself emerged as the innovator. Evidently, what he meant by dogmatism was the Party's blind emulation of all things Soviet; it did not include the rigid implementation of Mao's own dogma. It is now clear that Mao never thought of himself or the Chinese Communist Party under his leadership as having erred in any basic way. He was lost in complacency, aiming to increase his own prestige by the new ideas and tactics as put forward in his speeches and writings, such as "On the Ten Great Relationships," and "On the Correct Handling of Contradictions among the People," and the speech where he articulated the "hundred flowers" policy. He was, in fact, aspiring to the position of leadership in the world Communist movement. Even in his attack on Zhong Dianfei's article, one could see that he was absolutely intolerant of the slightest criticism, of any difference of opinion. And we, poor fools, went ahead with eyes open and still unseeing.

After my trip up north, I wanted to stay on in Beijing for a while. But something momentous happened that made me change my mind. At a meeting of our editorial board, the editor-in-chief, Zhang Liqun, informed us of a directive from Liu Shaoqi, who ranked second only to Mao on the Politburo. The *People's Daily* and *China Youth News* were to report on the strikes in the Shanghai cotton mills.

According to the orthodox view, a strike was the way the working class fought against capitalists—and thus if workers struck against a Communist government (or even a manager) it would mean a loss of face for the latter. Moreover, it was dangerous, since it displayed to the public at large the mistakes of the Party. So when the Party decided to make the strikes public, it meant that it had enough confidence to acknowledge its mistakes and overcome the growing alienation between the Party and the people. I was greatly buoyed by this prospect and all the more overjoyed that the task of reporting had been placed on my shoulders. I set out for Shanghai in the company of my colleague Chen Bohong, our Shanghai correspondent.

As soon as we arrived in Shanghai, Bohong and I headed straight for the Yunda Cotton Mill, whose workers were on strike. We had a deadline to meet. Apart from my interest in publishing a report that was sure to create a stir, I was anxious to understand why some Party organizations had deteriorated within a few years from being unanimously supported by the workers to becoming objects of hatred.

A day or two after we arrived in Shanghai, the Central Committee of the CCP announced its decision to conduct a Party rectification campaign nationwide. The "speaking-out"* sessions, as part of the campaign, were in full swing and were followed closely by all the big papers; criticism of the Party had begun. I felt that the Party now had a good opportunity to rectify its mistakes and overcome its bureaucratism, sectarianism, and dogmatism, and that China would move forward at a faster rate. For several nights in a row, I was so excited I couldn't sleep. I would drop off and wake up again, my head bursting with ideas. Often I would sit up and start writing at a furious rate. Thus in rapid succession I produced a short satire of officious political opportunists of the day, an essay on the rights of reporters and their existing situation, and a report on the current speaking-out sessions in Shanghai.

The day after I reached Shanghai, I reported to the municipal Party headquarters. I was met by the deputy head of the propaganda department, himself a writer. I introduced myself and explained my business, but he remained totally expressionless. At the time I assumed it was either his temperament or that he did not like my works, since our styles were so different. Ten days later, I met Yao Wenyuan, a man who had not yet attained his later high position, but who still managed to make a name for himself based on the strength of praise from Mao Zedong for one of his articles. He also was expressionless. I inquired about the "speaking-out" sessions in Shanghai art and literature circles, but he made no comment.

*Literally "bloom and contend," from Mao's "let a hundred flowers bloom, and a hundred schools of thought contend." These sessions were part of the Party rectification program, when the masses were called on to "speak out" in criticism at meetings convened for the purpose.

It was a most unpleasant meeting. We parted without touching the tea on the table.

Yunda Cotton Mill had about two hundred woman workers. Bohong and I spent two weeks interviewing workers and cadres of varying attitudes, some of them Communists, some not. We came to the conclusion that the crisis within the Party branch of this particular factory was of universal significance in that it called attention to the dangers that the Party faced in wielding power over the country. Only two years had passed since the workers had welcomed the establishment of joint ownership and had accepted the state representatives; now they were on strike and were holding the state representatives under house arrest as hostages. Only two years.

It was an interesting phenomenon: after the mill changed from private to public ownership (which was what joint ownership amounted to), production had decreased; the mill, formerly profitable, was now losing money. The workers had less say than before on factory affairs, the appointed representatives were inefficient and unpopular, and the "elected" chairman of the workers' union was distrusted.

Since the Communist Party members were not representing the interest of the workers, a non-Party person was—namely, the accountant, Ding Xikang. He was accused of instigating the strike. When the mill was still privately owned, this man had, in the interest of workers, kept an eye on the financial dealings of the capitalists and had been declared a madman by them. Now, following the socialist transformation, the Communist cadres declared him a madman as well. Ding was an orphan; after 1949, he was the first person at the mill to join the union, and had also applied to join the Party. In the same spirit that he had once confronted the capitalists, he now "stood alone against an organization," "in a state of war against the Party and the Youth League."

And what did the Party branch in the mill think of the situation? "Due to adverse international influences," it said, "the state of ideology within the mill has deteriorated, and political indoctrination should be reinforced"; "elements [that is, Ding] within the ranks of the workers who are spreading reactionary ideology should be isolated." Under such circumstances, what could the workers do except strike to make themselves heard by the higher leadership and attract the attention of the public?

A few months later, China entered another era, during which strikes were virtually illegal. Crises similar to that of the Yunda Cotton Mill were to occur in hundreds and thousands of factories all over the country, but they would never disturb the equanimity of the higher-ups, because they did not turn into strikes, but took on the silent form of protracted low productivity. Only later was I to understand that the proletarian Party, more attached to appearances and its own peace of mind, prefers this, as it does not disrupt social stability and would not make the Party lose face. It was a silent corrosive.

I have never been so eager to get to the papers as during that period. Of course, there was no time to read through everything, but just scanning the headlines was enough to give you the feel of things. People were rethinking a lot of issues, from the economy to the political system. Through the "speaking-out" sessions, people from every walk of life voiced their criticism of the social restrictions on their creativity. Life could have become more enjoyable; people could have become happier, and their relations with each other closer, less tense. But this was not to be. The rigidity of the Party's policies, the transformation of the Party cadres from public servants to a privileged clique, and the Party's clannish insolence toward non-Party people, and intellectuals in particular, isolated it from the masses of the people. Until then, nothing had been able to stop this vicious trend. But now, for the first time, the newspapers had become the mouthpiece of public opinion, and could voice the dissatisfaction, the doubts, and the aspirations of the people.

A young reporter from Radio Shanghai repeatedly invited me to give a talk to the staff there. I was undecided. It was getting on toward the end of May. The ominous tones and gloomy looks of the Shanghai Party leadership did not bode well. I had seen these unpropitious signs and did not want to give them ammunition to use against me. On the other hand, my reporter's instinct impelled me to the broadcasting station, where, I was told, the political conflict was acute and complex. Besides, the young reporters and editors were so earnest in their invitation that I could hardly refuse.

About a hundred people attended the talk; the atmosphere was warm and sympathetic. I talked about my experiences as a journalist and the issues I had been thinking over; I also told them about Poland's reforms in journalism. The audience raised many questions, which I answered.

On that occasion, my old weakness, of which I will probably never free myself, got the better of me once again. As I answered, reason repeatedly warned me to be cautious, but my emotions were hard to control. I could not bring myself to prevaricate, to say what I did not mean.

One question was, What obstacles had *China Youth News* confronted in its efforts to carry on open criticism over the last few years? Answering this fully would mean dragging in the names of senior Party cadres, which was to be avoided at all costs, but I still could not help saying, "One could write a book about the vicissitudes of our paper, but the biggest problem is conservative opposition from within the Party." I just managed to keep from mentioning names, but I went on to say that although Hu Yaobang, secretary of the Youth League Central, was not among those conservatives, they were in the majority and he was not in a position to support us.

The next question was, To what extent was the Central Committee of the CCP committed to carrying on the "speaking-out" sessions and the Party rectification campaign? I was treading on thin ice and only said, "There is no doubt Chairman Mao is fully committed." I should have stopped there, but I felt it was not a full answer, and therefore not a truthful answer. I remembered how provincial and municipal leaders had set themselves against Mao's directives; I remembered Mao saying in a speech to the State Council, "Among the leading cadres, nine out of ten are opposed to the policy of letting 'a hundred flowers bloom and a hundred schools of thought contend,' or at least have doubts about it. Only a minority support it." How could I not mention such an important point? So I added, after a slight pause, "As for other members of the Central Committee, we must wait and see. A group of leading cadres within the Party is opposed to the rectification campaign." I could not help but succumb to the friendly faces and expectant looks in the audience, and finally just let myself go. "In the past, when I heard that Chairman Mao himself had said that nine out of ten of the leading cadres were opposed to the 'hundred flowers' policy, I always thought it was an exaggeration. Now that I think of it, I realize that during the last few years, the opposition that our paper has met has come from the same lot. They are in a special position; you can't touch them. Newspapers can't criticize anyone above the head of a government ministry, and even that is hard to do. Comrade Liu Shaoqi has said that we must eradicate the feudal caste system. But I am not so optimistic. The problem is that those who most need supervision are beyond supervision. From the factory level to the Central Committee, a privileged stratum has already formed. Some might not have intended to become privileged individuals, but once you are in that position, it is easy to adapt."

Before I had finished, a folded note was passed to me. It read, "Hearing you talk, I realize you are the person I have been seeking. Can you give me a little of your time?"

Once the crowd had dispersed, a handsome woman walked over to me and asked for a private interview. We walked to a nearby coffee shop and talked. Tears came to her eyes as she told me about the misfortunes of her husband, the well-known literary critic He Manzi, who had been labeled a member of the Hu Feng clique in 1955, sentenced to prison, and later released but not cleared. His whole family suffered discrimination on his account. All I could do was offer her words of sympathy; within months she herself had also been labeled a rightist.

Meanwhile, the situation in Shanghai became unstable. Unrest in the factories continued to spread, strikes occurred every week, and every day dozens of workers marched to the municipal Party headquarters to petition. Of the state representatives sent to jointly owned factories, five had been beaten up. The Party Committee issued an emergency directive that the workers' unrest must be put down in ten days. The newspapers had stopped reporting on the "speaking-out" sessions. Rumor had it that Ke Qingshi, secretary of the Shanghai Party Committee, was on his way to Beijing to report to Mao. It was also said that Mao himself was planning to make his pronouncement on the current issues on June 1 at a meeting of the State Council. I guessed that Ke Qingshi would advise Mao to put on the brakes. If that happened, the current trend of democratization would be reversed.

At that meeting, I had also said, "We must not underestimate the strength of conservatives within the Party; they have ways to sway the leadership in their direction. But we should not underestimate ourselves either. We can influence the leadership with our pen. Chairman Mao reads the newspaper *Wenhui Bao*. The situation at the grass-roots level could be made known to those at the top." My heart full of foreboding, I sat up all night, in the basement room of the broadcasting station where I was staying, and wrote a letter to Chairman Mao, appealing directly to him not to reverse the trend. My letter read as follows:

The Central Committee of the Chinese Communist Party
General Office
Most respected Chairman Mao,
    I am a Communist Party member, a reporter for China Youth News. *For the last few years I have traveled through the northeast, northwest, and various provinces of the south, and the irregularities in the Party and abnormalities in*

our society that I have seen leave me unquiet. I wholeheartedly support the decision to expand democracy and conduct rectification. A wise man in ancient Rome once said, "To make fire, one cannot avoid smoke. The wise man puts out smoke and makes a fire; the fool would put out both fire and smoke." There is no lack of such fools within our Party. There are even those who would put out a cooking fire, so great is their fear of fire. You must know that the conservatives within the Party will oppose the current measures for rectification. I sincerely hope you will not believe their reports or be swayed by their opinions; they represent neither the Party nor the people. The situation in Shanghai has its adverse side, but the basic situation is good. Please take note that:

1. A privileged clique has formed itself within the Party. Its members are above supervision by the Party or the people, and have evolved into a new aristocracy.
2. In the majority of factories and industrial enterprises, Party organizations have become paralyzed. In some factories in the northeast, less than a quarter of the Party members are a credit to the Party. In government units, healthy tendencies are crushed; the dogmatists and the sectarianists have the upper hand. Over one third of the leading cadres have lost their political enthusiasm.
3. "Chameleons" exist among leading cadres; they are always changing color, and they are always on the safe side. The present rectification campaign cannot touch them. . . .

As for the deterioration of relationships between the Party and the people, it is so apparent to everyone that I need not dwell upon it.

I write about these things, of which you are probably aware, out of a sense of urgency. In Shanghai and Harbin, in my contact with leading cadres, I feel strongly that they are hostile to the Central Committee of the Party and the masses, yet they hold the reins of power. The ideas of the Party organization at the grass-roots level and the masses do not carry weight. What is needed are measures from the Central Committee. . . .

Actually there was no need for anyone to influence him—Mao's mind had already been made up and the stage all set. And my own fate had been decided by him personally about two weeks before. One of my early pieces about the "speaking-out" sessions in Shanghai, entitled "Shanghai Lost in Thought," had been published on May 12, and Mao had read it. He made a note: "Evidently, some people are interested not in solving problems, but in stirring up confusion."

The word *confusion* carries a lot of weight. He meant that I was instigating a Hungarian-style revolt in China. How could he have taken my article so seriously? That piece of writing mainly dealt with the Party's management of art and literature. It posed the question, "Why was it that under reactionary rule, Shanghai had produced the greatest number of books and plays and talented people, while after the liberation, the cultural scene became so bleak?" Obviously, this was offensive, but what had enraged him most must have been the ending:

The "speaking-out" sessions in Shanghai have just begun. But some people refuse to talk; others who have spoken still hold back something. They are afraid of being trapped, of being reported on behind their backs, of having to recant; others are doubtful that any real changes could be effected. . . . People cannot help but follow every move of the leading cadres, who are present at meetings but never open their mouths, their faces remaining expressionless. Nobody knows what they have up their sleeve. Considering how often the Party has gone back on its word, you cannot blame the masses for having reservations.

After finishing the letter to Mao, I made my way back to Beijing with a heavy heart. On the train, I read a denunciation of Professor Ge Peiqi, of People's University, in the pages of the *People's Daily*. The article said that Ge had been a high-ranking official in the Kuomintang army, and out of hate for the Communist Party had launched a vicious attack during a "speaking-out" session and even vowed to personally kill Communist Party members. It was the first time I had ever heard of such naked hatred for the Party, and I was shocked, yet at the time I never doubted the truth of the report. It was only after twenty years that the truth of Ge's case came to light. He was actually an old Party member, working under cover in the Kuomintang army. He never said a word about killing Communist Party members. What he actually said was that he had seen how the Kuomintang had risen to power and then been toppled, and by the way Communist Party members were going, he feared that they would follow in the footsteps of the Kuomintang.

On June 1, the *People's Daily* published an editorial titled "What Is the Reason Behind All This?" The editorial made reference to an anonymous letter that had been sent to Lu Yuwen, member of the Kuomintang Revolutionary Committee,* after he had spoken at a meeting of the

---

*This committee was a splinter group of the Kuomintang that supported the Communist Party before liberation in 1949, and then became one of the various democratic parties that continued a nominal existence in the People's Republic.

committee in defense of the Communist Party. The editorial cited this incident as a sign that "class struggle was not over" and that rightists were making use of the present situation to overthrow the Party. Two days later, the paper published another editorial, "The Workers Speak Up"; it sent out an official call to the masses to "repel the attacks of the bourgeois rightists." Already, as the two editorials were appearing, mass rallies were being held in Beijing, Tianjin, Shanghai, Shenyang, and other big cities to denounce the anti-Communist, anti-socialist attacks of the rightists. Everything was being carefully staged.

Denunciations were being heaped on the heads of leading figures of the "democratic" parties, accusing them of "anti-Party and antisocialist" words and deeds. The logic was that although these figures had indeed opposed the Kuomintang regime in the old days, they had become resentful of the Party leadership when they did not get a share of the spoils of power. The papers also exposed their various plots and machinations. One of the most notorious groups was the "Zhang Bojun–Luo Longji League," as it was decried, named after leading figures of the democratic parties. I was convinced that these people were rightists in the true sense of the word. But even so, I felt that some of their resentment was not totally unfounded, as when Chu Anping (editor-in-chief of their newspaper, the *Guangming Daily*) referred to "the Party-monopolized country." As the attacks escalated, so did my own disquiet. If this continues, I thought, all the hopes of China's democratization will be gone; we will revert to the old ways.

At the time, I had an intuition that any Communist Party member who shared my views was within the range of these attacks. I was sure we couldn't be labeled rightists, but recalling the discussion of Wang Meng's short story, I had a premonition that we would have to answer for our words and our writings if people started questioning them.

I was restless. What was to be done? All the papers were speaking in one voice. There was no room for expressing my private convictions.

Some of the younger editors on our staff shared my restlessness. We talked it over; acting with a sense of urgency, we decided to call a meeting of Party members to continue with the "speaking-out" sessions. Looking back, it is clear that we had overrated our own ability to command the situation. I had been elected Party secretary of the No. 2 Party cell a few months previously. The deputy secretary, a young woman reporter, agreed with the decision. So one evening in the latter part of June, a Party cell meeting was held in the meeting hall of our office building.

It was a half-hearted affair. The ongoing antirightist drive had made people timid. I, on the contrary, had gained courage from the heightened sense of danger. I stood and spoke, encouraging others to speak up. "Don't be afraid, we are speaking at the behest of Chairman Mao. Of course there are people within the Party opposed to rectification, who close their ears to criticism. Well, all the more reason for rectification. If the existing bureaucratism and special privileges continue, the Party itself will be endangered. Anyway, if we Party members are afraid to speak up, how can we expect non-Party people to express themselves?"

My words worked. Some members pointed out the mistakes of the Party Committee during the campaign to purge counterrevolutionary elements on the staff. Some of those who had been unjustly targeted during that campaign spoke; understandably they were agitated. To my surprise, my colleague Feng Yuqing, a veteran member who had always been more cautious than I was, spoke up sharply against the lack of democracy within the Party.

After the meeting, several comrades suggested that we write a summary of the speeches at the meeting and put it up as a wall poster, to give a push to the flagging Party rectification program. Others thought this a rash idea. After a slight hesitation, I seconded the proposal, and we went ahead. This of course was an unusual step, and an added risk, apart from the meeting itself.

Several days later, at another meeting, Hu Yaobang, then secretary of the Youth League, came to our editorial office to hear what we had to say, and again I unreservedly spoke my mind and voiced sharp criticism. I raised the question, "Now, how do we distinguish between 'right' and 'left' anyway? As I see it, those who support progress and oppose bureaucratism and conservatism should be classed as 'leftist.' Why then are they labeled 'rightist' while those who oppose reform and want to continue with the old ways are honored as 'leftist'? Why this strange inversion?"

This was the last such speech I made as a Party member in the 1950s.

On the evening of July 8, a meeting of the entire staff was called at the big mess hall. As usual, I sauntered in, fan in hand. She Shiguang, secretary of the Party organization of our paper, took the chair, and said, "The antirightist campaign has been going on for a while, and a number of anti-Communist, antisocialist rightist elements have been exposed. Some say that there are no rightists on the staff of the Youth

League or at *China Youth News*. Well, let's face it. Are there, or aren't there, rightists among us?" And he answered himself: "Yes, there are, and Liu Binyan is one."

My heart gave a thump and nearly stopped beating. Could this be true? Was I dreaming? For a few seconds, I felt my head spinning. But I quickly got hold of myself. I realized that I faced a monstrous threat. Although I sensed its full enormity, part of me could not accept the reality. I thought, "It is a misunderstanding. Something must have gone wrong somewhere. How could I be an enemy?"

The second person to stand up and denounce me was a worker—a tall, bulky fellow from the printing section. He agreed completely with the words of the secretary of the Party Committee and added: "There's not an ounce of the Communist in Liu Binyan. He's crooked. You can smell it a mile away." I was shocked. Just two days before, my family and I had met him while we were out for a stroll on Wangfujing Street. He was friendliness itself and had insisted on taking a photo of my children! But on second thought, however, I realized that there was nothing strange about it. All the early speakers, as they rose one by one to denounce me, must have been coached. A few others also stood up to speak, but they could not work themselves up to the proper pitch. In fact, they even said some things in my favor after criticizing my faults, which was not to the taste of the leftists.

At the time, I never imagined that it was all the result of careful planning. I thought it a misunderstanding. Finally it was my chance to speak.

Slowly I rose to my feet. I was sitting in the front, to the left of the audience, and all eyes were turned on me as I stood up. I controlled my agitation and began to speak. I said that the meeting was a shock and a surprise not only to myself but to many others, and that I had never been regarded in this light before. I admitted that I had many faults, but did that make me a rightist like Zhang Bojun or Luo Longji? I refuted some of the accusations, such as the contention that I was interested only in smearing the Party in my writings. I insisted that I had written out of concern for the Party. I wanted to lay out all my thoughts, all my actions, so that people could judge me fairly.

I knew that according to usual practices, my case would be all over the papers the next day. By then, my fate would be irrevocable. So I said, "I hope this won't get go into the papers." Someone in the crowd shouted,

"That's one of his tricks. Let's not be taken in!" But it turned out his warning went unheeded, and several days indeed passed before the news appeared in the papers.

Even after the meeting had ended, I couldn't believe that my case had been decided upon. I still hoped to find a sympathetic ear, someone who believed that I was not a rightist. My greatest cause of concern was my wife. I knew that she had been present at the meeting although I had not tried to catch her eye. She must have been terribly shocked. I wanted to say a few words of comfort to her.

As I walked out of the hall, nobody spoke to me. Only Zhu Hong waited for me at the door. I told her I was going to look up Luo Yi, a secretary of the Youth League Central who was in charge of this campaign. She told me not to worry. She was sure everything would be cleared up.

I got on my bike and headed straight for Luo Yi's residence in Guandongdian, in the eastern part of the city. I had known Luo Yi since 1950–1951 when he was part of the delegation of Chinese youth visiting the Soviet Union. He received me kindly, as if nothing had happened. I laid my case before him. I told him it must be a mistake. How could I possibly be a rightist? I begged him to review my case. Luo Yi was all affability; he told me not to worry and to put my trust in the Party. He said the Party would see to it that no one would be unjustly accused. I believed him and calmed down.

It was not until ten years later that I realized my fate had already been sealed by Mao Zedong himself in May, sealed in a way that no human effort could reverse. Luo Yi was simply repeating empty words.

It was midnight when I left Luo Yi's house. Halfway home, I met my wife. She was out looking for me. She said a friend had advised her to keep an eye on me in case I couldn't bear the strain and did something rash. She was alarmed and ran out to find me. I laughed at the idea. How could I think of anything like that? I, who was clearly innocent!

Endless meetings were held, one after the other, in deliberations over my case. They were small ones in the meeting room on the second story of our office building, where I had undergone interrogation as a suspected counterrevolutionary back in 1955.

The first change in my life was that people stopped talking to me. My acquaintances would avert their eyes when our paths crossed, or I would turn the other way if I happened to catch their eye. But I did not see hostility or contempt in their expressions. It is not easy to turn a man into a villain overnight, in spite of the omnipotence of the Party. But the wall separating the Chinese people and me had been erected; it would only be a matter of time before it would block me out entirely.

The courtyard of our office building was filled with big-character posters hanging everywhere. I was too listless to inspect them. On the red brick building of *Young Vanguard,* the newspaper for children where my wife worked as one of the editors, a huge poster had been hung above the entrance: "Rightist Liu Binyan, bow down your head and acknowledge your guilt!"

The papers started to expose and denounce me, first in individual articles, then in entire sections of the paper. The atmosphere around me grew more and more tense, in keeping with the trend.

At the small meetings, however, with around twenty people attending, I could still defend myself. I pointed out to my accusers that during the height of the "speaking-out" sessions in Shanghai, I never once tried to take part, never once tried to interview the people who were now being labeled rightists. I stressed that I had immersed myself wholeheartedly in my assigned job: to report on the situation in the mills. I pointed this out to prove myself innocent of any anti-Party activities.

Large meetings were held, and then even larger ones. A young woman reporter who had worked in my section and who had been my most ardent follower, took the lead in denouncing me. I could understand her behavior. I simply would not believe that she meant all she said, or that she had changed so quickly, but I understood that she had to make a public statement, to dissociate herself from me, or she herself would have been in trouble.

The only person I could talk to was my wife. At the time, many families were being broken up; when someone was accused of being a rightist, the spouse would immediately ask for a divorce. In my family, however, my wife Zhu Hong became my guardian angel.

Later, when she was put under pressure to "draw a line" between us, she had no choice but to put out big-character posters to expose me. She had nothing to hide, and so it was impossible for her to expose my nonexistent plots against the Party. Sometimes I would help her out, reminding her of some details that she might use for exposure.

Zhu Hong tried to cheer me up, asking me not to worry over what could not be mended, adding that luckily she was independent and would not be implicated by me. But how could I believe that?

Only our children, our four-year-old son and our three-year-old daughter, were still living in blissful ignorance. Only with them could I forget my grief for a moment. But then the question rose in my mind: What was going to happen to them? The disgrace of their father would be brought to bear sooner or later. And the thought struck a note of terror in my heart.

Zhu Hong did not tell me what she had planned to do, but it turned out we had thought along the same lines. She turned all my letters to her over to the Party leadership as evidence of my political loyalty. A couple of years later, these letters were returned to me. One of them had been written in Hubei. Zhu Hong had underlined the part where I had expressed indignation at some of the atrocities committed against security officers during the Hungarian Uprising.

At the small meetings, the participants listened to me patiently without saying a word. They never interrupted me. Among them were members of the editorial board, members of the Party Committee, and several department heads, all Party members, of course. Of those present, two or three might have had an interest in seeing me labeled a rightist. As for the majority, some had reservations about the campaign altogether, while others, such as the editor-in-chief Zhang Liqun, must have been spending sleepless nights over their own precarious positions. But whatever they thought they kept to themselves, except for a handful of militant activists who followed the Party "faithfully."

I admitted that I had gone too far in Shanghai, that my articles and speeches could have been used by anti-Party rightists. But my belief in Marxism and socialism had been shaped before the liberation. Besides, my whole family and I stood to gain in material terms and social prestige with the liberation. Why should I oppose the Communist Party and socialism? Still, neither my sincerity nor my litany of facts moved my listeners. All I got in return for my efforts were further denunciations and accusations.

In contrast to the practice of the Cultural Revolution nine years later, there was no shouting of personal insults or physical abuse. The participants at the meeting spoke out against me or interrogated me, but I was allowed to defend myself without interruption. Behind this façade of leniency and flexibility, however, lay an inexorable fate.

By now the media were full of denunciations against rightists, who allegedly were full of malice against the Party. It surpassed all the preceding political campaigns in scale and stridency of tone. My own case, enhanced with exposures and denunciatory articles, made headlines in *China Youth News*.

I knew very well that when the working class was supposed to be "speaking up," workers in at least thirty factories in Shanghai were on strike, certainly not in support of the Central Committee of the Party. Anyway, how many workers were there who really understood the rift between the Party and the intellectuals and had decided to side with the Party? Judging from the papers, it looked as though the workers stood behind the Party as one against the so-called rightists.

As a reporter, I was not taken in by all the bombast in the media. I was an insider. Take, for example, the denunciation against me "written" by an illiterate old woman whom I knew in Tianjin—I could easily imagine the way it was concocted. Nevertheless, the sheer scale of the campaign in the press and my own isolation were enough to intimidate me.

Days had passed since I was first denounced as a rightist. One after another, members of the *China Youth News* staff were declared rightists. The combined prestige of Mao Zedong and the Communist Party was enough to sway public opinion and make them anathema.

As for myself, I had become notorious throughout the nation. None of the others labeled as rightists could compare with me in this respect. I had been made into such a rightist that if the official line on me had changed, the campaign might have faltered. If I were not a rightist, then nobody could legitimately be called a rightist—and then how could this campaign launched by Mao himself be justified?

I began to lose self-confidence. Was I without a fault? Of course not. And all my faults, in the final analysis, boiled down to bourgeois individualism. Could I honestly say that I had joined the Party solely for the liberation of the Chinese people, with no ulterior motives? Of course not. There was at least some element of self-fulfillment. And then there was my writing. Could I honestly say that I never had any eye on the publicity and the profit? Of course not.

The meetings dragged on and on. I would not admit to anti-Party or antisocialist sentiments. I went so far as to admit that some of my words and deeds were in line with those of the rightists. But that did not mean that I myself was a rightist, I argued. My judges went on to quote Chairman Mao's dictum on the correlation of motive and result. Being part of the result, how could you disengage yourself from the motive? But I couldn't accept this kind of reasoning. I knew my own motives better than anybody else.

At the same time, in the office building of the *Beijing Daily*, meetings sponsored by the Association of Chinese Journalists to "criticize rightists in media circles" from all over Beijing were going on. I had attended one such meeting there two months ago, before I had been denounced. At the time, the target of the attack was Wang Yunsheng, a non-Party political figure and director of *Da Gong Bao*, a daily that survived from before 1949. Later, the man was listed as belonging to a category of people "under special protection," and the charges against him were dropped. I still remember that I had met Deng Tuo of the *People's Daily* during a break at that meeting. He was quite glum, evidently disturbed at the way things were going. Earlier on, in May, I had mailed him one of my articles written in Shanghai, airing the grievances of reporters. According to practice, he should have sent it to the Party Committee of the paper, to disengage himself from me and my dangerous views. But he had chosen to give it back to me instead.

Now, at the present session of the "criticism of rightists in media circles," euphemistically called "discussions of issues within the media," I had become the centerpiece. It was my turn to make public confessions, criticize myself, and accept criticism from the masses. Compared to the previous sessions, the attendance had shot up ten times. The hall was packed, almost bursting.

Like a drowning man, still worried that a stone in the river might hurt him, I was annoyed at a young woman, the Youth League secretary for the *Beijing Daily*. At her insistence, I had given a talk to Youth Leaguers at the *Beijing Daily* a year ago, and now she had the cheek to stand up and accuse me of worming my way into the *Beijing Daily* to poison the minds of the youth! I made up my mind then and there never to give any more public talks. It was, of course, an absurd fantasy. Refuse imaginary invitations indeed!

At that meeting, I had noticed a wave of consternation sweep through the audience as I walked into the room. After the meeting, I learned that someone had jumped to his death from an upper floor of the same building. Later I learned that it was my friend Qi Xueyi, who had jumped from the fifth floor to his death in an act of protest against the campaign and against the victimization of myself. Qi had been an underground Party member in his student days. After the liberation, he was expelled from the Party for individualism. In 1956, he had come to work under me at *China Youth News*. The political atmosphere at the time was favorable, and he had hopes of having his Party membership restored. He was in good spirits and worked very hard. As we thought along the same lines, we became close personal friends, and he had also written articles praising my work as a writer. After I was labeled a rightist, he became very tense; he felt the same fate awaited him and decided to anticipate his fate and add his corpse to China's crushed hopes.

Qi Xueyi had no relatives in Beijing. His body was soon cremated. He had called at my apartment a few days earlier, and we had talked late into the night; he had left his jacket still hanging on the wall in my bedroom. It hung there a long time, right until my own political fate was finally sealed.

To display the inflexible will of the Party and the inescapable clutch of its power, Qi Xueyi was posthumously labeled an anti-Party, antisocialist rightist.

Within the walls of *China Youth News*, the criticism against me dragged on. Following in my footsteps, one staff member after the other was singled out as a target. Sometimes people were here one day to denounce me, and gone the next morning, only to resurface at another meeting to be denounced themselves. In all, seventeen people on the paper were accused of being rightists. Without exception, their offenses were less serious than mine. The last one to be dragged into the net was the painter on our staff, Lu Xikun. He was labeled a rightist solely because he had disobeyed a reassignment order to work in the provinces.

I must convince myself, I kept saying, for I couldn't really accept that I was a rightist. But if I were not a rightist, none of the other sixteen people would qualify as a rightist. None of the hundred or so rightists in the entire Youth League headquarters, to which *China Youth News* was affiliated, would qualify as a rightist. None of their offenses could compare to mine. Because of those two articles and my talks all over the place, I had acquired considerable influence in press circles and among the young. Many people considered me avant-garde; some of the young wanted to follow my example. Later on, many of them were labeled rightists for writing works similar to mine, for praising my works, or for merely expressing sympathy for me.

The antirightist campaign was personally launched and led by Mao himself. Since it was a political campaign, it had to have targets. Only the presence of enemy targets could justify such a campaign, and I had been picked out to serve as an enemy. In other words, my fate was sealed. The finality of the whole thing was as clear as day. And so, what was the point of these exhausting meetings day after day?

We reached a deadlock over the question of motive. No amount of criticism or analysis could convince me that I had consciously opposed the Party and socialism. Then, under endless verbal attack, I did some hard thinking on my own and began to see the light. At one of the last meetings, I said, "My mind is steeped in bourgeois ideology and individualism. All my words and deeds originate in my mind, and since my mind is completely poisoned, how can anything good come out of it? Probably what I consider good is its exact opposite." As I said these words, both the audience and I gave a sigh of relief.

Still, the business of making me into a rightist was not over. The deputy secretary of the Party Committee, the man who controlled my fate, hurled a command at me: "Confess the political ambition behind all your rightist words and deeds!" I had known this man since 1946, but because of a difference of temperament, we had never been close. He suspected me of basing Ma Wenyuan, a character in "Inside Story," on him and had always borne me a grudge. Now his face was grimmer than ever as he spoke to me.

I was shocked. This was not only a further attack; it was political extortion! He wanted me to confess that I was out to overthrow the leadership of the Party. This was going too far! I refused point-blank.

The meetings of the successive days were protracted squabbles over this issue. I would not give in, and the deputy secretary would not back down from his accusation. It gradually dawned on me that he needed this last confession of political ambition to pin me down in a certain category in anticipation of the punishment that was to be handed down later.

The speechifying eventually focused on the definition of the term "ambition." One person said, "There must be a purpose behind your words and deeds." I replied, "Of course. When I speak, I am trying to influence others with my own ideas." "Right," the deputy secretary shot back; "and that is exactly what is meant by 'political ambition'!" I asked, "But doesn't that mean that all speech, all preaching, all teaching, all agitation, beginning with Confucius, was political ambition?" But he held to his own logic. I realized that this man had a job to do; what was the point of arguing? Suddenly, I just let go. "What's the use?" I said to myself. "The knife is coming down anyway. What does it matter if a little more or less blood is spilled?" And so, I acknowledged that I was motivated by "political ambition" in the sense that I had tried to "influence others by my own words." Only in 1988 did I fully realize that his task was to label me an extreme rightist. And to accomplish this, he had to have me acknowledge that I had political ambition.

The job was finally over and done with. Both sides felt a sense of relief. After that, I was left undisturbed. Every day, I would go to my office and read at my desk, while others were busying themselves over my political corpse.

I do not boast of great strength of character. Later on I learned that many people did not bow down to their verdict, accepting a harsher treatment rather than knuckling under. But not I. When I saw so many people who had done much less and said much less than I being labeled rightists, I began to convince myself: between Mao and myself, there could only be one wrong, and since he was beyond wrong, it could only be me. Thus I accepted my fate.

The official verdict was handed down six months later.

On March 5, 1958, I signed my name to five copies of a three-thousand-word verdict on my case; in other words, I signed my own political death warrant. To my own surprise, I was completely calm. My guilt was sixfold:

1. I had viciously attacked the Central Committee of the Party and various echelons of Party leadership, distorted the image of Party cadres, and villified the political life of the Party.
2. I had denied the achievements of the Party in directing art and literature.
3. I had villified the policy of eliminating counterrevolutionary elements and enacting socialist democratic centralization; I had spread the slander that "human rights are trampled, human dignity is insulted."
4. I had denied the Party's achievements in directing the work of *China Youth News,* trying to divert the paper into bourgeois trends.
5. I had denied the Party's achievements in its orientation of China's youth, opposing the Party's political indoctrination of the young generation.
6. I had stirred up unrest during the speaking-out sessions, conducting a series of anti-Party activities.

The last entry included my letter to Mao Zedong. The relevant passage ran thus: "He feared that the 'speaking-out' sessions would stop, so he spent a whole night writing a letter to Chairman Mao, arrogantly trying to influence Chairman Mao with his own vicious thinking."

A few months later, I learned that my elder sister, a primary-school teacher, had been labeled a rightist for defending me—an extreme rightist at that. That was the hardest blow of all.

Hearing of my fate, my friend the Soviet writer Valentine Ovechkin wrote me, angry and perplexed at my treatment. He said he would not believe that people like the woman writer and veteran Party member Ding Ling and I could oppose socialism. I wrote back assuring him that although I had no such intention, my words and deeds coincided with those of the rightists, and that I therefore accepted my punishment and asked him not to protest on my behalf. Still, he was not convinced.

I continued to correspond with Ovechkin until September of the same year, when I was sent to the countryside for reform through manual labor. Then suddenly his letters stopped. I presumed that he must have been disciplined for corresponding with a Chinese rightist. It was not until 1962 that I learned that he had written to the Chinese Communist Party's Central Committee on my behalf, and that Zhou Enlai, the premier, had lost his temper over the affair. It was what I had feared most. My Chinese compatriots could guess immediately what the Central Committee would think of such a letter—that I had begged a Russian to intercede on my behalf. It was also said that the removal of my rightist label was delayed on this account.

After a while, I began to have an inkling of the overwhelming scale of that antirightist campaign. At the time, the official figure for the number of rightists the campaign had uncovered was five hundred and fifty thousand. The actual figure exceeded one million. And of them, less than a hundred had ever published any rightist material. For the vast majority, the grounds for conviction were but a few words of criticism at meetings where criticism had been invited, or a few words spoken in private. For others, there weren't any speeches or words to go by; they were simply dragged in to fill the quota handed down from above. According to practice, the cadres in charge had to exceed the quota as a sign of dedication and efficiency.

These rightists were trapped in various ways. For instance, after the heat of the campaign was over, people were requested to report on their thoughts, and some poor innocent would admit to having sympathized with a particular rightist point of view, or to have doubted the campaign altogether at one point, though these deviations had now been resolved. Well, if the quota needed filling, even such harmless thoughts were enough to damn you. More curious still were the cases of those who had not said a word or shown any sign of being rightists. They were the ones accused of "stopping up their mouths like bottles in their hate and distrust of the Party," and that was reason enough to slap the label on them.

There were also more than a few cases of people in power using this opportunity to pursue private ends. Thus, some people languished under the "rightist" label for twenty years, were forced to divorce their spouses, and had their family broken, only to find that when the moment for rehabilitation came, there was but a slip of paper in their files, that the process of labeling had never been completed, and that therefore, legally, they had never been rightists at all. Later I came across a case in Henan where the principal of an elementary school had had his eye on the pretty wife of the physical-education teacher, but could not lay hands on her. He had condemned the teacher as a rightist and had engineered the couple's divorce; then the woman became his.

The antirightist campaign inflicted irremediable damage to the Party and to the country as a whole. From then on, intellectuals and ordinary cadres no longer dared to raise their voices in criticism of the Party or the government. Decadent trends within the Party and erroneous policies of the Central Committee and of Mao were allowed to go unchecked; the adulation of Mao grew out of bounds. As for democracy within the Party and society as a whole, it was steadily whittled down to nothing. Following the Great Leap Forward, the man-made economic disaster of 1958–1960, and by the man-made political disaster of 1966–1976, China lay stagnant, surpassed in output by other less developed countries. Even after the Cultural Revolution, China was still forced to taste the bitter fruits of these disasters, paying heavily for each step forward. For all this, the Antirightist campaign of 1957–1958 was the starting point.

chapter seven

Prison without Walls

Of all creatures, man is the most adaptable. I had been at the height of my popularity, "in the vanguard of our age," and overnight, I became the detested "enemy of the people." And yet I went on living. The world around me suddenly turned strange and hostile. Nobody spoke to me. If I saw an acquaintance walking toward me on the street, I would cross to the other side, to save us both embarrassment. All the sunshine had faded from my life, and all sounds of laughter were banished to another world.

I did not think of death—that thought came ten years later. What was it that kept me alive? It was my wife's undying love, and my son and daughter, whom I loved more than my own life. But there was something else that kept me going: the conviction that this setback was not final. The stubborn urge to make something of myself that I felt when I had to leave school now seized me again. I admitted to myself that I was beaten, but not for good; something in me told me that I would survive.

In the early part of 1958, the final details of my punishment were determined: I was labeled an extreme rightist. Rightists were divided into six categories; those in the first three categories were all extreme rightists, with varying degrees of punishment. Those in the first and second categories were struck off the payroll. I was in the third category, which meant that I was suspended from public office and allowed 20 yuan for living expenses, barely enough money for food and cheap cigarettes. The rightists in the fourth and fifth categories had their pay reduced from one to four grades on the salary scale; only those in the sixth category retained their original salaries. In the actual implementation, the penalties were often exceeded. And of course, all rightists who were Party members were to be expelled from the Party without exception.

Everything that I could call my own vanished—credit for years of service, salary, and status, even the right to work according to my ability— all were denied me. I was stripped of everything. And what's more, my family and I were weighed down with the stigma of my being labeled an enemy of the people. Only my life was spared, thanks to the "overflowing mercy of the leader"—a fate much better than the one I would have suffered under Stalin.

Of the staff of over a hundred at *China Youth News,* seventeen were labeled rightists. In March, these seventeen, under the escort of "good" comrades, were sent to the countryside in Shanxi Province for reform through manual labor. It was in the Taihang Mountains, and as far as living and working conditions were concerned, it was the most remote area in China.

As the truck carrying us crawled up the mountains, the sky darkened, and snow drifted silently over us. We sat motionless in the truck, like figures of stone. A year before, these same men had been so elated, caught up in the expectations of democratization, as promised by Mao Zedong. They had had such visions of the future, such enthusiasm to live life to the fullest, such determination to leave a mark on history. And now, they were being sent into exile, a herd of dumb creatures, their souls left behind. We sat facing each other, our eyes averted, careful to hide all expression from our faces. Only last year, some of us had been close friends, but now none of us so much as broke the silence during the long ride. Each of us bid farewell to a former life with its illusions of hope and love and happiness, and now waited in a daze for whatever was to come. On the surface, each of us had succumbed to our fates, admitted to being opposed to socialism and the Party. But as I gauged the others through my own feelings, I doubted they had really given in. Since I, the worst offender, did not in my heart of hearts acknowledge guilt, how could they, convicted on such flimsy evidence, acknowledge as much?

That spring was a turning-point in Chinese history. Hundreds of thousands of Chinese intellectuals had been labeled rightists and driven to the farms for ideological reform; others who were labeled counterrevolutionaries as well as rightists had been sent to labor camps, where many of them perished. Meanwhile, the antirightist campaign was still forging ahead; several hundred thousand would follow in our wake wearing the rightist label.

Looking back three decades later, I ask myself: Did Mao really believe that so many people were opposed to him? Compared to other political movements launched by the Party, the antirightist campaign was the most ruthless. Why? Even from my own humble position I could see that the campaign was going to impose a reign of terror over the whole population. Could Mao not see it as well?

Perhaps that is precisely what Mao had set out to achieve. At least that was what it was, judging by the overall effect. Following the clampdown on intellectuals came the policy of forcing the peasants into communes and all of the resulting regimentation.

As to the group of us sitting in the truck, if we had not been labeled rightists at the time, we would have later become avowed opponents of the Great Leap Forward and the People's Commune, and would have been punished anyway.

I suddenly had a fantasy that in an hour's time, a special messenger from the Central Committee would come and announce that the antirightist campaign was a mistake, and all present would rise up like one to protest their innocence. This quietly faded as the entire population of Yanjingdi village came out to inspect this group of cadres from Beijing. At first sight, it looked as though one side of the mountain was overflowing with people, but on a closer inspection, I realized that the families were standing outside their own doors—they lived in cave dwellings, cut out of the mountain.

In the beginning, as a gesture of magnanimity, our political identities were not revealed, but the peasants soon figured out that we were political exiles. They did not, however, show any contempt for us. On the contrary, they became more friendly. And we soon found out why. Liu Erhai, the middle-aged bachelor with whom I was lodging, told me that during the Anti-Japanese War, there was a very good man working there who was shot on account of political slander. The peasants put two and two together and guessed we were victims of the same fate: "You spoke the truth, and they didn't like it."

I was thirty-three years old; until then, I had never done manual labor, let alone farm work. This part of the country was all terraced fields. In spring, one had to carry all the seeds, all the manure, and all the water needed for planting up to the terraces in vessels balanced on poles carried across the shoulders. In fall, all the harvest had to be carried down. The peasants mercifully made us carry less than sixty pounds at a time. But by fall, I could shoulder more than twice that weight and walk nonstop for a mile or two.

Only on rare occasions—for instance, when a goat was killed in an accident—did we have a taste of meat. Even cooking oil was a rarity. At first, I could hardly swallow the coarse food prepared in such a strange way. But the peasants were happy to have their bellies filled. They were mostly descendants of peasants from Honan Province who had been driven into the mountains by famine. By the sweat of several generations, they had managed to carve terraced fields out of the mountainsides, which could withstand drought. In fall, the trees were laden with fruit. These peasants had not made the transition from mutual-aid teams to cooperatives voluntarily, but orders were orders, and they made the best of the situation. When we first arrived, every family had a bank account. The peasants had a great fear of poverty and saved every penny they could. As the farmers planned it, productivity would grow, and the value of a day's work would increase to a yuan and a half. It was a realistic goal that they could have attained if our "Great Leader Chairman Mao" had not launched the Great Leap Forward and the People's Commune campaign.

When we left Beijing, I had thought that I would take my punishment and start over again, minus a Party card, but as a cadre nevertheless. At the first meeting of the rightists in the countryside, I spoke my mind and was immediately admonished by the "good" comrades in charge of us: "Don't forget your rightist label." Only then did I realize not only that I would have to bury myself in the countryside, but that I would be branded forever with a rightist label.

If we had known at the time that we would have to bear that label for twenty-one years (the removal of the tag in the early sixties converted us into "rightists with labels removed"), I wonder how many of us would have gone on living. At the beginning of 1958, when the general secretary of the Youth League saw us off at the railway station and said that we must brace ourselves for a three-year to five-year period in the country, I had thought it intolerable. But actually, I labored in the countryside, separated from my wife and children, off and on, for thirteen years in all. What was harder to bear was the stigma we carried with us, invisible yet apparent to the world, a stigma that seemed branded in our flesh, worse than that of a downright criminal. We were truly untouchables.

Mao was much cleverer than Stalin. Why kill off your enemies? Crush them under a label, and if that doesn't work, there's the reformatory, and after that, jail. If Mao had killed off all his political opponents, all the landlords and all the rich, then his rallying cry of four years later—"class struggle must be kept in mind, year in and year out, month in and month out, day in and day out"—would have been pointless. And eight years later, during the Cultural Revolution, the Red Guards would have had no targets on which to focus their revolutionary ardor. The label also served to stir up competition among the rightists themselves. Beginning in 1959, a few were "unlabeled" every year, and this spurred the remaining ones to improve their performance. And what better way than to report on their fellow victims? That is exactly what happened. From the very beginning, there were those who reported on or even slandered their own kind. So there was a lot of mutual criticism among us seventeen rightists: "You have the wrong attitude," "you are persisting in your reactionary point of view," and so on. All these were very effective in adding to our load of guilt.

All this sounds ridiculous, of course, but at the time it was conducted in all seriousness. The absurdity lies in the fact that we were rightists, each and every one of us, enemies of the people and political outcasts. Yet, in criticizing one another, we judged each other by the criteria of Communist Party members. The object of criticism, whoever it happened to be at the moment, also measured himself by the same high standards. Thus, the criteria we set out with were grandiose, but in the end, it always boiled down to "insufficient awareness of one's own guilt," "insufficient resolution to undergo thorough and complete reform of the self," as was in keeping with our rightist status. Or worse, we could end our self-criticism with confessions of being "hostile to the Party," "hoping to regain a lost paradise," and so on.

Being the most "serious" criminal of the lot, I came in for the harshest criticism. My self-criticism had to be even more soul-racking than that of the others. I, of course, also had to criticize others without mercy as part of my own reform.

These meetings would go on for days. All of us would go about it very seriously, no hint of play-acting. Of course, the desire to get the approval of the Party was always at the back of our minds, which tended to make the criticism of others severe and the self-criticism lacerating. But after each meeting, we were again fellow sufferers sharing the same fate, no offense taken.

I found it harder to accept the attack on "independent thinking," for which I was criticized. Was it possible to be human and at the same time simply repeat what the Party said without using one's own judgment? Soon after settling in the countryside, I read a *Beijing Daily* editorial entitled "Communist Party Members Should Be Pliant Tools of the Party." I was even more confused. According to current practices, what was required of Party members was also required of the masses. We rightists were not exempt either. The Chinese people have had more than enough of their share of conformity! I saw before me a life lived as an instrument, a tool. What dreariness, what monotony, what misery was in store for me!

But man is a complex animal. Even the invincible thoughts of Mao Zedong could not snuff out a man's innate sense of right and wrong. As soon as the thunderous denunciations died down, another voice inside would softly ask, "Are you really guilty? Perhaps not."

I took a lot of books with me to the country. The *Complete Works of Belinski,* each volume as thick as a brick, and the equally heavy four volumes of *Russian Authors on the Writer and His Work.* All in the original. I pored over them, trying to find an answer to the question, Why is it that as soon as the revolution is over, literature is restricted to singing praises?

My ostensible submission was motivated in large part by my hope of casting off that rightist label and resuming normal work, and especially of freeing my wife and children from the degrading involvement with a rightist, to mend the wrong that I had done them. Of our group, I was considered the most extreme rightist, so it would be harder for me to win my way back to normalcy than for the others.

Actually, I did not act on my decision to commit myself to the Party's mandated program of reform and thus win an early exoneration. In my heart, I was defiant, I did not accept defeat, and I still believed in myself. After a day's hard work in the fields, I would read Tolstoy's *War and Peace* by the light of a little oil lamp. I also opened up a third window to the outside world—in that year, by making use of the breaks during work, I began to memorize an English-Japanese dictionary.

What really kept me from reforming my thought was not my own lack of sincerity, as I was often told, but the Central Committee of the Communist Party itself. It had condemned me and ordered me to reform, but its own colossal mistakes during that one year of the Great Leap Forward proved that I was not so wrong after all.

The various "highest directives" that were handed down during this momentous campaign insulted the common sense of the peasants. What were they to do with those orders—to increase the corn crop, to introduce the sweet potato, to plow deep and plant close—all carried to ridiculous lengths, and forced on them from on high? Pushing everyone into communes invaded the last inch of freedom in their lives—they had to give up their family plots and eat in the communal kitchens. Work points were abolished; everybody was paid the same—that is, if they were paid at all. My landlord Liu Erhai was assigned a "specialty," as it was called—haircutting. Thus the cave dwelling that I shared with him became a sort of club for the peasants. Every evening, as I leaned against the wall reading *War and Peace,* the peasants chattered around me. They commented on the long and short of the policies handed down to them, often complaining bitterly. They had no inhibitions at all about talking in front of me; in fact, once they even asked me to write a letter of protest in their name.

I had doubts that I should write it, but they trusted me more than the cadres, and clearly did not hold it against me that I was a rightist. So I wrote down their complaints—of the problems with the government directives to grow sweet potatoes in pursuit of high production figures, only to see them rot because they lacked proper storage facilities. Even the pigs could not eat them. They were forced to grow corn instead of the millet they liked. They hated the abolishment of the work-point system, and they disliked the communal dining room.

Absurdities abounded. There was no underground water in the mountain village, but orders came for a fountain to be set up on Main Street. The people rarely ever had a scrap of meat, but were ordered to carve out cave dwellings on the mountainsides to house a zoo containing tigers and lions. Their carefully tended terraced fields were destroyed to erect a miniature Summer Palace. Then, the entire work force was assigned the unprecedented task of making iron in makeshift backyard furnaces, while a harvest of corn was left to rot in the fields.

At the end of the year, the whole community paraded with gongs and cymbals and drums to a nearby town to celebrate the setting up of the communes. Each commune member was given a red envelope. When the envelope was opened at home, the contents fell out—a one-yuan banknote. That was the reward for one year's work.

That same night, back in our cave dwelling, my landlord took out his account book, with its record of the haircuts he had given, and pored over it inconsolably under a little oil lamp. He had long suspected that this record was a waste of time and that he would never see the money. I tried to give him what comfort I could. That night, I could not sleep. Listening to the moaning of the wind, I asked myself: "Is this the voice of the peasants?"

Between 1958 and 1960, I worked in three counties in Shanxi and Shandong and experienced firsthand the disastrous consequences of Mao's false hope of overtaking all the Western countries in the twinkling of an eye. The rural economy, just getting back on its feet after the war, was a shambles. The commune movement had taken the life blood of the peasants, while the three years of famine had drained them of their strength and taken tens of millions of lives.

In 1960, I spent the third year of my thought reform in Gaotang County in Shandong. As I entered the village where I had been assigned work, I came upon a scene of complete devastation. The wind swept through the village, a whirlwind of dust and sand. The whole place was littered with manure. The courtyards were filled with dirt, and there was not a soul in sight. It was like a ghost town. The peasants have lost interest in life, I thought to myself.

From 1959 onward, the starving peasants resorted to the only legal form of protest in China—a work slowdown—and they would continue to do this for the next thirty years. Every morning and every afternoon, as we set out to work collectively, we would sit down and chat for half an hour upon reaching the fields. After starting work, we often stood still, leaning on our hoes and chatting for another half-hour. Then when the regular break arrived, the peasants would take out their pipes and smoke for an hour. Time in China slipped away like that.

And from this universal lethargy and depression, the Chinese character has deteriorated into one of submission to order and hostility toward all initiative. Shandong Province had one of the highest rates of death from starvation. The survivors were so emaciated they had no energy to make love. Once in a while, a few women would get pregnant, but would soon start menstruating again. The peasants said, "The fetus has dissolved itself"; but what really happened was that it was aborted spontaneously due to lack of nutrition. The great wave of stealing was in full swing. Peasants stole public property, from the state or the collective, which was their way of revolting against the state.

The cadres sent down from the cities suffered terribly. As for myself, both my legs were swollen. I was so weak I could hardly climb a slope; every step seemed to drain my last drop of energy. I was preoccupied by the problem of getting enough to eat, making me forget all shame. I stole half-ripe tomatoes from the vine. Dragging a manure cart through the streets, I could not resist spending the few cents and coupons I had to buy myself a bit of stale pastry, although I knew that I was taking this from the mouths of my children. I discovered that only a thin line divided man from beast, a line that could be crossed with only one step.

Faced with this widespread famine and high death tolls, the Chinese Communist Party decided to retrench; a policy was implemented that was more suitable to the level of production at that time. There was also a loosening of politics and ideology. Those labeled as "right opportunists" in 1959 for opposing Mao's policies were being rehabilitated. And for a short while, in the province of Anhui, rightists were also being screened for rehabilitation. About one-third of the rightists in that province had their cases reversed. The matter was brought to Mao's attention, however, and he laid down the iron rule: "There are no grounds for the rehabilitation of rightists," and thus the matter was brought to an end. What was even worse, those who had been requested to apply for rehabilitation were convicted of "trying to overturn their verdict" and were therefore found doubly guilty.

chapter eight

Agony

There is a saying in Chinese that "festivals sharpen the longing for family." The Lunar New Year is the most important festival in China. In 1959, we rightists spent the Lunar New Year tortured by separation and longing. The non-rightists among us, the wholesome comrades, left before the New Year for family reunions. We rightists, who were scattered throughout the countryside, not only suffered from separation but were beset by a thousand sad thoughts. This was not an ordinary separation; I was being treated like a criminal. What were my wife and children thinking? Almost a year had passed since we had last seen each other; I was truly guilty only insofar as they were concerned. I knew my wife would be putting on a forced gaiety to cheer up the children. It was a sad New Year, and looking toward the future, I wondered how many more such New Years there were in store for me.

The bachelor with whom I was boarding, Liu Erhai, had already shared several meals of noodles with me, and generously scooped up the last remains of his precious flour to make dumplings stuffed with minced lamb and carrots. That was our New Year feast. He even managed to procure some wine. He talked to me incessantly, trying to keep up my spirits. I tried not to disappoint him, but I just couldn't bring myself to match his mood.

I had been designated an extreme rightist, so my monthly stipend was barely enough to keep me alive. Furthermore, I was completely discredited in people's eyes through remorseless vilification at meetings and in the press. But in one sense, I gained from this. I distanced myself from the other rightists. I absolutely gave up all hope of the future and threw my lot in with the peasants. Thus during the Great Leap Forward, when the papers were predicting the amount of meat, milk, and fruit available to every peasant in the near future, I assumed that that would be my share as well. With them, I deplored the decrease in their income since the elimination of the work-point system. With them, I lamented the imposition of the common dining rooms where it was proclaimed the famished would "swell out their bellies and eat their full." With them, I grieved for the crops left rotting in the fields while everyone was ordered to make iron in back-yard furnaces.

By this time, I understood their dialect, and they could follow me when I spoke. My status as a rightist earned me their sympathy; they treated me like one of them. They spoke openly in front of me and even made bawdy jokes. I learned that the peasants were not really confined by traditional concepts of behavior. They had a free-and-easy attitude toward sex.

After the New Year, we rightists were suddenly ordered to return to Beijing. The peasants were glad for us, but they also regretted my leaving. To my surprise, many people came to see me off at my cave dwelling; they brought me presents—boiled eggs, already quite a rarity by then. I was very touched by the sincerity of their good wishes.

During my brief holiday in Beijing, I had no time to relax. Like a soldier just back from the front, I had to get myself in shape for new combat. In meetings, I had to sum up all my progress during the year's thought reform and discuss and develop new plans for the future. Actually, we had gone through all this before, but there was no harm in repetition, I suppose, as such meetings continued to be held at regular intervals.

The procedure was as follows: first, you made a self-confession. Then the others in the group had a go at you, and could criticize you or even expose anything you had failed to mention. As far as the individual speakers were concerned, you could not say that they were insincere—yet it was still play-acting, to a certain degree. All in all, this type of criticism and exposure was a hoax from beginning to end. The whole matter was the greatest violation of justice since the founding of the People's Republic. These people had acted out of patriotism, they had been encouraged by the chairman of the Party, Mao Zedong himself, to speak up, and they had spoken the truth. But by a perversity of circumstances, they were now treated as criminals to be spat upon. And now by order of the revolution they were indeed lying. They had put on a mask: in their hearts, they knew they were innocent, but they had to go on repeating how bad they were and throw themselves into the thought-reform process; they outdid each other in the harshness of their self-criticism and the criticism of each other. Some cried while making their self-criticism. If one could have analyzed those tears chemically, I think the result would have been 50 percent tears of self-pity, 25 percent tears of despair over being labeled rightists, and the remaining 25 percent tears of remorse.

Actually, my fellow rightists should have deemed themselves lucky for having me among them. I was the arch-rightist, the one who was least reformed and furthest removed from any hope of exoneration. To the extent that I was the chief culprit, my fellow rightists' situations were ameliorated. If they were not properly reformed, well, so much less was I; if they confessed to harboring illusions about the future, well, so much more did I, though actually I had none at all. As everybody confessed to fearing hardships in the countryside, I of course feared them more. At the summing-up, everyone acted a part. You couldn't say they were lying. They all used trite political terms to criticize each other, but the criticism could still hurt.

Of the criticism leveled at me during those sessions in 1959, I only remember one accusation that really hurt.

Two fellow rightists and I had gone to the kindergarten to visit our children. My own two appeared, and stood on either side of me. How I longed to embrace them, my darlings! But they stood there stonily, looking away from me, as if they feared my presence or wanted to distance themselves from me. I could not hold back the tears. I felt guilty in front of them. I knew they must have suffered from discrimination.

At my summing-up sessions, someone actually asked why I had cried when I saw my children. Was it out of hatred for the Party? I refused to answer that question.

My own misfortune affected everybody connected with me, first and foremost my wife and children. But what they actually suffered I will never know. In our brief meetings, Zhu Hong never mentioned these things. As for my children, I thought they would understand their suffering better when they grew up and looked back on their childhood. Although I had to keep repeating my crimes to the Party, I only felt guilty in front of my wife and children.

China had moved forward, for one man's crime no longer implicated his kith and kin to the ninth degree, and his entire family was not beheaded with him. But what about the mental torture and spiritual oppression that left no one untouched?

Consider, for example, the problem of joining the Party. Following liberation, it was considered an honor and a sign of raised consciousness to join the Party. Even people who did not seek office, such as members of the intelligentsia, aspired to join the Party. To be rejected by the Party reflected badly on one's political standing. That was why an honored few were posthumously honored with the title of Party member. That was why many members of the intelligentsia kept applying and handing in reports on their ideological progress month after month, year after year. Preposterous as it may sound, the title of Party member had become an end in itself. It was the norm at the time. It was also a form of discrimination against the families of rightists. My wife, Zhu Hong, was a professionally ambitious woman with an awareness of her worth. Since the early fifties, she had applied for Party membership. But the Party had strict rules about one's family background and overseas ties, and thus her application had been shelved. As a result of my label, her chances of joining the Party were gone for good.

At the time, she was already a middle-ranking cadre on the editorial staff of *Young Vanguard.* Everybody at that level was a Party member except her. Given her abilities and her dedication to work, she could have gone far, had I not stood in her way. Moreover, she was continually asked to expose me and reveal my inner thoughts. In 1957, she had sympathized with me and was thus guilty of "not drawing a line" between herself and the "class enemy." To make amends for that offense, she had to make extra efforts to criticize and expose me. But she loved me; how could she satisfy all their demands?

I was tortured with all these thoughts during the three years of my reform in the countryside. I realized that when misfortune was shared by loved ones, that pain was not decreased by half but doubled for both.

In the spring of 1961, I was returned to Beijing, where I was to cart night soil from the city to a farm run by *China Youth News.* I would drag a two-wheeled cart with a big wooden tub into the city by the Dongzhi Gate. I would leave the cart and container in the yard of our office building and go home. Early the next morning, I would go and open the lids to all the sewage pits in the precincts of our work unit and the surrounding area, ladle out the contents into the empty tub on my cart. After filling it, I would drag the cart with its six-hundred-pound load back to the farm.

Carting manure was the worst job on the farm. I didn't resent having to do it, but the smell always stayed with me. I would change my clothes the minute I got home, but the smell still clung to me. I was afraid that this would bother Zhu Hong, but she didn't seem to mind. She was glad that I could come home oftener with this job. When my children came back from school, they would see father sitting at home. The atmosphere in our family improved.

Gradually I learned the truth about our finances. The one thousand yuan that we had had in the bank in 1957 was gone. Zhu Hong was supporting a family of five, not including me—herself, our two children, and the two daughters of my elder sister, who were attending middle school. At holidays, money also had to be sent to my father in the Northeast. Zhu Hong had cut expenses to the minimum. Clothes for the children and stockings for the whole family kept her forever mending and sewing. All the same, she was second to none in her work; she worked overtime, and even worked when she was ill, but she got no acknowledgment in return. And all because of me. At night when the children were asleep, she must have shed countless tears for the slights and insults she had suffered during the day or for having to criticize me against her will.

Zhu Hong also had to cope with the problem of feeding us during those years of scarcity. At the time, all families with an average income bought high-priced pastries and candies to compensate for the deficiency in basic nutrition. Our neighbor would buy a leg of lamb on the free market every few days. But our family had only the regular allowances to keep going. Every Sunday morning, Zhu Hong would hand out to each of us a piece of the coarse cake made from our monthly ration, always leaving an extra piece on my plate, since I was doing heavy manual labor. I found it hard to swallow.

Zhu Hong was never harsh with the children. Only once did she hit our son Dahong. Egged on by his classmates, he had taken some money lying on the table at home to buy expensive candy. She knew the boy was hungry and couldn't resist the temptation when all the other boys had such candies in their pockets. She didn't mind the five yuan, although that was a considerable sum for our family. She was strict about the children's education, especially after my misfortune. She didn't want them to make any more "mistakes."

As our son grew up, he also began to bear insults on my account. Once I heard him quarreling with some neighborhood children. Another boy said, "Your father is a rightist," and my son was effectively silenced.

In the fall of 1961, thought reform of rightists came to an end, and we were allowed to go back to our work units.

I was assigned to the files of the international section of our paper. My job was to cut clippings from the papers, classify them, and take care of the library. The foreign-language papers were also in my charge. Sometimes I was asked to translate certain articles from Russian, Japanese, or

English-language papers to be published in *China Youth News*.

With economic problems looming larger and larger, political tensions relaxed. Thus the distinctions between rightists and regular comrades faded. We began to be treated like human beings again; the artificial label began to lose its hold. Two former rightists were actually named heads of departments. One of the two was elected model worker, and his enlarged photo was hung in the hall of the Youth League Central. My colleagues at the international section were friendly toward me; two of them asked me to teach them Russian.

But this new openness also had its problems. People would forget that I was still labeled a rightist, and would ask me to meetings that I had no right to attend. Sometimes, an alert comrade would discover this alien among "wholesome" comrades and suddenly shout: "Liu Binyan, leave at once!" And I would have to make my way to the door under dozens or even hundreds of pairs of eyes. I still remember the humiliation on those occasions; after all these years, I can still feel it.

On the last day of December 1961, I was leaving work for the day and walking down the stairs when I saw a big poster on the wall. It read: "According to a decision of the Party Committee of the Youth League Central, the rightist label has been removed from the following comrades," followed by a list of names. My heart pounded wildly. My eyes swept over the list of names. My heart nearly stopped beating. I went over the list again. No, my name was not there. All the others were on the list. I was the only exception.

That piece of paper was like a ball of fire, which seemed to scorch me. I rushed away in a daze. I left the building, walked across the yard into the familiar streets, not knowing where I was going.

How could I go home and tell the news to my wife? She had been waiting for the day to come when we would no longer be pariahs. She had been waiting for four years. Until that time, twelve of us had borne the "rightist" label, but from then on, I would have to carry the burden alone. The political pressure on her shoulders would be multiplied a dozen times. How could I account for this; what words of comfort could I offer her?

Neither of us was prepared for such a blow. The Youth League Central and the leading cadres of *China Youth News* had more than once expressed satisfaction with my thought-reform performance and hinted that the day of my deliverance was not far off.

Had I known that across the country there were tens of thousands of rightists still bearing the detested label until 1978 or even 1979, I might not have been so staggered. But during the last night of 1961, I had only one thought: Of the entire *China Youth News* staff, there is only a single rightist, and that is you!

This thought haunted me for a long time. I couldn't find out why I had not been rehabilitated. Party leaders at the Youth League Central and *China Youth News* gave evasive answers when I asked for an explanation.

I would often wake up in the middle of the night, seized by the thought that I was the only one, the only remaining rightist. Next, my thoughts would drift to my wife by me, then to the children in the next room. For the last four years I had felt guilty towards them. My guilt would keep on accumulating as time passed. I knew that this was something I could not change, but I couldn't keep my thoughts off the problem. I even began losing my hair; bald patches appeared here and there on my head.

During the day, I went to work as usual, silently clipping newspapers, silently performing any manual-labor assignments in the international section. Invariably, the "wholesome" comrades would be unavailable for these assignments, and I would be given the tasks instead; sometimes they were indispensable for the work on hand, though not always. In any event there I was, the only one who could never refuse an order.

The beginning of 1962 saw a glimmer of hope for China. At the time, I did not know of the meeting of seven thousand leading cadres in late January, and that at the meeting Mao Zedong had acknowledged his mistake that had led to the famine in the wake of the 1958 Great Leap Forward and the People's Commune movement. I also did not know that all the cadres above the seventeenth level of Party membership were undergoing special training, actually to review the mistakes of the Party since 1958 and speak their minds.

I attended a gathering to hear a tape recording of a speech given by Politburo member Chen Yi ; I had been invited by someone who had forgotten my rightist identity. Only then did I get some inkling of the change in the political climate. Speaking at a meeting in Guangdong on problems in drama, Chen Yi called for an end to the "hat-and-stick" policy with respect to intellectuals—that is, putting incriminatory labels on them like duncecaps or bludgeoning them with critical attacks. He said issues of art and literature should be discussed freely. He also announced that from then on, members of the intelligentsia should be "unhatted" and "crowned"—in other words, divested of the universally applied stigma of "bourgeois intellectuals" and crowned with the title of "proletarian intellectuals."

I was beside myself with joy. Soon the *People's Daily* published an editorial stating that "art and literature should serve all the people" and not just "workers, peasants, and soldiers" according to the old formulation. *People's Literature* published a short story by Wang Meng, and *China Youth News* published another by Fan Zhi; both former rightists, they had already been unhatted of course, but it was still a sign of change. This made me think of my own future: once I was unhatted, could I begin writing again? I pondered the question from all angles and decided against it. My name stank with all the vilification that had been poured on it; I would carry the stigma all my life.

Once again, sticks of fried dough appeared on the streets of Beijing. The famine was over. Zhu Hong returned from business trips in the provinces and reported that food was now more plentiful in the markets.

And then Mao decided to tighten the reins of "class struggle" once again. The Chinese people summed it up as follows: "Whenever you get your belly filled, another political campaign will overtake you."

The struggle against the revisionists was directed against Khrushchev and the Soviet Union. It was also directed against the so-called bourgeoisie. Hadn't the bourgeoisie been eliminated as a class seven years before? Well, that was not enough. It still existed in people's heads. And, in any case, during the three years of famine, bourgeois revisionism had resurfaced.

Once again my rightist label was overlooked, and I was able to attend the reading of a document about the launching of the "five-anti" campaign, aimed at repelling the attack of the bourgeoisie. One example of this attack caught my attention during the reading: two young girls in the Xuanwumen district of Beijing could not find employment after finishing middle school. So they banded together with a few other jobless young people and started a copying workshop for a living. This was branded as an "evil underground factory, an attempt to restore capitalism." I trembled for the fate of these poor young people. How could this be considered capitalism?

I didn't pursue the issue, however, for I had been cut off from the world too long. The papers were flooded with articles condemning Soviet revisionism and extolling what the masses could learn from emulating such model figures as Lei Feng and Wang Jie, both young soldiers. These two campaigns converged and focused on one theme—"revolutionization." The demands of the campaigns could be summed up as follows: suppress all desires, resist all nonproletarian culture, uphold the tenets of "fear no hardship, fear no death," and live a politically saturated life.

I was intrigued by this propaganda. Thinking back, one couldn't help but admire Mao's astuteness. He knew that once the people were mindlessly geared to revolution and political struggle, they could be manipulated at will, and the press was a willing tool in this process. But I did have my doubts. For instance, the papers said that the peasants were "tilling the soil for the revolution." I had lived in the country for four years, and as far as I could tell, the peasants had lost all interest in living, not to mention making revolution.

During the Lunar New Year festival in 1963, the Chinese Writers' Association held an evening party. Nothing terrible happened; the women simply dressed up, and the lights dimmed during the dancing. A poet with more than the usual share of political vigilance was alerted at once. In a letter to Mao, he reported on the affair, adding that in his judgment the Writers' Association was steeped in revisionism. In reply, Mao scrawled out these words across the letter: "Another step and the Writers' Association will have degenerated into a Petőfi Club," as if it were on the brink of a counterrevolutionary uprising. This effectively ignited the antirevisionist campaign in artistic and literary circles, which continued right up to the outbreak of the Cultural Revolution.

In 1964, a deputy editor-in-chief of *China Youth News* was about to leave for another job. Before he left, I called on him and asked him what was preventing my rightist label from being removed. I imagine he was touched by my earnestness and hinted at the true reason. He said that my problem was not in the hands of *China Youth News,* and not even of the Youth League Central. He hinted that the resolution of my case was being held up somewhere in the Central Committee of the Party. That was as far as he went. Only then did I realize that whether I was ever unhatted or not did not depend on my own performance. Perhaps it was imperative to retain a few die-hard rightists as a justification for the movement.

Finally, though, in February 1966, a secretary of the Youth League Central came to our office for a meeting. We ran into each other afterward, and he passed on the news that my rightist label would soon be removed.

I rushed home and told my wife the news. We had waited so long. Of the past nine years, this was the best day in our lives. Late that night, Zhu Hong said: "Our poor children have suffered so much! When your problem is solved, let's start another baby and call him Xin [new]. We'll have a new beginning. And our new baby will never be allowed to suffer like that."

That year I was forty-one years old, but I felt that I was already old. The following March, however, when my rightist label was officially removed, I felt myself grow young again. My heart sang as I rode on my bike through the streets and alleys of Beijing on my way to the Institute of International Studies, an official letter of recommendation in my pocket. All my pent-up energies were wakened and struggled for release. But when I really thought about it, I realized that I was merely being given the right to return to normal life. Actually, I was not even given that, for I was an unhatted rightist. Even if the rightist tag had been removed without a trace, I still had lost my Party membership. And in the China of those days, you were not a complete man without membership in the Party. So why, I asked myself, was I rejoicing? Under such circumstances, I suppose I was easily satisfied. In the spring of that same year, *China Youth News* organized an outing to the Summer Palace. Fortunately, my younger sister, who worked in Shenyang, was in Beijing on a business trip, so our whole family went along. In the soothing warmth of early spring, my children seemed so lovely. The cloud over my wife's face had disappeared. We took many pictures that day; we wanted to capture that spring and keep it with us always.

But that spring was short-lived. How could I have known that fate had lifted my spirits, only to dash me to the ground?

chapter nine

Drained of the Milk of Human Kindness

Every evening after I left work, a woman Communist Party member sitting opposite me would open a drawer in my desk, take out the three volumes of diaries written during my years in the country, nearly a decade earlier, and copy them. One morning in early June 1966, I walked into the office building to see a whole wall plastered with big-character posters and a huge title reading: "Liu Binyan has not retreated from his anti-Party stand!" My diary accounts of problems arising from the Great Leap Forward and the policy of communalization were, at the time of writing, all part of my own thought-reform program. Now they were being made public and used as proof of my anti-Party stand.

I was shocked into immobility. This blow was even more surprising than the one in 1957. At that time, I had already had a premonition that disaster awaited me. But now, during the early stages of the Cultural Revolution, Wu Han, Deng Tuo, and company initially seemed to be the exclusive targets. By no stretch of the imagination could I have foreseen that they would pick on me, a political corpse of nine years' standing. Only three months before, I had been declared acceptable by the authorities.

I realized at once that this was a premeditated move on the part of the leadership, but I couldn't understand it. All I knew was that I was perfectly innocent. The offending quotations on the big-character posters were all taken from my diaries of long ago, when I had wrestled with my own thoughts to convince myself of my mistakes. "This is despicable," I said to myself. But I was completely helpless and could do nothing but wait for the iron fist of the Party to come down on my head.

Further "exposures" in the big-character posters revealed the true extent of the plot. The fact was that the Cultural Revolution, unlike all other campaigns, had not been a policy decided upon by the full leadership, but had been launched by Mao, with the knowledge of only a few close associates. Nobody knew what he had up his sleeve. The leadership at the Youth League Central, sensing that their own positions were endangered, decided to act fast, and picked out their targets. They made out a list of fifteen people among the *China Youth News* editorial staff as the first group of victims, or in their words, "targets of the revolution." Most of the fifteen had been, in 1957, labeled rightists or semi-rightists who had managed to escape the ultimate label. Foremost among this group was the former deputy editor-in-chief Zhong Peizhang (who had been labeled a rightist in 1958). I was also one of this first group.

Since 1957, I had thought that I was the lowest of the low, that I couldn't sink any lower. But the first few days of June 1966 dispelled these illusions.

Again I was deprived of freedom and ordered to confess my sins. In the international section, staff members met to develop a plan of attack. In the neighboring office, big-character posters were being made.

I knew that I was perfectly innocent; even so, the tense atmosphere, the rustling of paper in the next room sent chills through my heart. I knew that this time, the attack would be more merciless than the preceding one. The less righteous the cause, the more ferocious the attack.

At last, I was summoned to stand trial. To mark the change in my status, even my name was pronounced with a vicious twist.

Seven of my colleagues sat behind their desks in that all too familiar room. There I was, standing in the middle of the room, one accused facing seven judges. Judging from the political history and personal character of the presiding judge, I knew I was lost. This was a great chance for him to prove himself at my expense. Over the years, the expression on his face and the tilt of his voice had always shifted with the changing winds. Just as I had foreseen, he began the interrogation with a resounding bang on the table. "Liu Binyan!" he shouted. "Off with your mask! Confess your recent anti-Party, antisocialist activities!"

I kept my head and said: "Since 1957, I have not committed any such crimes. Otherwise, the Youth League Central would not have unhatted me."

At this, a shrill female voice screamed at me: "Wretched rightist Liu Binyan! Don't go deluding yourself! Don't think you can cheat us! We know all your tricks!"

I answered, "You have decided that I was qualified to be unhatted. Without the agreement of all of you present here, the Youth League Central could not have made the decision." In my heart, I wondered at the ferocity of the woman. Unlike the presiding judge, she was not a political activist. We lived in the same compound and were on friendly terms. There was no reason for her to make such a display of animosity. She was further incensed at my reply: "Don't try to be too clever! We all know someone was protecting you. Unhatted, indeed! Just you wait and see! If you go on in this way, you'll be smashed to smithereens!" And so it went on.

All seven ranted and raved, but I could see through them perfectly. One of the other women shouting at me was applying for Party membership, but was dragged down by a bad family background and a rightist husband. Another editor had a mother who had studied in the United States and a father of questionable background. His extremist attitude was understandable. But another young woman, just demobilized from the army, who had previously seemed quite extremist, was quite moderate compared to the other two. Another woman, the wife of a rightist, was also more restrained than the rest.

The interrogation dragged on. They had proof of nothing, but I was put into the enemy category all the same. This was the way the dictatorship of the proletariat worked. Finally, they laid down a few rules that I was to follow and sent me home to think over my sins.

Later, I was ordered to hand over my diary. Not satisfied with that, they came again and took away all my bulky notebooks, as well as my newspaper clippings about the Soviet Union. And later still, two men came to my house and took away all the letters I had accumulated since the fifties. Luckily, I had already torn out a few pages that could have been used against me. Meanwhile, the siege of big-character posters continued, just a lot of bluff and bluster.

With the beginning of the Cultural Revolution, all the rightists on the staff of *China Youth News,* whether unlabeled or not, were grouped into a labor gang. The men in leadership positions at the time had planned to convict the fifteen of us as counterrevolutionaries and make us the main target of the Cultural Revolution. Before they could accomplish this, however, they themselves were toppled from power, and the Red Guards had taken over their unfinished work. In August 1966, it was decided that I was to be relabeled a rightist and assigned to labor under surveillance.

My relabeling was to take place in the big mess hall, where I had first been accused. On that occasion, my wife had been sitting in the audience; this time, in addition to my wife, my thirteen-year-old son was in the crowd. He had walked in with a couple of friends to see what all the excitement was about, just in time to see his father publicly disgraced. On both occasions, my family had to witness my disgrace, which made it all the more painful.

My son was in a quandary. To prove himself a true Red Guard, he had to make a clean break with his father. Egged on by his companions, he made a black label with the words "rightist element Liu Binyan"; most "bad elements" had to wear such labels over their chests. But my son could not stifle his natural feelings for his father. He couldn't bring himself to pin that label on my chest, and instead he simply ended by putting a notice over the door, "Liu Binyan, confess your offenses, go to work and return on time, be on your good behavior."

My twelve-year-old daughter joined the neighborhood children's Red Guard group and ran about happily for the first few days. But one night I came back home and found her in tears. I asked her what was the matter. She told me between sobs that she had been discharged from the Red Guards because her father was a rightist. I grieved with her, although I knew very well that the red armband was completely worthless.

The attack on me also affected Zhu Hong. She resisted pressure from her own unit, the editorial staff of *Young Vanguard*, for a few days, keeping an obstinate silence, but finally she had to give in. She had to write a big-character poster, ordering me to confess my sins, and that was the end of it.

After I had been unhatted, my father had come to stay with us in Beijing. Who would have thought that a few days after he arrived, the Cultural Revolution would begin? We kept things from him, and he didn't see through our forced gaiety. But then my salary was stopped; we were in financial straits and had to send him back.

I was a main target of the Cultural Revolution from the very beginning, but I developed an interest in it not at all in keeping with my own circumstances. Although the ultra-leftist turn of its ideology repelled me, its attack on bureaucratism, corruption, and special privileges within the Party seemed to point to a road of regeneration for China.

The "wiping away of the four olds" campaign of 1966 was in full swing in the streets and alleys of Beijing. This campaign was directed against obsolete ideas, culture, customs, and habits. I learned of many incidents through the conversations of the typesetters during the lunch break. The

Red Guards arrested anybody who had been an official of the old regime, a landlord, a capitalist, a remnant of the imperial dynasty, a collaborator with the Japanese, or a brothel owner—in other words, anybody who had a stain on his or her history and had paid for it. Then they went after everybody who had been working loyally for the new regime but was now classed as being in one of the "three privileged categories" (defined on the basis of fame and income), chiefly artists and writers. The Red Guards dragged these people from their homes, hung signs proclaiming their offenses over them, made them kneel in public, and paraded them along the streets. Then they ransacked their dwellings, took all the valuables they could lay hands on, and destroyed their precious scrolls of inscriptions, calligraphy, and painting. Some of the victims could not bear the humiliation; others could not stand the endless torture and took their own lives. I heard one worker ask another whether he had passed by the moat. He said there were so many corpses that the water was backed up.

Being a "class enemy," I was of course not qualified to join a group, or put up big-character posters, but I would often roam around the main streets of Beijing and the campus of Beijing Normal University to read the posters on their walls. As far as my means allowed, I would buy the papers published by the various groups. In other words, I followed the situation closely. I hailed the publication of the article by the student Yu Luoke that refuted the theory of judging people by their class background, and I mourned his later execution. I was intrigued by the rise and fall of the ideologues of the Cultural Revolution—Guan Feng, Wang Li, and Qi Benyu—but frankly, I did not concern myself with the power struggle at the top, or the fates of the toppled senior cadres. The question that occupied my thoughts was how the fact that the masses of the people were now enjoying unprecedented freedom would affect the political life of the society as a whole. I expected and hoped it would bring about democracy.

What I actually saw, however, was unprecedented confusion, infighting, and mass killings. Furthermore, I knew that what I saw was but a fraction of the whole situation, and it was frightful. The army, intervening in the infighting and siding with one faction against another, was a crucial factor, of course. I also think that factions within the army had an excellent knowledge of how to manipulate the unarmed crowd by appealing to the worst traits in the Chinese character. The masses were divided into groups, all evoking the name and teaching of Mao, and fell to fighting each other in the bid for power.

I was puzzled. How was it that these young people, who had never seen
a fascist face to face or gone through a war, could be so ruthless? There
was only one possible answer, and that was the cumulative result of all the
indoctrination and practices of class struggle that had been conducted
since 1949.

As the Cultural Revolution progressed, the staffs of *China Youth News*
and *Young Vanguard* grouped under the banner "Kindling Spark," and
the workers in the printing section grouped under the banner "Revolutionary Team." By this time, both sides had lost interest in us, long
overthrown, and directed their attention to the live targets, the
"capitalist-roaders." So after the work of the day was done—cleaning the
building and the latrines—I was free to get on my bike and go down to
Wangfujing Street to look at the big-character posters along the streets,
and to buy the newspapers printed by various revolutionary groups all over
the country.

During the summer and fall of 1966, group after group of Red Guards
would stomp into the courtyard of our offices and "struggle" against the
capitalist-roaders. I was sometimes dragged in to play a supportive role,
standing beside the main culprits. To avoid that humiliation, I often
escaped into the file room and locked myself in. From the window I could
see what was going on in the courtyard. Those young people were not
necessarily bullies and hooligans. Sometimes they would hold a debate with
the heads of our newspaper. Their spirit of rebellion, self-assertiveness, and
critical acumen made me think of my own youth. That was the same spirit
in which I had entered the Community Party. But for the last dozen years,
the Communist Party had used every means in its power to stifle that spirit
until the Party itself finally became the target of that kind of critical spirit.

Mao's call to oppose the "reactionary bourgeois line" and his assertion
of the right to rebel mobilized a group of people who had always been
victimized by the authorities in past political campaigns. They were the
people who had always been repressed because of their political views,
family background, or other reasons. But now, political organizations,
pamphlets, and papers had sprung up all over the country, giving people
a sense of political liberty and freedom of speech for the first time since
1949. They flaunted Mao's revolutionary line, but they were actually
attacking Mao's longstanding policy of suppressing democracy and upholding inner Party privileges. Posters all over the country exposed the mistakes
and dark side of the Party. Even secret documents and details of Mao's
private life were made public. For the first time, the Chinese people had

a look inside the workings of the Party. Its veil of sanctity was torn apart. Some rightists clamored for a reversal of their verdicts. Some even went so far as to establish their own organization and start their own paper.

In the month of June 1968, I was sent to the farm and held in detention in the "cowshed"—a small, crude hut for the worst offenders—for further investigation: in addition to being a rightist, I was now suspected of being a Soviet spy and renegade of the Party, the latter because it was mistakenly thought that I had once been arrested. The inmates of the cowshed came from two backgrounds. One group had been politically discriminated against and suppressed since the 1950s; the other was the handful of men in power who were directly responsible for their discrimination and suppression. But both groups were equal before the Cultural Revolution. They were herded together like cattle and chased hither and thither to attend endless struggle sessions; each was allotted a small, square table on which to write his confession. They were ordered to stand together in front of Mao's image every morning and every night to show contrition for their sins, and to recite Mao's quotations; they were punished if they made a mistake.

These people were divided into two new categories—those who could go home for the night and those who couldn't. I was one of those forbidden to go home even on Sundays and holidays. That lasted a year; then I would be sent to Henan Province, to spend eight years planting rice, making adobe bricks, and raising pigs.

For twenty-two years I was labeled a "rightist." Compared to those who were hounded to death, were sentenced to long jail terms, or saw their families broken up, I was lucky. The greatest damage done to me was the loss of twenty-two years of my life and the psychological scar left by prolonged humiliation. Looking back, I realize that I was not brooding over my own condition all the time; that was clearly not possible. But I was preoccupied with a sense of humiliation, silently reminding me that I was the lowest of the low, that I had injured my wife and children, that I had no hope of exoneration in this life.

Over the years, people were gradually sent back to normal work, but not I. As late as 1977, not even the translating of chemical-engineering manuals could be entrusted to a man named Liu Binyan.

During the winter of 1968, I was in the depths of despair. The whole country was engulfed in factional wars; many of the best of China's youth had been killed or had died under torture. My own future lay in complete darkness. I had lost personal liberty, and was tormented by daily humiliation. I suffered from insomnia and lost over twenty-five pounds.

Every morning I had to clean the office building housing *China Young Vanguard.* I often walked to the top of the building and looked east, where my home was. I longed for my children. On the day I had been ordered to the cowshed for further investigation, my son and daughter had seen me off. It was raining, and my daughter was crying. She was afraid that we would never see each other again. Where were they at this moment, and what were they thinking of? And my wife, who was working in the building where I was standing—did she still believe in my innocence?

For the first time in my life I thought of death. Ten years before, I had gone on living with the hope of a better life. But now, although I still clung to my wife and children, I had lost all pleasure in living, all hope for the future. But if I were to die without my name being cleared, it would be harder for them. Two of the inmates of the cowshed had already tried to kill themselves—one had broken his leg, and the other had ruined all his teeth. Eventually I gave up the idea of ending my life by my own hand.

In April 1969, I was given seven days off to go home and prepare myself for the May Seventh Cadre School in Henan, where the staffs of our papers were to go for reeducation.

After an entire year of investigation, the authorities had still not made up their minds whether I was or was not a renegade of the Party or a Soviet spy. At that time, political considerations outweighed everything else in the world, so much so that it was stifling. I was a husband and a father who might, or might not, be an enemy to his own family. Under these strange and strained circumstances, I met with my family. We were all quite tense. The children had grown up, and the room seemed desolate.

My wife Zhu Hong's role was the most difficult. Although she may have had some halfhearted doubts about my being entirely innocent of the accusations against me, still she was much too mature to give in to those doubts. How should she talk to the children about their father? It was hard. I realized that this time my daughter would not cry as much as she had when I left nine months ago.

My wife was to go with her work unit to the cadre school; she decided to take our son with her to keep him from acquiring bad habits during the social unrest. We decided our daughter would stay on in Beijing and attend middle school. We had to pack clothes to last the year. Our finances were strained to the utmost. Even Zhu Hong, who had lived on so little over the years, was at a loss. We had to cut up the mattress covering to make padded clothing for winter.

As we said our final farewells in Beijing, the workers and editors in power did not forgo their last chance to humiliate us. We who were targets of the revolutionary dictatorship were put in one end of the train. When my son came over to give me a message from my wife, who was in the front cars, he was rudely ordered away. The train was ready to leave when we were suddenly ordered out of the car. We were made to stand in line on the platform and listen to one last lecture. The routine was familiar, but on such an occasion, it was particularly galling. It was also an emotional trial for our families, who could not help but see us through the windows of their cars.

Our May Seventh Cadre School was located in Huang Chuan County, which is in the Xinyang district of Henan Province, five hundred miles south of Beijing. The area had formerly been grasslands used for grazing, but now the land had been converted to rice paddies without consideration for costs. So there they were, a thousand cadres being paid their full salaries, doing manual labor ten times less efficiently than rural laborers, who could have been hired for a fraction of the cost. This was Mao's idea of "paying dues" for the thought-reform of these cadres. At the same time, he had said that these people had been trained under an obsolete educational system and were perfectly useless.

At the cadre school, I lived and worked apart from the peasants; and even in my own working group, I was herded with others of my own kind in the cowshed reserved for "demons and monsters," and was thus cut off from my own colleagues. There were no books at the cadre school, and so these years were devoid of intellectual and literary stimulation. But even in this narrow world, I could feel how the pernicious political struggles had released all the baseness in human nature. Some of my longstanding colleagues at *China Youth News*, people who really knew me, changed their tune overnight. I was a handy tool for them: to prove their revolutionary zeal, to outdo their opponents in political mudslinging. Shouts, insults, banging on tables, and stamping of feet became part of the burden I had to bear; this became the means by which Party members demonstrated their class and Party loyalty, non-Party members demonstrated their solidarity with the Party as a steppingstone to membership, and those from bad social backgrounds demonstrated their change of class allegiance.

The capitalist-roaders left the cowshed one by one, while those of us who had been blacklisted remained targets of the proletarian dictatorship.

The members of the May Seventh Cadre School did not let go of the class struggle even in the midst of all the farm work. They had to weed out new class enemies while keeping tight rein on the old ones. There was no lack of excuses for holding struggle sessions against me. I had read the works of Marx and Engels; that was good enough reason for one session. I was asked, Why had I not read the works of Chairman Mao? And why had I read the Marxist classics in a Japanese edition? Once I happened to say, "Mankind is so helpless, we can't even get rid of mosquitoes!" That of course offered itself as another subject for a struggle session, at which I was reminded that "Our great leader Chairman Mao has taught us that the people, and only the people, are the motivating force."

By now, these struggle sessions had taken on the nature of performances. I could not refuse to attend, and I had no choice but to bow my head. But as far as confessing was concerned, I insisted on speaking the truth. Of course, all I got in return was a barrage of abuse—"Death and destruction to the class enemy" and so on—and the performance would be over. I was stripped of everything and had nothing to fear. Except for torture, they had run out of means to deal with me.

I had never been beaten or physically abused. But I know from experience that personal insult is worse than physical abuse and leaves a deeper scar.

I enjoyed a short respite only when I was with the peasants. They did not worry about political standards in dealing with people. Their sympathy for all the unfortunates like myself often moved me to tears. But the minute I was back among my own kind, it was another story.

During the entire course of the Cultural Revolution, the person who hurt me most was not an army representative or a leader of one of the revolutionary factions, who had all taken over power at different periods. It was an intellectual, a certain Jiang, an editor and painter, with two university degrees. I became the target of his sadistic attacks.

I remember an incident with several youngsters who came to stay with their parents during the holidays and shared our room. Once they asked me whether I thought that science-fiction novels, which were forbidden, would be permitted again. I answered that I thought they probably would. That same night, Jiang staged a struggle session against me in our room

and accused me of exposing the children's minds to "revisionist poison."
On another occasion, I saw some kids torturing a cat; they tried to scorch
her by holding her over the flames in an iron stove. I persuaded them to
let her go, saying, "Don't torment the poor animal." When Jiang got wind
of this, he staged another struggle session. He asked me what I meant by
torment and whether I was insinuating that the revolutionary masses were
tormenting me. From that incident, I realized that he had made those
children spy and report on me. He had also instigated another youngster
to pour black ink over my new mosquito net and write insulting words on
my bed sheet.

Jiang had a manly exterior. Through him I learned the truth of the
phrase, "Don't judge a man by his appearance." I discovered that a manly
form could house a mean and pitiable spirit.

Under such circumstances, a smile, a few words of kindness would bring
warmth to my heart. Once when I returned from work, I went to get my
quilt, which I had laid out under the sun. When I picked it up, a bank
note dropped from its folds, a brand-new ten-yuan note. What a godsend!
A few days before, I had had to borrow five yuan to go to the clinic in the
county seat. Who could have stuffed this money into the folds of my quilt?
My fellow sufferers in the cowshed guessed that it could only have been
my wife.

My wife and son and I were working at the same May Seventh Cadre
School, and often met each other on the road or while working, but we
were not allowed to speak to each other. My wife probably knew that I
was hard up and had quietly stuffed the money into my quilt. Seventeen
years later, I happened to mention the incident to her, and only then did
I discover it had not been she. Who, then, was my anonymous benefactor?
Apart from the inmates of the cowshed, I did not have a friend. In those
feverish days of class struggle, people were full of suspicions and grudges.
Who would have risked having compassion for me, an object of universal
contempt? It remains a riddle.

Those of us who were finally left in the cowshed were considered to be
the lowest of the low. Our group also included an old man, a former
Japanese collaborator, and a former Party member who had joined in the
early 1940s and had later been expelled for falling in love with a landlord's
daughter during land reform, and who therefore was repeatedly attacked.
But though we were continually insulted, we thought quite well of our-

selves and each other, and developed a bond of friendship that was to last. After we were released, every January, if I was in Beijing, we would get together and have a dinner at the old man's house. The friendship that developed among us then gave me a renewed strength and belief in my fellow man.

Sometimes there were moments of respite. We always had to clean up the cadres' offices, and we were able to read the "internal reference news," which contained some real information about the world. We discussed the news; indeed, we had no secrets from each other, and no fear that any of us would speak to the authorities about our own comments.

Once we were chatting, talking about the mole that was so prominently evident on Mao's face. The old collaborator smiled and said that he had one, too—on his bottom. And he took off his pants to show us. Unfortunately, our merriment was somehow overheard. Six or seven of the revolutionaries came to interrogate us, to figure out what had happened, and though they never quite figured it out, we were punished by having to stand for long periods reciting Mao's words from the Little Red Book.

Finally, even the representative of the army in charge of us affirmed that I should be "liberated." But instead, my colleagues, though they knew I was innocent, insisted that I was unregenerated, thus putting back by a whole year my restoration to freedom.

Six years passed by. In the spring of 1972 I was finally given back the status at *China Youth News* that I had held from March to June 1966, but I was stripped of my charge over the newspapers and magazines of the international section. All the ex-rightists, ex-counterrevolutionaries, and other "bad elements" had to stay on at the May Seventh Cadre School until all the "wholesome" comrades had been assigned to new jobs. None of us knew whether we would ever be given regular jobs again. And of those left behind I would be the last to be reassigned. Of one thing I was certain, my "unhatted rightist" label would stick to me to my dying day. I would not be allowed to write, and even if I were allowed to return to regular employment, it would be to some menial job in which I would not be permitted to comment on affairs of state.

Strangely, the minute I was released from the cowshed, my political and theoretical interests soared. Only my early teenage enthusiasm for politics and theory could compare to my renewed absorption with the subject. After work every day, in the heat of the summer night, I would sit in the dorm, take out my magnifying glass, and pore over the works of Marx, Engels, Hegel, Plekhanov, and Lenin, in search of answers. I asked myself how China had ended up in such an appalling situation. What had gone wrong? What role had Lin Biao, Jiang Qing, and ideological dictators such as Kang Sheng played in all this? How could China escape this impasse? I read the ancient book *Mirror for Rulers* looking for an answer.

What, exactly, were the connections between the theories of Lin Biao, Zhang Chunqiao, and Mao himself?

My whole body would be soaked in sweat in an hour's time. I would go outside and let the midnight breeze cool me down and then resume my studies. I shared that dorm with a dozen other men, who were absorbed in chess or poker. Only another young editor and I pursued our studies. Unlike me, he, however, was a young Communist Party member with a promising career ahead of him.

In 1975, the last dregs of the May Seventh Cadre School were finally allowed to return to Beijing to look for jobs, after Deng Xiaoping was rehabilitated. After twenty years of life as a pariah, I felt as if I were returning from the dead. I had some hope. Everything seemed new and exciting.

I got back on my old Hungarian bike, which I had bought in the early fifties, and went riding through the streets and lanes of Beijing, visiting with friends, assiduously collecting back-alley news, as if I were being paid to do so. At the time, rumor was rife; a new crisis seemed to be brewing. Deng Xiaoping bickered openly with Jiang Qing, Mao's wife. An American writer's biography of Jiang Qing had given Deng Xiaoping's associates the opportunity to attack her.

Then in September 1975 I heard that, after a period of silence, Jiang Qing had made an appearance at a model commune, Dazhai, claiming that Mao had expressed his sympathy for her. Having established backing from above, she went on to criticize those in the Politburo whom she referred to as Song Jiang–like figures (alluding to a character in the Chinese classical novel *Heroes of the Marshes*, which she meant as a veiled attack on the pragmatic Zhou Enlai), and vowed to combat their kind to the bitter end. The campaign to repulse the "right reversionist trend" followed closely thereafter, with Deng Xiaoping as the main target. The instigators were Jiang Qing and her three cohorts, the Gang of Four. I was terribly downcast by the news.

I passed that winter in deep dejection, but the spontaneous commemoration of the death of Zhou Enlai at Tiananmen Square raised my hopes again. It was evident that people were using the commemoration to express their dissatisfaction with Mao's policies and the Cultural Revolution. On April 2, 1976, I went to Tiananmen and witnessed that moving sight. People from all over China laid wreaths at the foot of the memorial for the heroes of the revolution in the middle of the square. I edged my way through the crowd, trying to have a look at the prose and verse had posted to the people eulogize Zhou and express their own feelings. Many people stood up to read their writings through loudspeakers, while those behind them took down their words. Others made impassioned speeches. I could not help but admire those courageous young people and regret that my days of political involvement had been cut short in 1957.

Of course, from the official point of view, the events in Tiananmen Square were totally unacceptable. It was the first time that the Chinese people had staged a mass protest movement on their own in contempt of the Party.

The Tiananmen Square demonstrations made me jubilant; they were the first sign of an awakening of the Chinese people in twenty-seven years. Mao's new call for a campaign to "criticize Deng" was slowed down, which was also an encouraging sign. For over twenty years, Mao had always been followed whenever he initiated a campaign, even if unwillingly. Now he had started this new campaign to "criticize Deng and repulse the rightist reversionary trend," but his words no longer worked. I viewed this as a new turn in China's history. The ticket sellers on the buses in Beijing cursed Jiang Qing loudly and freely, something that would have been absolutely unthinkable in the old days.

If it had not been for Zhu Hong's warnings, I would have gone to the square every day. It was said that the secret police were taking photos and videotapes of the activists down there, and so people like me had best be careful.

On April 5, Mao finally decided on an armed crackdown, the Tiananmen Square incident that shocked the nation.

Once again I was returned to the May Seventh Cadre School. It was a sad April for me. We were repeatedly required to clarify our position on the Tiananmen Square incident and on the movement to criticize Deng. I always managed to refrain from speaking until the time was up. But I did have to prepare a speech, evading the main issue myself, but quoting from some passages I had copied from *Red Flag* to comply with the requirements.

When would these dark ages come to an end? How would China emerge from this decade-long disaster? I racked my brains over the problem.

I was still at the May Seventh Cadre School when Mao's death was announced. We were all made to sit in solemn silence and listen to the broadcast. I shed no tears. I said to myself, "Dead at last! Without your death, China would have gone to pieces." As far as I know, many people had exactly the same reaction.

One month later, news filtered down that the Gang of Four had been toppled; this had the same impact on people as the great earthquake that had shaken parts of the country the previous summer. Nobody had foreseen that the downfall of the gang would follow so closely on the death of Mao. I felt that this was a time for celebration. At our group meeting, recalling the disaster that the gang had wrought on our country, I could not help but cry for the people who had died at their hands. Soon, I discovered that many Communist Party members, Party secretaries in particular, were on guard, preserving a cautious silence. It was also said that my words at the group meeting had been reported to the Party branch. The fact was that many people found it impossible to believe that the Gang of Four was really gone for good, and that the followers of the gang were not actually planning a comeback coup. Thus the wait-and-see attitude of the Party members was easily explained. It was also perfectly understandable that they would use a rightist, who had been unlabeled ten years before, as a target to practice their political vigilance. Nine months later, an article in *People's Daily* was distributed to the whole country through the Xinhua News Agency. The title of the article was "On the Two-Faced Reactionary Yao Wenyuan," and it denounced Liu Binyan the rightist by name in the same breath that it denounced Yao Wenyuan.

The article appeared simultaneously in all the major newspapers throughout the country. I was denounced as the "rightist Liu Binyan"; that is to say, my unlabeling was once again reversed. I seemed to come under nationwide attack every ten years. The first time was in 1957. The second time was in the mid-sixties, when Yao Wenyuan, in a long article "On the Two-Faced Reactionary Zhou Yang," listed the fact that he had shielded the rightist Liu Binyan among Zhou Yang's crimes. Ten years later, it was Yao Wenynan's turn to be denounced—and among the damning evidence of his two-facedness cited in the May 1977 article was the fact that Yao had a "high regard" for my writings. I never imagined that the cycle would be repeated again.

chapter ten

Return to
a Strange
World

In the autumn of 1978, word was going around Beijing that the rightists would see a change for the better, perhaps even official rehabilitation. There had been talk about this back in 1972, but nothing had come of it. Now again, this topic, which was so close to the hearts of us rightists, became the center of heated discussion. I, for one, believed that rehabilitation was probably on the agenda, but my guess was that even if only 10 percent were retained as rightists, I would be among them. After all, my case had been decided on by Mao Zedong himself, and it had been one of the most notorious cases. Rehabilitation for me would imply a virtual reversal of the whole campaign, and would even have cast doubt on Mao himself. Apparently the time was not yet ripe for that.

Nevertheless, I was as deeply engrossed as my more hopeful fellow victims and followed developments closely. There were rumors of a directive that circumspectly ordered a "correction" of "wrong decisions" in certain cases, but in practice, this would mean rehabilitating the great majority of rightists. I felt this was very likely; the guarded wording of the document was intended to appease those in the Party who were opposed to any of the rightists being rehabilitated. As I said, I realized that the odds were against me, but I still hoped against hope.

By early 1979, it was confirmed that I too would be rehabilitated. I assumed it was Hu Yaobang, then head of the Central Committee's Organization Department, who had put in a good word for me.

On January 24, I completed all the formalities with *China Youth News* for my rehabilitation. It was an ordinary, clear winter day; nothing about the day itself holds any special memories. But the date is now engraved in my memory, because eight years later, to the day, the Central Broadcasting Station and the Central TV Station broadcast the news of my second expulsion from the Communist Party.

Of course I was elated by the news of my rehabilitation. None of us rightists had ever dreamt of a thorough rehabilitation. The last few months of intense hope and anxiety, however, had left us emotionally drained, and my joy was therefore somewhat restrained.

The real moment of exhilaration came in Shanghai. I was assigned by *China Youth News* to interview Cao Tianyu, who belonged to the generation after me. In 1957, he was a junior middle school student, but even then was condemned as a "mini-rightist" without being formally labeled. At the university, he was targeted as a "reactionary student" and sent to a labor camp. During the Cultural Revolution, the denunciations against him were escalated, and he ended up labeled an "active counterrevolutionary element" and placed under political surveillance. He was near forty, neither cadre nor student, neither worker nor peasant, and still living with his old mother. Cao was exceptionally talented. He loved literature, had majored in aesthetics and philosophy, and had been a top student. In the labor camp, he realized that he would never be able to pursue any calling connected with the social sciences or the humanities, and so he continued his studies in physics through all of his hardships. Under his tutelage, his younger sister Cao Nanwei had passed the national examinations and was enrolled in the graduate school of the Chinese Academy of Sciences. She had done it entirely through self-study, with no formal education. Her feat was widely publicized in the papers, but the older brother who helped make it possible remained under a shadow.

I did a thorough investigation of the string of misfortunes that had followed Cao Tianyu all his life. Beijing University, which had been responsible for his label of "reactionary student," was unwilling to reverse the verdict, so his current university in Shanghai, in its turn, would not clear him of the later charge of being an "active counterrevolutionary element," and from this, it followed that his case could not be openly publicized. All I could do with my investigative report was to publish it in the internal publication of *China Youth News.* It did its part in pushing for an amelioration of the man's condition. It struck me as quite symbolic that the first piece of investigative reporting I wrote after resuming my political rights was about someone whose plight was worse than mine.

From that point on, I was the self-appointed mouthpiece of these people. At the same time, the fact that Cao Tianyu's full rehabilitation was still being blocked made me realize that the overthrow of the Gang of Four in October 1976 had not solved all of China's problems. The heart of the problems lay in the fact that the Party itself had changed so much since 1957 that there were many people within its ranks whom I would disdain to address as "comrade." Why, then, rejoin the Party? To reform it, of course.

It is a reality in China that without Party membership it is almost impossible to participate on the political stage. I had acquired a relatively high status in the official hierarchy, so my words would carry more weight.

On March 16, I walked into the Great Hall of the People for the first time. Built in 1959, it housed China's supreme authority. That day ten thousand others and I gathered there to hear Deng Xiaoping speak.

It was at that time that Deng Xiaoping first discussed the problem of the "Four Cardinal Principles" (uphold the leadership of the Party, socialism, the proletarian dictatorship, and Marxism–Leninism–Mao Zedong Thought) and the drive against "bourgeois liberalization." Everyone realized that this meant a slowdown of the "emancipation of the mind" movement, which had been taking place in intellectual circles since the previous winter.

This was also a signal that the critique of the cult of Mao Zedong and the general overhaul of all the fallacious theories of the last two decades, which had begun at the meetings for the "exchange of views on questions of theory" at the beginning of the year, would come to a halt. It was precisely at these meetings that our group of middle-aged theorists, foremost among them Wang Ruoshui, Guo Luoji, Li Honglin, Zhang Xianyang, and Ruan Ming, had shown their mettle. After 1981, all were successively stripped of their jobs and most expelled from the Party.

Needless to say, Deng's talk poured a cold shower on those intellectuals who were pushing for reform. Two months later, when I was in Heilongjiang Province, I found that many people were still recovering from the effects of that cold blast.

I was inclined to be optimistic. I felt that the "Four Cardinal Principles" were not Deng's own convictions, that they were just lip service, inserted to appease the conservatives within the Party. The events of the following eight years proved me only partly right.

In May, I was invited to attend the Conference of Young Writers of Heilongjiang, held in the city of Harbin. I had been away from Harbin, my home town, for twenty-two years. As in Shanghai, the streets and buildings in the city had not changed much, but the population had swollen; crowds were everywhere, noisy and jostling.

The beautiful Byzantine-Russian railway station had disappeared. In its

stead stood an ugly square building, grimy with soot, testimony to the
Great Leap Forward of 1958, when the old station had been demolished
in a furor against all things foreign, and this monstrous thing had been put
up in its place. Due to budgetary and design problems, it had been left
half-finished.

Emerging from the station, I looked for the wooden Russian Orthodox
church across the street, which had been one of the sights of old Harbin.
It, too, had disappeared, thanks to the Cultural Revolution and the combined efforts of the antirevisionist and antireligious drives.

But I was soon to taste the aftereffects of the Cultural Revolution in
another way. I suppose some people in Harbin still remembered me from
the forties and fifties; in any case, the meeting room was more packed than
usual when it was my turn to speak. It was my first public speech since
reattaining my political rights. For the first time in twenty-two years, I was
standing in front of several hundred people as the speaker, not as the
accused.

The early summer sun cast its rays over the meeting room, lighting up
the brightly polished windowpanes and the neatly arranged tables and
chairs. All eyes were fixed on me in expectation and friendly encouragement. "I must not disappoint them," I said to myself. "I must speak my
own thoughts in my own words. I must offer them something new, something they haven't heard before."

At the time, the Central Committee of the Party had not yet made any
official statements on the Cultural Revolution, so it was not permitted to
speculate on the long and short of the matter. But this point somehow
escaped me. I began, "We have done what no other nation in history has
done; in the name of revolution, we have brought about the colossal
disaster of the Cultural Revolution. We are paying a price unprecedented
in human history for this, and because of social forces (real, not just
ideological) that refuse to face the facts and draw a lesson, we are continuing to pay a price. How was this disaster allowed to happen in the first
place?"

I looked back at history and pointed out a few sets of contradictions.
First, the Chinese Communist Party seemed to lay great stress on the
human factor, emphasizing the subjective as a motivating force; at least
it did in its theories and slogans. But in reality, in China, human beings
were of little importance. Ideas such as the freedom and welfare of the
individual had become taboo, giving rise to a situation where the masses

had become completely apathetic to public affairs, and the workers, the so-called masters of the enterprises, were totally uninterested in their work. Second, the Party was making high claims for ideology, or what it called class struggle on the political and ideological front, yet studies in philosophy and the social sciences were languishing, while the ethical standards of the Chinese people had dropped to an all-time low. Finally, immediately after Mao Zedong called for the correct handling of internal contradictions among the people, repeated political campaigns converted millions of innocents into class enemies. "The more you stir up class struggle, the more class enemies appear from nowhere. Why is that?"

The reason, I thought, was our ignorance about our own society, which I ascribed to the fact that for the last several decades, the complicated job of understanding China had been entrusted to one man and one alone—Mao Zedong. And meanwhile, certain social forces had formed in China, special-interest groups that were not interested in seeing China as it really was, because as Marx said, "Understanding is full of terror, if he who understands cannot benefit therefrom."

I talked about humanism, though five years later, it was still a taboo subject. I pointed out that Mao had deviated from the Communist Manifesto, that he had not expanded, but limited, the freedom of the individual. . . .

My talk was being recorded, of course, as all my talks would be during the following years. The fact is, I had always overestimated the amount of freedom that was allowed. I thought my talk was quite within bounds, and I felt secure. My audience was much more vigilant. As I talked on, they applauded repeatedly while keeping a close eye on a man and a woman sitting on either side of me, busily taking notes, as if a bit uneasy about their intentions. I had also seen the pair. I had thought they were busy taking notes in appreciation of my talk.

My audience had the right intuition after all. That very same night, the leading cadre from the provincial federation of art and literature rushed to my room and told me that the two deputy secretaries of the provincial Youth League who had been taking notes had reported me to the provincial Party Committee, saying that I had attacked Chairman Mao. They had also said that I had attacked Daqing, the model oil field then viewed as something holy.

I was speechless. I had thought my talk had been very mild, with no passing shot at Mao, much less at Daqing. The accusation was totally unfounded. Even so, I was a bit tense. That was the first time I had been in such a situation since my rehabilitation. I was far from being inured—twenty-two years as a pariah had left their mark. My sense of inferiority surfaced; I felt as if I were back in the cowshed of the May Seventh Cadre School, and anybody could take note of anything I said and call a meeting to denounce me.

I recalled everything I had said and realized that any criticism of the past two decades, especially any criticism of the Cultural Revolution, could be taken as an attack on Mao. As for the matter of Daqing, it had been a complete misunderstanding. I had spoken negatively of the slogan: "Work hard during the eight working hours and make extra contributions during the remaining hours!" I had said that people are flesh and blood after all, and should be left alone to enjoy some spare time. I had read this slogan when I was in the countryside and had assumed that it was a Dazhai slogan, and as Dazhai, the model farm, was by then open to criticism, I had brought up the subject. Unfortunately, the slogan came from Daqing, which had been set up by Mao himself as a model enterprise for universal emulation. Daqing had not yet been dislodged from its pedestal, and criticism was not tolerated.

It had become part of the scheme of things in Heilongjiang that all the leading positions at organs of the Party, the Youth League, the government administration, the union, and the federation of women must be filled by people sent out from Daqing. The man who had reported on me was deputy secretary of the provincial Youth League and a product of Daqing. I later learned that he had started out as a temporary worker, but was transferred to the permanent staff, then elevated to cadre status, then appointed secretary of the Youth League of the Daqing oil fields, and finally named secretary of the provincial Youth League. This was of course beyond the expectations of any ordinary worker and was certainly not to be achieved through plain hard work. Every rung on the ladder upward had been climbed with the help of toadyism accompanied by "revolutionary" activities—that is to say, ultra-leftist excesses. The female deputy secretary had made it by the same route. Both were beneficiaries of the Cultural Revolution, and my appearance in Heilongjiang had given them a unique chance to distinguish themselves.

Soon rumors spread that the provincial Party Committee was going to examine the report of my speech, and that a copy would be sent to Beijing for inspection. In that case it would be sent to the very man who had actually set up the Daqing model. They could not pin down anything incriminatory in my talk, but I was aware that at that very moment, there was a heated debate going on at the very top about the road that China was to take: reform or the beaten track of the sixties. Against such a background there was always the possibility of someone blowing the incident out of proportion to put pressure on Hu Yaobang, who strongly supported reform. Understandably, I was feeling a bit low. The next day, the delegates from other provinces were taken on an outing to Mirror Lake, one of the main attractions in Heilongjiang, but I did not join them.

When the young writers at the meeting heard of the unfair report against me, they were furious. They wanted to confront the informers. The woman poet Linzi said: "If they're going to put a label on you again, I'd rather wear it in your stead!"

Rightist labels could, of course, not be passed around so easily, but we began to discuss what would happen if another antirightist campaign were launched.

I said, "There are three possibilities. One, the people will be dragged to those struggle sessions again, but will refuse to speak, which is what I call passive resistance. Two, the people will simply refuse to attend those meetings. Or three, the people will take over the stage and have it out with the instigators of those movements. History will move closer and closer to the third possibility." As I said those words, though, I asked myself whether I was being too optimistic again.

At the time, the biggest case of embezzlement of public funds since the founding of the People's Republic, which had taken place in Binxian County just thirty miles outside Harbin, was no longer news. The case had been cracked in 1978, and it had been widely covered in the media. However, I had always felt that the full story had never been told. Something was being held back. Having been an outcast for twenty-two years, I also had a great unsatisfied curiosity about our society. What, exactly, had happened during those years? I felt that the damage of the Cultural Revolution had not been adequately exposed, and of what had been exposed, we had no real understanding.

Two things led to my decision to investigate the case of Wang Shouxin of Binxian. One was the fact that all the culprits were Communist Party members. The second was the fact that although Wang, the leader, was already under arrest, she had not really been discredited—she was still affectionately called "old Mrs. Wang" by the locals, while the people who had helped to uncover the crime were treated like dirt. Some of them had even tried to dissociate themselves completely from the case. What was the secret behind this strange state of affairs? I hoped that unraveling the mystery would tell us something about society after the Cultural Revolution and about the state of the Party.

The first person to give me an interview was the secretary of the Binxian Party Committee, a woman in her forties named Liang Weiling. She talked for a whole evening, primarily to explain that although she and Wang had been next-door neighbors, she had never had any financial dealings with her. Then she complained that the county Party Committee had been instrumental in uncovering the crime, but that the Songhuajiang prefectural committee, their direct superiors, had taken all the credit themselves. I was greatly disappointed. It was not the kind of material I was looking for. Only six months later, when Liang had become my avowed political opponent, did I realize that even a local Party secretary would show her claws if caught in a mistake. All they really wanted to hear was adulation.

What intrigued me, however, was this: How could this case of embezzlement, record-breaking in terms of the sums involved, take place in a land under thirty-three years of Communist rule? How was it that these criminals were so free to act after thirty-three years of class struggle and political campaigns? I was looking for the historical and social roots of this evil, and so I did not limit myself to the case as such. Luckily for me, the very next person who looked me up at the guest house brought my attention straight to the heart of Binxian society.

I can still see the man in front of me, Liu Zhonghou, about fifty years old, with the looks and manners of a peasant—the last person one would connect with any kind of sex scandal. He was the head of the Binxian winery. In the spring of 1977, during the crackdown on economic crimes, he was arrested, without a legal warrant of course, as a prime suspect in a major case. But in handling the case, the work team of the county government pounced on the issue of illicit sex. They accused him of having relations with his own niece, and set up a private court to judge him. They sent out police cars to the neighboring county, where his niece worked, to arrest the girl. They were questioned separately, and torture was used to extract confessions. Liu refused to confess, and the room in which he was detained was sealed and sprayed with insecticide. At the same time, his examiners had found a witness who claimed to have seen them copulating in the fields, while another witness claimed that he had been asked to look after their bastard child. What had actually happened was the exact opposite. Liu Zhonghou had come across a man copulating in the fields, and then, worse luck, came across the same man again in the same act, this time indoors with a different woman. Liu bore no personal grudge against the man and never mentioned the matter, but evidently, the other man decided to take no chances. And—unfortunately as it turned out for Liu—that man was not just anybody; he was head of the industry department of the county government. What's worse, his actual power far exceeded his position. Acting on the principle of "Always be the first to strike," he had fabricated the whole case against Liu Zhonghou.

I had many callers. I would receive one group before breakfast, and talk to one or two other groups after breakfast. My afternoons and evenings were also tightly packed. Binxian County seemed to be a book with all the answers to my questions about Chinese society, and every new caller turned a new page of the book. It didn't matter whether it was reporting a case of persecution, bringing up a petition for justice, exposing political corruption, or offering a clue to the case of Wang Shouxin. Everything interested me. Everything was new, coming as I did from my sealed existence.

I called on the main officials of the county government and the Party Committee. I also visited the local archives and read through the records of all the meetings of the standing committees of the county Party organization over the last dozen years.

I finally found the answer to the question of how Wang Shouxin, an uneducated woman, had become an important figure on the political stage of Binxian, as well as how she managed to embezzle 440,000 yuan.

Binxian was the site of one of the earliest Communist bases in northeast China. The Northeast Bureau, headed by Chen Yun, had once been headquartered there. It was here that land reform was first tried out in 1945. That is to say, it was here that the poor peasants first seized power. The feudal land ownership had ended—but it had been revived in a new form through the Party's political structure and the so-called socialistic public ownership controlled by Party officials. Meanwhile, because unending cycles of political campaigns had poisoned human relationships, various groups had been formed for self-protection or promotion of interests. And with the Cultural Revolution, new groups had been formed. People were motivated not by ethical or revolutionary ideals, but by political or economic interests.

Thus in Binxian the so-called "planned economy" was in practice nothing but a continuous flow of public resources into the private pockets of the power-holders. Whatever was spent on economic development was mainly to solve local problems, to ease unemployment, for instance, or to balance their budget, with no consideration for economic losses, which were all palmed off on the state. For instance, of the thirteen factories operating in Binxian, twelve were operating at severe losses and were causing great fuel shortages in the county as well. What Wang did to gain her special foothold in the county was to get surplus coal for the county from the provincial authorities. She took advantage of the scarcity of food and made offerings of fancy food to county officials, establishing a special form of exchange between material resources and political power, peculiar to our nation. She freely disposed of coal and food products, nominally under "public ownership," while the officials who received these goods used their power, nominally belonging to the "dictatorship of the proletariat," to cover her illegal activities. The Party had made itself caretaker of all aspects of the country and the society, but then sat back and let itself deteriorate from day to day.

In my report "People or Monsters?" I exposed that network of relationships, that reciprocal exchange of power and cash. I examined the fates of a succession of Party secretaries, who had been faced with two choices, either to fight the corruption—which two of them did, only to be ousted— or to join in, preserve power, and lose personal integrity.

I told my readers finally that under these conditions, any talk of socialism, or the leadership of the Party, or the "Four Cardinal Principles," was hypocritical nonsense.

When I was a child, my elders had read my palm more than once, and the tangled mass of lines on my palms always left them aghast. "This boy," they foretold, "has many trials and tribulations ahead of him, more than an ordinary man's lot."

Perhaps my fate had been sealed from the start. But I think my troubles have risen more from my own overpowering curiosity. Having been isolated from society from 1957 to 1979, I returned to a seemingly alien world. The changes that had transpired did not strike others as they struck me. To them, these changes were barely noticeable, or simply taken for granted, but to me, they were preposterous, inexplicable, and unbearable. What I saw in Harbin, for instance, was a shock. The Chinese Communist Party and the society as a whole seemed gravely deteriorated. Mao's misguided drives had plunged the Party and the society into chaos, achieving the opposite of their slogans and promises.

Heilongjiang, for instance, the province with the richest soil, the most open space, and a low population, was so poor that the peasants could not afford matting for their beds, or salt, and in some cases, not even warm clothing for winter.

This brand of socialism had not come close to wiping out class and class oppression; on the contrary, new parasites were cropping up on all sides. Public ownership of property had become a joke. A popular ditty put it this way:

> First-class men are the secretaries,
> Also their descendants and accessories;
> Second-class become captains of the team,
> An endless round of food and drink;
> Third are members of the committee,
> All kith and kin may share their luck;
> Fourth we have the bookkeeper,
> Tinkering with the books is just child's play;
> Fifth comes the keeper of the storeroom,
> Grain and wheat he could carry home;
> Sixth in line is the accountant,
> Plenty of cash to play around with;
> Seventh in line is the "diplomat,"
> Strutting around with an expense account;
> Eighth is the driver in his seat,
> Farmwork never soils his hands and feet;
> Ninth is the elder sitting in his home,
> Wagging his tongue to settle right and wrong;
> Last is the member of the People's Commune,
> Lowest of the low, shouldering the burden.

This picture of the countryside is, in fact, replicated throughout our whole society. Each member of the society gets a little something from the "dictatorship of the proletariat" and the "socialist system of public ownership" through the bit of power he wields. The common people at the bottom must survive on what little remains.

I came across something that may be called a social throwback. Abject poverty had brought back certain aspects of slave society. In times of scarcity, the peasants must still turn in a fixed amount of grain as tax to the state, and depend on government subsidies later. The distribution of these subsidies was in the hands of the Party secretaries, and since these subsidies were a matter of life and death to poor peasant families, the Party secretary could pick and choose any girl from destitute families to sleep with him, in return for food subsidies, a practice not tolerated even under feudalism.

Mao's excesses and mistakes had turned the so-called leadership of the Party into a mechanism whereby a handful of people could fatten themselves while oppressing their opponents. The Cultural Revolution had pushed this state of things to an extreme, but the end of the Cultural Revolution did not really bring about a change for the better in this respect. Things had reached the point where a provincial Party Committee could not even solve as relatively minor a problem as the theft of public property from a factory or the rape of a girl by a policeman. Ordinary people could only stand by and look on helplessly.

In the government and Party apparatus, conscientious officials were helpless against those usurpers of power, because the latter had protection from above and kept climbing the hierarchical ladder. Thus, violations of law and discipline got completely out of hand.

The impact of "People or Monsters?" was unprecedented. *People's Literature,* the major literary magazine in China, has a circulation of 1.4 million. Copies of the September 1979 issue, which contained my report, were in such great demand that readers in public libraries were only allowed to borrow copies for a few hours; in a few instances, a copy was read out loud. The article was also reprinted in many papers and broadcast over the radio in several provinces.

During that year, works of literature became part of people's lives for the first time. Much of the fiction writing exposed negative aspects of the Cultural Revolution or delved into social problems affecting people's lives and were welcomed by intellectuals and ordinary readers alike. But "People or Monsters?" was the first work to candidly describe and analyze corruption within the Party—corruption that was going on under our very eyes. It also discussed the problem in documentary form, without shrouding it in the cloak of fiction. It answered the questions that had been weighing on people's hearts. Letters from readers said, "You write about Binxian, but the same thing is happening right here where we are!"

The reactions from the Binxian Party Committee and the provincial Party Committee were equally strong. The Binxian Party secretary flew into fits of rage and denounced me at countless meetings, large and small. She also went to the secretary of the provincial Party Committee to attack me, and he, in turn, denounced me to the Central Committee in Beijing.

And what did they hold against me? Their reasoning seemed to run as follows: Since the downfall of the Gang of Four, the situation in Binxian had been very good, but the appearance of "People or Monsters?" created dire confusion among the cadres and the masses, disrupting the stable situation, and the county Party Committee found itself paralyzed. Another objection was that my report was fallacious. Well, if this were true, I thought, the masses of Binxian would see through the lies and stand behind the Party Committee. How was it possible that the same committee that had reigned for thirty-four years could be paralyzed by a pack of lies?

At the time, the Central Committee of the CCP did not commit itself, nor did it comment on my talks, which had been taped and reported to them. I regarded this silence as tacit approval.

During the rest of that year, I gave dozens of talks in Heilongjiang, Liaoning, and Beijing, with the audiences averaging over a thousand at every talk. I continued to expose and analyze Mao's mistakes and their disastrous effects on the country, and I called for a thorough cleaning-up of ultra-leftist opportunism. I pointed out that the effects of political disasters were not to be compared to natural disasters such as earthquakes; that they left behind more than debris. They brought forth a breed of special-interest groups who fattened themselves and flourished on the debris. I warned that we should not underestimate their destructiveness, then or in years to come.

chapter eleven

A First
Glimpse of
the Fangs

The Third Congress of the Writers' Association, which was convened in late 1979, was a landmark event. The delegates looked back at the unjust treatment of the arts and literature since the fifties and commended the new tide. A group of writers, including myself, who had been silenced since 1957, who were now middle-aged, were at the center of the cultural scene and at the center of the congress.

In my speech at the meeting, I talked about the lessons I had drawn from my own experiences during the Great Leap Forward: "I saw with my own eyes how the papers said one thing while the feelings of the peasants were the exact opposite; it was as if there were two truths sitting side by side. My heart was torn. Now I know that, in such cases, we should always listen to what the people want, for they represent history." I reminded the meeting, "Our several thousand years of feudal tradition, poverty, and ignorance have prepared the ground for extremist policies. Special-interest groups are against reform; they just want to keep on the old tracks." I added, "In our time, the first priority for literature is to be concerned with major issues related to the fate of our people. I'll pursue the course I've chosen. Of course there are difficulties, even dangers, but my mind is made up. The article I just published is enough to label me 'rightist'; if I write a hundred articles like that, it will be nothing but a 'rightist' label over and over again. So why not go on writing?" The audience laughed. I had sat up the night before to write my speech, but after the first few words I put aside the draft and was swept away by the force of my own convictions without thinking of the consequences.

The months from late 1978 to 1979 was the most open time ever since the founding of the People's Republic. It was also the year when I gave the most speeches—fifteen speeches in five provinces, six of them at universities. Tape recordings of these speeches were widely distributed.

But some found my talks highly objectionable. To them, the antirightist campaign was still a living memory, and not as a source of self-reproach.

Their hands were itching to strike again as soon as they heard intellectuals speaking their minds. Hua Guofeng, still chairman of the Central Committee of the Party at the time, had threatened, "We have no intention of conducting another antirightist campaign, but we are ready to repeat it if challenged."

Bai Hua, Wang Ruowang, Wang Meng, Ding Ling, and I, all former rightists, had all spoken at the congress; and the Council of the Writers' Association and the governing body elected by the council included not a few former rightists in their ranks.

Soon after this meeting, there was a change of climate; a cold blast swept over Beijing and several provinces. People in influential positions spread the word that "the meeting of the Writers' Association had been a meeting of rightists overthrowing their verdicts," that "the rightists had taken over the platform; others had not had a chance to speak," and that the "newly elected members of the governing board were all rightists."

Actually, everyone had had an equal chance to speak at the meeting; many old writers were on the agenda, but once things had been set in motion, they withdrew their talks, feeling that no one would care to listen to them. It was the way things were going. They would be further provoked, and their works would be rejected by publishers. These hitherto much-sought-after writers complained bitterly that the former "rightists" and young writers were monopolizing the scene.

Art and literature were then under the direction of Hu Yaobang. Inevitably, a lot of pressure was brought to bear on him, particularly in the case of the play *If I Were Real* and the filmscript *In the Archives of Society*.

If I Were Real, by the young Shanghai dramatist Sha Yexin, was a satire about a young man masquerading as the son of a leading cadre who makes his way into the inner circles of society. He receives favors from all sides, and a young woman even volunteers to marry him, all because he is believed to be the son of someone important. Finally, he is exposed and brought before the law. The play provoked a controversy, and could only be staged for limited audiences. The writer made several revisions, but not enough to satisfy the critics, so it was never staged for a general audience. The filmscript of Wang Jing's *In the Archives of Society* is about corruption in the army—and a high-ranking army official and his son's sexual abuse of the same girl. Opposition to this script came primarily from the army.

Hu Yaobang scheduled a meeting for January 1980 on issues relating to the drama. This decision was made in late 1979, when the climate was still favorable, but by the time the meeting actually took place, the situation had changed considerably. A week before the meeting, Hu Yaobang had planned to announce that with some further alterations, the play and the script could both be shown to the public. Then just two days before the meeting, he changed his mind. People speculated that he must have been under great pressure.

At the same time, I had also become a target. In November of 1979, I became a reporter for the *People's Daily*. In early 1980, I was just about to go to Sichuan on assignment when an old friend told me that Hu Yaobang had criticized me. Later, other friends sent the same warning.

At the time, Hu Yaobang was only the head of the Propaganda Department of the Central Committee, but he was regarded as the standard-bearer for the reform movement, second only to Deng Xiaoping. The fact that he would speak against me was completely unexpected. Was he denying his attitude in general? My spirits, buoyed by the meeting of the Writer's Association, were dampened. Piecing information together, I finally made out facts.

At a regular working meeting of the propaganda department, a woman cadre from the high-level Communist Party Central Advanced Training Center complained that I had given a talk at the People's University wherein I had spoken on behalf of the rightist Lin Xiling. At the end of the working meeting, when Hu Yaobang was doing the summing up, Yang Shijie, deputy head of the Organization Department of the Central Committee, interrupted him and said, "There is a certain person who is going around saying that he is not a Party member, even though his 'rightist' label has been removed and his Party membership restored. He persists in saying that socialism is inferior to capitalism, that the Communist Party is inferior to the Kuomintang, and that the mainland is inferior to Taiwan. As with most of his kind, his ultimate goal is to get to the United States. This person is no other than Liu Binyan!" At the time, Hu Yaobang did not acknowledge the interruption but went on with his summary. But he must have realized that two such mentions of Liu Binyan were no coincidence, and that their significance was not limited to me personally. He could not avoid acknowledging the remarks in some way, so at the end of his speech, he said, "I know of Liu Binyan. In 1957, when he was labeled a rightist, I had my reservations. Last year, I gave my full support to his rehabilitation. Of course he has his faults."

When my friends sat down and studied this remark in full context, they thought there was no cause to worry; it was apparent that Hu was protecting me.

A few years later, when I had occasion to think of this remark again, I felt that he was doing more than just protecting me. What he was saying was: "I don't see much wrong with Liu. I supported him twenty-two years ago, as I do now. If he has his faults, they are certainly no greater than those of you who are attacking him." This was the first time that Hu Yaobang had spoken more or less openly in support of me. Later on, he again mentioned me under different circumstances in more or less the same terms, with slight modifications.

At that point, however, I realized that I must be careful not to give my opponents any reason to attack me or my comrades. I talked things over with my wife, and we decided that on this visit to Sichuan, I would not give any public talks. Happily, this coincided with the decision of the provincial federation of art and literature of Sichuan, which had declared that "Sichuan will not provide any platform for Liu Binyan!" So we were in complete agreement.

When I went to Sichuan, therefore, I tried to be unusually circumspect. I did not go home to Beijing for the Lunar New Year, but decided instead to use the holiday to look up an old craftsman, who was an expert shoemaker. What had struck me about him was that during the Cultural Revolution, when he had lost his job and was in a very bad way, he had written a book on shoemaking and published it at his own expense (it later became the first texbook for the shoemakers' training course). We made an appointment to meet on the first day of the New Year.

When I arrived, he was not in. His wife and elder son received me politely, saying that he had been called away unexpectedly. I believed them and waited, chatting with the mother and son, trying to find out more about the shoemaker's work. When it was noon, and the old man had still not returned, I had to go. His son insisted on seeing me all the way back to my hotel. I thought he was being overly polite, but actually he was acting out of guilt. He told me that his father had heard that I was going to be attacked and severely punished and so did not want to get involved with me. Actually, at the moment, the cloud over me was not cleared. The son had not been given his father's permission to speak, but he told me the truth anyway. He need not have done it, but my sincerity must have touched him; he was convinced I could not be a bad man.

Later, the old craftsman deeply regretted having avoided me, and he would call on me every time he came to Beijing, bringing presents from his home town, but we never had a chance to go into his story. From this incident and others that followed, I realized that I was the victim of widespread rumors—that I was "under house arrest and being interrogated," that I had been "banished from Beijing," and that I had been "expelled from the Party."

At that time, I was just undergoing a first wave of rumors, which was to recur every year until January 1987, when the rumors turned to reality. The political climate of China changed with the same frequency. My political fortunes had become a barometer by which to gauge these changes.

Rumors greeted me when I returned to Beijing, rumors of a serious nature. The moment I arrived at the *People's Daily,* the current editor-in-chief, Hu Jiwei, called me into his office and asked me, "What have you been making speeches about in Sichuan?"

I answered, "Nothing; I never talked."

"But I have heard that you were speaking in public and that a student handed you a note asking, 'Can we go out into the street to demonstrate?' and you said, 'Of course. The students of People's University in Beijing have done it!' " I insisted that I had said nothing of the sort and demanded that they investigate.

I found out later that the man who had slandered me to Hu Jiwei was none other than the deputy chief of the Organization Department of the Central Committee, Yang Shijie, the man who had attacked me in front of Hu Yaobang. I did not know him personally. We did not bear any grudge against each other, so I wondered why he kept stabbing me in the back. Had it not been for this encounter, I would not have known that he had once been Party secretary for the city of Anshan in Liaoning Province. Had he fabricated those rumors himself, or had they been provided by Sichuan Province?

In any case, I did not pursue the matter. At the time, we did not have a set of civil laws, and so I could not have prosecuted Yang, and even if I had, he would have gotten protection from certain quarters. Still, I should have kept in mind that I had made enemies not only among the various provincial Party Committees that I had offended by my report, but also within the Central Committee itself in Beijing. I did not pursue the matter, and soon forgot about it.

Two or three years later, however, I found out that others did not forget as easily and had their eyes on me all along. They instinctively felt that I was an alien, a threat. They carefully hoarded all my publications, all recordings of my talks, all letters of accusation against me by people I had exposed, all letters informing against me. They hoarded all of these, biding their time.

Still I remained confident that the Party and Deng Xiaoping would understand that my goals were the same as theirs, that all my talks and publications were in their interest, that we were fighting on the same front.

This series of attacks by "leftist" opponents only served to provoke my anger, and I decided to take them on. That same year, the Central Committee had warned that some lingering elements of the Gang of Four might try to work their way back into power through administrative readjustments designed to make room for younger men. I felt sure that exposing their kind would be supported by the Central Committee.

In July 1980, I went to Yinan County in Shandong Province, accompanied by Li Chunguang, a special writer for the *People's Daily*. My family's home county, Linyi, is near Yinan. This was the first time I had set foot on the soil that my grandfather had left at the beginning of the century in search of life in the Northeast. Seventy years had passed; of these, thirty years had been spent under the leadership of the Communist Party, but the area was as poor as ever. The peasants still went on begging and still left for the northeastern provinces such as Heilongjiang, as my grandfather had done.

In Yinan County, we found that the members of the clique that had seized power during the Cultural Revolution held it. During the Cultural Revolution, many people had died directly at their hands or during the armed violence that they had instigated. Many had also been tortured during infighting, and if they managed to escape alive, they were later labeled as political offenders and, along with their families, were systematically victimized and deprived of means of living. After the Cultural Revolution, the power-wielders used the movement to weed out remnants of the Gang of Four for their own ends, and again turned the attack on their former victims, causing more violence and death.

During this visit, we found that from the Cultural Revolution right up to the present, the peasants remained as docile as they had been since 1949, always accepting the leadership of the Communist Party and fascist rule in the name of the "dictatorship of the proletariat." They continued to elect as people's delegates the candidates hand-picked by the leaders; those attending the various levels of the People's Congress invariably clapped and approved the list of candidates for government positions handed down by the Party Committee. In their everyday lives, the peasants would go and work in the fields, following orders from the Party secretary who had been picked by the higher-ups, and at the end of the year they received an inadequate supply of grain and a pitiful payment in cash that was not enough to to compensate for the deficiency. The bureaucrats were more unscrupulous than ever in exploiting the peasants, fearing no consequences, for they expected the current Central Committee of the CCP to step down soon. Having the support of certain high-ranking officials behind them, they even went so far as to vilify Deng Xiaoping and Hu Yaobang by name and refused to implement the responsibility system in the rural areas under their jurisdiction.

My report exposing this Yinan clique, "A Long and Weary Road," stung them to the quick. I received an anonymous letter accusing me of being a "hireling of Nagy and others trying to restore capitalism in China"; it said that I had a "long history of anti-Party and antisocialist activities" and was now "selling myself to Nagy in order to restore capitalism." (During the campaign to criticize Deng Xiaoping, the Gang of Four had compared him to Imre Nagy, who led the short-lived coalition government at the time of the Hungarian uprising of 1956, and was executed by the Russians. Here, "Nagy" means "Deng"; the letter-writer did not dare criticize Deng by name.) Furthermore, the letter accused me of acting under the orders of "certain people in power" to "discredit the Party Committee of Yinan County." It also stated that "some people in power are worse than the most treacherous prime ministers in Chinese history, such as Wang Mang, Liang Ji, Dong Zhuo, Li Linfu, Qin Kuai, Jia Sidao, Wei Zhongxian, and the like" and ended by saying, "As long as these traitors are left unexposed, there will be no peace for the country!" These denunciations, too, were clearly aimed at Deng Xiaoping, as well as Hu Yaobang and other leading comrades who were pushing ahead with reforms. Evidently this clique in Yinan County did not even feel the need to camouflage its political stance.

In order to discredit me thoroughly, they falsely attacked my morals, saying that "the evil-minded Liu Binyan had on several occasions forced a girl attendant of the guest house to sleep with him, causing pregnancy and no end of misery to the poor girl. " Luckily, I had shared a room with

Li Chunguang, and since we worked together in the daytime, I would have had no chance to force a girl attendant to sleep with me; otherwise it would have been even more difficult to defend myself.

This anonymous letter was turned over to the Ministry of Public Security, which requested that the department of Public Security of Shandong Province track its writer down, but the latter didn't lift a finger. This was in itself very revealing about the struggles within the Party.

My friends felt that the anonymous attack on me proved that I was on Deng's side. They surmised that when Party members in Shandong conducted their attack on me, Deng would not side with them.

In August 1980, I returned to Shenyang, the capital of Liaoning Province. I was brought there by a wish still unfulfilled.

Ever since the case of Zhang Zhixin, a young woman who had been executed some years earlier for opposing Mao and the Cultural Revolution, had been made public in 1979, it had been gnawing at my heart. That summer, many writers had gone to Shenyang to write on the subject. On my way back to Beijing from conference in Harbin, I too had made a stop at Shenyang and read over some of the files on Zhang's case and looked up some of her former associates.

Many articles had been published on Zhang Zhixin, but none was very satisfactory. An idea occurred to me: Zhang was dead, dozens of volumes of her diary had been destroyed, yet the subject of Mao and the Cultural Revolution remained taboo. I didn't want to write about Zhang's death as a personal tragedy. I wanted to write from another angle, to write about the people around Zhang, how they, under the circumstances of the seventies, each in his or her own way, contributed to her death. I wanted to write about the political conditions existing since 1949 that made it inevitable that a person like Zhang Zhixin must die. I thought this kind of writing might help the Chinese people come to terms with the thirty-odd years of their contemporary history and with Mao's mistakes.

And so I returned to Shenyang in the summer of 1980 to bury myself in the records of Zhang Zhixin's trial, and to retrace her path to execution.

Yet I received little help from those who had survived her. Some even tried to defame her. All of the people who were in one way or another responsible for her death, from the prime culprit to the last on the list, had escaped punishment. The poet Xie Tingyu disclosed that before her execution, Zhang's larynx had been cut to prevent her from shouting slogans in front of the firing squad. For this, the poor man was roundly abused by the authorities, as if he had committed a crime himself.

The whole affair led me to examine the question of the criminals of the Cultural Revolution. At the time, the ground had been well prepared for the takeover by Jiang Qing and company in Liaoning Province. One of the leading members of Jiang's clique, Li Buoqiu, had said that once Jiang Qing took over, all the cadres above county Party secretary level in Liaoning could be trusted to carry out their policies. I was curious as to the whereabouts of these trustworthy people.

Liaoning actually had conducted a thorough investigation of all associates and followers of the Gang of Four in 1977–78. They had even conducted a follow-up investigation later on. In Liaoning, in contrast to Shandong Province, the leaders were launching a campaign to round up those criminals of the Cultural Revolution who had managed to elude detection. But I encountered a preposterous situation. I saw that while many upright cadres were conscientiously conducting the campaign, others even more powerful were feverishly trying to cover up. During the 1977–79 campaign to round up holdovers of the Gang of Four, the Party was completely split over the issue. The protectors eventually gained the upper hand, so the ongoing campaign could not win much support. Even the former victims were, having lost confidence in the campaign altogether, reluctant to stand up for themselves.

When I attended a three-day meeting in Liaoning to hear reports of the results, I was appalled by what I heard. In the counties and factory units where dozens or even hundreds of people had been killed or driven to commit suicide, not a single follower of the gang had been uncovered! Some of those who were guilty of various crimes during the Cultural Revolution were still in positions of power in Party Committees, security bureaus, personnel offices, and even the official Party paper, the *Liaoning Daily*. Those who had been victimized for opposing Lin Biao, Jiang Qing, and company, by contrast, were still being victimized.

I felt compelled to do something. I put Zhang Zhixin's files aside and continued investigating on my own. I looked up friends who could give me information and others in charge of the investigation of the followers of the Gang of Four.

In Liaoning, as in Shangdong, one faction took over power after the Cultural Revolution, namely, the faction supported by the army. It was comprised mostly of workers. Strangely, this faction had violently opposed the provincial Party leaders and the Northeast Bureau of the Central Committee, but the latter, once reinstalled, did not seek retribution against their previous persecutors, nor did they offer protection to the opposing faction (composed mostly of members of the intelligentsia) who had suffered for protecting them.

Gradually, I realized there was something unique about the nature of the Cultural Revolution, which differed from all previous campaigns. It was established that the Gang of Four was counterrevolutionary, but Mao, who started the Cultural Revolution, was not touched. The chaos had been created by leaders of the Central Committee in the first place, many of them had been in seats of power during the Cultural Revolution, and now they were given credit for ending it and were as firmly installed as ever. They were "veterans of three dynasties." Of the people promoted after the Cultural Revolution, most had already been in office before. They were targets at the outbreak of the confusion, but soon afterward joined the gang and pursued its policies. As for the veteran cadres, they had long-standing relations with old associates in Beijing who were in positions of power, and they were linked to lower- and middle-ranking cadres by bonds of mutual interest. In 1979, I had spotted an intricate network of economic relations in Binxian, but what stood out in Liaoning was the network of political relations. Through this network, cadres who found it too danger-ous to stay on were discreetly reassigned to escape investigation. Through this double network, the abuse of power, graft and embezzlement, and violation of human rights were rampant.

Economic reforms were forging ahead in Liaoning, and the papers were full of positive reports in this respect. I suspected, however, that a political crisis was brewing. If injustices were not righted, how would the people get their share of the fruits of this reform?

With this in mind, I wrote a piece entitled "Good People, Why Are You So Weak?"

My writing went well that summer. Besides "Good People," I also wrote "The Hampered Flight," about the remarkable reformer Li Risheng, head of the Bureau of Light Industry of the city of Dandong in Liaoning Province, and "Seeing Beyond and Behind the Crime," about a case of injustice against a peasant girl. I returned to Beijing with a light heart.

But soon, a new round of angry and factually inaccurate accusations came from Shandong, then from Liaoning. The Liaoning Party Committee even contended that except for the mention that a history of the Cultural Revolution was being written in Liaoning Province, everything I had written about Liaoning was a pack of lies.

Where had I gone wrong? I reread my writings and compared them with others. Over a hundred articles praising Li Risheng had been published. The problem was that my report touched on some of the obstacles in the man's way. This inevitably involved other people—in this case, none other than the veteran of three dynasties, the man who had been deputy Party secretary of Dandong during the Cultural Revolution and was still in office, secure in the midst of a nest of relations. When I went to interview him, he was just about to retire. People shook their heads when his name was mentioned. The most recent scandal around him related to his son's appropriation of a couple's private house and the subsequent suicide of the wife.

As soon as my article was published, however, the Party secretary was made into a hero. He was made the official representative to welcome an honored guest at the harbor. There he was, seated among the members of the Presidium at the provincial People's Congress, and interviewed on TV. It seemed like a demonstration directed against my article. And before I arrived in Dandong, Li Risheng, the reformer, had been about to be promoted. But after my article appeared, he was subjected to investigation. One team after another descended on his work unit to probe into his problems. All of the accomplishments that I had affirmed in my article were disputed by the municipal Party Committee.

I began to doubt myself. Could I have been taken in? Was Li Risheng a fake? Apparently not. Two years later, the deputy minister of light industry of the central government conducted a long and thorough investigation and reinstated Li Risheng and his reforms, and appointed him head of the Department of Light Industry of Liaoning Province.

My report "Seeing Beyond and Behind the Crime" concerned a young country girl from Liaoning, Wang Guangxiang, who had been wronged with respect to employment opportunities. She petitioned for a long time with no results, and the officer who was responsible for the injustice not only refused to help her, but met her with quips and insults. In desperation, she got hold of some dynamite and blasted away a corner of the man's living quarters and then reported herself to public security, to attract attention to her case. It was an isolated incident, but it was typical of the situation prevalent all over the country. Having no recourse to justice, the common people simply took the law into their own hands.

Thousands of peasants followed the trial of Wang Guangxiang. First, she was given three years, and then she was released on grounds of mental instability. The offending officer, however, was also quietly released.

Over eight thousand letters were received by the *People's Daily* in response to my article, the second one to elicit such a reaction since the founding of the paper. It was a warning to the authorities either to establish a legal system and work within its framework or bear the consequences.

Someday, victims like Wang Guangxiang who have been suffering mutely for years, in some cases, for dozens of years, will converge on Beijing. Then their piteous moans will change into an angry roar. I know that some have saved a copy of the *People's Daily* carrying my report, and often read it over to keep their fire of hope burning.

Still, the basic problem raised in "Looking Beyond and Behind the Crime" was ignored. Seven years later, Wang Guangxiang's style of retributive justice surfaced again, in the form of dynamite thrown at trains, at the Ministry of Public Security, and at Mao's mausoleum. Many figures like Wang Guangxiang have ended up as arsonists, murderers, or self-immolators.

I had become the target of concerted attacks by both Shandong and Liaoning provinces. They wrote to the Central Committee of the Party, saying my reports were false. Shandong had even set up investigation teams to fabricate their own versions, painting black white and white black. And of course I had to refute these accusations. This tug-of-war with Shandong dragged on until 1983, when the Party Congress exposed the mistakes of the former Party Committee, and the new Party secretary of the province announced that my report was based on fact and thus the debate was closed. And in Liaoning Province, an airliner was hijacked in 1983 by Zhuo Changren and company, who had used their connections with high provincial officials to shield themselves in their previous illegal dealings. Ultimately, the Party Committee had to admit in their report to the Central Committee that there were "alien elements" on the Party Committee, because the black dealings of the highjacker, which had long been known, had been covered up by various officials.

What struck me most, during my investigations on problems associated with the remnants of the Gang of Four that were still in power, was that many old cadres who had been victimized during the Cultural Revolution were on good terms with their former persecutors. In one way or another, the latter had wormed their way back into favor and were either back at their old posts or had been relocated to rule over the masses somewhere else. I heard those in charge of weeding out the remnants of the Gang of Four complain that no campaign had ever been so difficult to push forward. Of the former victims, some were, as I say, now reconciled; some, seeing their persecutors reinstalled, were afraid to speak up for fear of reprisal; and others had no confidence that the remnants of the gang would really be punished and therefore did not wish to come forward to denounce them.

There was a deeper reason for the leniency shown to former followers of the gang, but I only realized that in 1984. In the 1980s, I was struck by the different treatment that was given to the former rightists and the present leftists; the former continued to be treated harshly although they had suffered so long under false convictions and had been publicly rehabilitated. The damage wrought by the leftists, on the other hand, was still before our eyes—and yet they seemed immune from punishment.

The first film based on the rightist theme, *The Tianyun Shan Story,* was an example of this. It was released in 1980 and was favorably received by the general audience, but resented by many cadres, from the grass roots to the Central Committee. In fact, the resentment was so strong that the film had to close for a time. What offended them was the fact that the negative character in the film, Wu Yao, was a person who climbed the political ladder by trampling on others and by getting them labeled rightist; the Party critics of the film felt that this was a smear of all Party members. Evidently, they identified themselves with Wu. The positive character in the film, Luo Chun, who was unjustly labeled a rightist, however, was also a Communist Party member, and I wondered why these people didn't identify themselves with him. The answer was that they sympathized with Wu Yao, and not with Luo Chun, because they themselves had either had a hand in getting people labeled or had profited from the leftists in power since 1957. Later, during the Cultural Revolution, these cadres were subjected to more or less the same kind of treatment as the former rightists, but even so, they reserved their hatred only for the particular people who persecuted them, and not for the basic political thinking of the Gang of Four. The latter was in line with their own long-held beliefs, only more extreme.

In 1980, several influential political groups began to surface.

The first group consisted of conservative elements within the Party. This group opposed Deng Xiaoping's policies of economic reform, such as doing away with the commune system, setting up the responsibility system (which allowed peasants to sell their surplus crops), and diminishing the Party secretary's power by establishing the managerial system. The still unchanged political structure and only slightly changed economic structure were favorable to their machinations, while Mao's school of thought constituted their ideological basis.

The second group consisted of the intellectuals who advocated reform of the political system, opposing Mao Zedong's ideology. They did not want to overthrow the Communist regime, but the conservatives within the Party saw no difference between them and the next group.

The third group were the radicals among the younger generation. These young people tried to continue operating the underground organizations and publications, even after the arrest of the dissident Wei Jingshen. At the time, college students were moving slowly in the direction of setting up an unofficial nationwide organization for democratization. Universities in Beijing had just elected their own deputies for the first time. Some of the candidates made sharp comments about the Communist Party in their campaign speeches and called for more democracy. They were hailed by their fellow students and were viewed with disquiet by the authorities. Meanwhile, the youth of Shanghai, who had been sent to Xinjiang army plantations, organized massive demonstrations, which went completely out of control.

And a final group is those who practice what is euphemistically called "unethical behavior"—in other words, corrupt Communist cadres', whose influence was still spreading.

In the early 1980's, Deng Xiaoping and his clique were opposed to all four groups. But the conservatives were lodged within the Party itself, although they opposed Deng's reform policies. They were basically from the same camp and shared many interests; therefore, the leadership at the time had to compromise with them. Treating them too harshly would only have abetted the radicals.

The Party leadership and the conservatives opposing reform were united in their hostility toward the second and third political forces, regarding them as the most dangerous threat to Communist rule, not to be tolerated on any account.

As for corruption within the Party, Chen Yun had once mentioned that eliminating it was a "matter of life and death for the ruling Party," but for one reason or another, no real effort had been made to curb it.

In our habitual terminology, the first group was regarded as "leftist," the second and third as "rightist." From 1979 onward, leftists constantly had to be fought against in economic matters, but the leftists themselves were never treated as enemies, and the battle was always treated as a family matter. The methods used were always persuasion and compromise, at worst a comfortable forced retirement or reassignment to another job. For years thereafter, the People's Political Consultative Conference and the People's Congress became the special shelters for the leftists.

In the field of ideology, by contrast, the leaders were always waging war on the right, regarding it as the main enemy. The only change from earlier campaigns against rightists was that now there were no more political labelings or arrests of rightist intellectuals. Their influence was limited by more subtle means, often by suspending their right to publish. Young people involved in underground organizations and publications, though, were invariably arrested and jailed.

chapter twelve

A
Perilous
Profession

The *People's Daily*, the official organ of the Chinese Communist Party, is the most important newspaper in China. People regard every article, every sentence in this paper as the voice of the Party. The position of a particular article on its pages, the kind of type used for its title, the order in which Party leaders are announced on its pages, and the number of times their names appear are all signals of the variable political climate.

Beginning in 1978—when all the other papers continued on the beaten path—the *People's Daily* underwent a great change. It sounded the notes of reform loud and clear, giving substantial support to Deng Xiaoping.

The years 1978 to 1980 were golden years for the *People's Daily*. Although there was no express policy allowing more freedom of expression at the time, the *People's Daily* expanded the scope of its reports much more than other papers, which continued to act as mouthpieces for worn-out orthodox policies. The *People's Daily* was able to do this because of the favorable political climate in Beijing and Hu Yaobang's stable position and positive influence. But it was also largely due to the moral courage of editor-in-chief Hu Jiwei and his deputy, the philosopher Wang Ruoshui, and their loyal staff. But even so, the *People's Daily* was often hemmed in or attacked by the conservatives. On occasion, it was forced to publish certain articles or suppress others. The editorial staff often received stern phone calls from people in positions of authority with specific warnings against certain articles, poems, or even the use of a particular word. At other times, really good articles, widely welcomed by readers, would draw fire from certain quarters.

In 1979, for instance, a story appeared about murders committed on an army-owned plantation in Shihezi, in Xinjiang. A young woman, Jiang Aizhen, beset by scandalous sexual rumors, met deaf ears on all sides when she asked for help from the leaders of her unit. Finally, in an act of desperation, she took a gun from the militia and killed three people who had been involved in spreading the malicious rumors about her. The

People's Daily published an article entitled, "Why Did Jiang Aizhen Resort to Murder?" which drew wide response from across the nation. The paper received ten thousand letters—a record-breaking figure—expressing sympathy and support for Jiang Aizhen and denouncing a political system that did not protect citizens' rights. This wave of support deterred the local court from handing down the death sentence according to usual practices. After long deliberations, in 1986 they finally sentenced her to fifteen years in prison.

Why was there such wide support for a murderess? The problem was worth investigation, but the official authorities completely ignored the issue. Instead, they accused the *People's Daily* of encouraging murder.

At the beginning of 1980, in keeping with the chill in the political climate, a secretary of the Youth League Central made a long speech to the Standing Committee of the People's Congress, attacking the *People's Daily* from beginning to end, but our paper was not intimidated.

By 1981, however, in light of the criticism against Bai Hua's filmscript *Bitter Love*, an exposé of Mao and the Cultural Revolution, the recurring attacks on "bourgeois liberalization," and the flag-waving of the "Four Cardinal Principles," the paper found itself in a tight corner.

That summer, the Propaganda Department of the Central Committee handed down a new regulation: newspapers had to obtain official approval from their supervising Party committees before they could publish any article of criticism. Actually, the provincial and municipal papers had already abandoned any attempts at criticism. Even at the *People's Daily*, reporters willing to take the risk of writing exposés were few and far between. They were threatened by letter or phone, and one reporter's child was beaten.

Clearly, if the Party shared the view that the newspapers should not be limited to singing praises and repeating slogans, but that they should expose corruption and protect citizens' rights, then logically the Party should move to expand freedom of expression and not set more limitations. Hadn't the Central Committee repeatedly called for rectification? Hadn't it reiterated that rectification was a matter of life and death for the Party? If so—and I did not want to doubt its sincerity—then there was all the more reason to upgrade the supervision of the process by the press, the form of supervision most feared by corrupt officials. Why, then, was the exact opposite done? As far as freedom of expression was concerned, that regulation did nothing but tighten the rope around the neck of a body already in shackles.

By this time, I had been pushed into a unique position by social forces. The trust people placed in me was more than most Party cadres could have ever expected, and even beyond what most writers and reporters could attain.

Readers all over the country sought my works. If my name appeared on the list of contributors, a magazine would be sold out in a flash. My books, which appeared in printings of only ten or twenty thousand copies a year (due to the limitations of the irrational book-distribution system in China), would be sold out in a week. My readers belonged to all levels of society and all age groups. Many of them had access to my works only through borrowed copies or even photocopies. Since corruption within the Party and the crisis in society were growing faster and faster while fewer and fewer critics dared to stand up to expose, analyze, and lead the attack, people with a social conscience or people who were suffering from official persecution pinned their hopes on me.

I received an average of twenty letters a day. Callers at the *People's Daily* numbered sixteen or seventeen every day. People at work did not give out my home address; nevertheless, an endless stream of people came to my home. Often, a caller would be sitting outside my door before I got out of bed. When I came back from work at noon, two would be sitting on the staircase. And in the evening, the moment I sat down to supper, sure enough, there would be the knock at the door before I picked up my bowl of rice.

While I was in Beijing, the main part of my working day consisted of receiving callers and taking notes. Every man's story opened another window to the outside world for me. I sat in my room but was in touch with the situation even in the remotest areas. Some of the accounts I heard were highly dramatic, more so than fiction could be. One might think that just listening was easy, but there is actually nothing more exhausting—you get swept away by the story, you are shocked, furious, then filled with pity and anxiety. I just could not go about it in a detached way.

From 1979 to 1984, Chai Shuzhen frequently climbed the stairway to my flat with the help of a walking stick. She was around forty, still unmarried. At the age of sixteen, when she was working at a papermaking factory in Qiqihar, Heilongjiang Province, she had been raped by a department head. Later, another cadre, to whom she had reported the incident, tried to take advantage of her as well. She petitioned for justice on all sides, only to become more deeply embroiled in scandal, and from that point on she became a victim of political libel. Eventually she ended up a political prisoner; during the Cultural Revolution, she was accused of "opposing the Core Committee of the Cultural Revolution," and after the Cultural Revolution subsided she was damned as a hanger-on of the Gang of Four. She was cast into a water hole, a cell flooded with water, where her legs became diseased and her eyesight deteriorated.

Deng Mingyuan, a man in his fifties, was a victim of another type. In 1955, when he was just out of technical school, he stumbled across a case of embezzlement involving the head of a lumber factory, and he reported it. For this, he was packed off to an insane asylum. The head of the lumber factory was later found guilty and given a fifteen-year sentence, but even after the man had served his sentence and was released, poor Deng Mingyuan had still not been cleared of the charge of mental instability. The head of the Ministry of Forestry had intervened in vain on his behalf, and so he ended up a tramp, homeless and jobless.

Teng Tianyu was yet another type, totally different. In 1947, he had been a reporter in the north Jiangsu Communist base area and had published a short article in a local paper, claiming that the county Party secretary had kept part of the spoils of the land reform for himself— clothes and household goods confiscated from the overthrown landlords— which should have gone to poor peasants. A few days after the article appeared, the criticized secretary himself went to Teng's home and under some false pretext had Teng's father, a teacher, arrested and executed. For the next forty years, Teng laboriously compiled evidence that his father was completely innocent and that the execution was purely an act of revenge on the part of the county secretary. The result of his unrelenting petitions for justice landed him in one predicament after another. By the time he looked me up, he was jobless. His enemy, meanwhile, had been steadily climbing the official ladder.

My callers were not all victims of notorious cases of injustice. As a matter of fact, some were people in high positions—members of standing committees of the National People's Congress, secretaries of municipal Party Committees, high-ranking army officers, model workers who had received wide publicity. Even they had not always been able to protect themselves—they had lost their jobs and positions and had been expelled from the Party. Some had even had found themselves in personal danger. Ironically, many of their predicaments came from following Party directives to protect public property or uphold reform, while the very Party and government units concerned—to which they were loyal—could not give them the protection they needed.

Not all of those who called on me asked for help. Some were the elite of the population, who came to me to discuss ways of regenerating the country. A young mathematician from Guiyang, in Guizhou Province, Jiang Guangdi, called and missed me four times in a row, having limped with a disabled leg across half the city. I was very sorry and made a special appointment to meet with him.

He spoke on behalf of a group of his friends and associates in Guiyang. "We have a suggestion for the Central Committee of the Party. The group of college students from the period between 1977 and 1979 are exceptionally valuable to the country. They have been through the Cultural Revolution. They have experienced everything from the initial stages of fanaticism to the later stages of disillusionment, and have finally settled down to some hard rethinking. They have been to the country, the factories, and the army, and they have gone through the thick and thin of life at the grass roots. They detest the ultra-leftist line and support reform; they are young, yet matured by life itself. It will be hard for this mass of talent to accomplish anything substantial if they are scattered across the country. Would it not be possible to set up special training centers, using the model of the Huangpu Military Academy of the 1920s, to give each batch of these graduates a period of training and then send them across the country to be the backbone of reform?" He added modestly, "If this project is too big, we could take one step at a time. Supposing we could select one county and test the reforms in this limited area, strictly in accordance with the spirit of the Third Plenary Session, would that do?"

Apparently, Jiang Guangdi and his associates had thought things through. They had seen a threat coming from the conservatives and had designed this program. A few months later, I heard the deputy Party secretary of Beijing University mention an identical project.

I was greatly touched by Jiang Guangdi's sincerity, and it was from my encounter with him that I became interested in Guizhou Province, one of the poorest in China. Its young generation was full of political enthusiasm. "A new generation of public men will emerge from this place," I said to myself.

I relayed Jiang Guangdi's written proposal to Hu Yaobang. Two years later, I received a letter from Jiang. In it, he told me that Hu had sent his proposal to the Organization Department of the Central Committee, which had relayed it to the Organization Department of the provincial Party Committee. The officials there held a discussion session at which

Jiang and his associates were given a chance to express their views. But the tale ended there.

I was saddened by the news and could imagine how disappointed Jiang must have been. But on the other hand, it was men like Jiang who kept my own hopes alive.

Sometimes, news from within the Party was encouraging. One day, a slim young fellow from Ciqi County in Hunan Province came to visit me. He was an office worker at the county Party headquarters, and he told me that several government and Party units in the county, including the head of the Security Bureau, supported reform and opposed the county Party secretary. No one, however, could touch him because he had support from his superior, the prefectur Party secretary. The young man said that he spoke not only for himself, but also for many others; they all wanted me to help them with my pen. I was moved and promised to write, but I had still not written by the time of his third visit. He was disappointed, but did not give up hope that I would eventually do so.

Other news from within the Party was not so heartening.

Three college graduates from the Party Committee of Yichuan County, Henan Province, all Communist Party members, wrote to me repeatedly, telling me about their struggle against the local Party secretary. The locality was famous for Dukan wine, and the Party secretary would appropriate several thousand bottles a year to buy favors from his network of contacts in the district, the province, and all the way up to the Central Committee. The writers said that while reform had been nominally going on for four years, it was so ineffective that local peasants would actually stop reporters' cars—even kneel down in front of their cars—to ask them to report on the persecution and extortion at the grass-roots level. The three young men also told me how they had struggled over the years, written letters of exposure to the newspapers and publications for internal circulation, but all to no avail. The three of them were simply reassigned to other jobs. As for the Party secretary, he was promoted to succeed his protector as prefectural secretary when the latter was promoted to provincial level. The story was depressing, but in one sense, it gave me heart. In the early days, the sixties, for instance, this kind of fight against one's superiors—and within the Party too—would have been unthinkable. I wanted to write their story. It would not be all exposé—weren't the three young men positive heroes in the fight against corruption in high places?

But I did not make the trip or write the story. My time and energy were limited, but that was not the main reason. The fact was that the provincial and district Party Committee would not approve publication of my report, as required by the new press regulation. Even if I could have gotten it published, it would only have led to new accusations that I was "disturbing the stable situation."

I was continuously plagued by the question of why the most popular newspaper reports always drew severe attacks from higher authorities. And why was it that the circulation of the *People's Daily* soared to seven million copies when it was the object of official criticism, yet dropped to less than half that number when praise was poured on it from above?

From 1956 to 1958, 15 to 30 percent of journalists in China were labeled rightists for publishing negative reports. But hadn't the debate of the last twenty years—a debate paid for with the blood and tears of reporters—proved that the disasters in this land of ours were not caused by too many negative reports? On the contrary, excessive cover-ups of mistakes were part of the problem. From 1958 to 1976, the newspapers were filled with lies and exaggerations of our glorious achievements, and that was precisely the period when China was moving toward the abyss!

After some hard thinking, I realized that since the Third Plenary Session of the Central Committee in 1979, calling for reform, things had moved forward in the economic field (both in theory and in practice) and in the literary field, where many taboos had been broken, whereas the field of journalism had seen little change.

Undeniably, this was to some extent due to differing views on the role of the media. The old leaders still held to the belief that newspapers were a tool with which the Party unified the masses under one uniform ideology. They didn't believe that the people had a right to information on issues of national interest or a right to share in policy-making. They themselves, of course, needed to know what was really going on, which they did through the various publications for internal circulation. But since they preferred not to hear any unpleasant news, even those internal publications became quite tame during the eighties.

There was also the problem of how we regarded the mass of our readers. I had seized every opportunity to maintain that readers would not be alarmed or disheartened by bad news. In fact, I pointed out that with only a few exceptions, my readers had all responded positively to critical reports. They said that they felt elated reading my works, because they saw in them some hope for overcoming evil. But some Party elders did not agree with this view. In their opinion, the only way to boost credibility with the masses was to deluge them with bulletins of our positive achievements, to sing a uniform song of praise and glory.

But of course the matter had other aspects. Why, for example, were some leaders so sensitive when our papers carried the news that Reagan's son had lined up among the unemployed or that the president of Italy and his wife lived very modestly? Why did they react the way they did, taking the editor-in-chief to task, demanding an explanation? Why? Because they feared that people would reflect on such examples, and ask questions about them.

For three full years, I could not publish what I wanted to in the pages of the *People's Daily.* I cautiously published my literary reportage in literary journals. But as a reporter for the *People's Daily,* I could write only positive reports about achievements in economic construction and the improvements they had brought about in people's lives and relationships. I was not unwilling to do this kind of story, and I did write a few. But information flowing in from all sides pointed to the crying need for a reform of the political structure and the Party itself. Thus my own attention was unswervingly focused on abuses in Chinese political life. The more the eight pages of our paper were devoted to fulsome praise, the more I felt that my mission was to disclose the impending crisis and get the message across to my readers.

Since I was allowed to write only positive reports, I tried to instill some awareness of the other side of the story between the lines. For instance, in my report on a successful reformer in Liaoning Province, I highlighted the obstacles he had overcome in his struggles with conservatives. Writing about Party rectification of ethics and behavior in Jiangsu Province, I described their achievements at the beginning and end of my article, but in the middle part, I concentrated on the tortuous paths they had gone through and pointed to some of the problems that remained unsolved. In writing the story of Zhu Boru, a model Party member held up by the Central Committee for nationwide emulation, I did not limit myself to his good works, as did some of the other reports. I stressed the environment in which he had to move—the general corruption that he could do nothing to change—and that he had accomplished what he did in spite of this environment. I stressed that twice his acts of philanthropy had taken place right outside the gates of the Party Committee building, and that he was in effect doing their job for them. Thus I tried to use Zhu Boru's story to point out that there was something corrupt about the state of the Party, and that if it was not attended to, ten thousand Zhu Borus would not be able to save the country from its present predicament. Some of the higher-ups were pretty alert and detected the "sting to the article." Of course there was a sting; it was right there for everyone to see.

The Chinese political structure had transformed reporters into officials who simply worked on specific subjects, handed out in accordance with Party need and Party ideology. Docility was prized and distinctive writing discouraged. Sensitivity, independence, and courage were viewed with suspicion, and the word *reporter* took on a new meaning.

Beginning in the eighties, courageous and innovative reporters were often disciplined or removed from their positions altogether by the Party apparatus on the appearance of any substantial or controversial piece of writing. And this, of course, served as an effective warning to others. Things came to such a pass that the *Heilongjiang Daily* had to assign a reporter to cook up harmless pieces of criticism for display now and then. But even so, the wife of this reporter kicked up such a row over the risk to the whole family that she had to be pacified with money.

But man is a special kind of animal, after all; even in prison he will be seized by a desire to dance about once in a while. Still, even without the freedom of reporting, staffs wanted to modify the appearance of their papers, at least to make them look less forbidding. Many papers, therefore, made an effort to make their title headings and special columns more appealing.

Another example of such an effort in "reform" was the suggestion put forward by the head of a department of reporters at the *People's Daily*. He suggested that our reporters write "reports with commentaries" and passed around examples of such pieces by Western journalists. At the meeting to discuss this measure, I said, rather impatiently, "Of course we can always 'emulate' others, but I doubt we could ever do the same in China. Why hasn't this type of report appeared in our papers for the last thirty years? Obviously, it is not just a problem of form and technique; it is a problem that has to do with the status and the state of mind of the reporter. In China, what a reporter writes and does not write, or even the way he chooses to approach a subject, is not for him to decide. A good part of the reporter's working life consists of hanging around official doorsteps waiting for approval for his pieces. Under such humiliating circumstances, how can you expect a reporter to be free to expound on the affairs of the world? His underdog position needs to be changed before anything else can be done!" Several years have passed since that meeting, and "reports with commentaries" have still not appeared in either the *People's Daily* or the other papers.

This state of affairs stifled three generations of reporters. As early as the fifties, people were asking why there were no famous reporters in our country. But the fact was that from 1949 to 1978, no reporter could say what he really thought. Even today, the situation has not changed much. After all these years, one would be hard put to find enough good newspaper articles to make up a book.

In the summer of 1983, I learned that there had been a change of personnel on the Party Committee of Heilongjiang Province. The Party secretary who had so harassed me for my report "People or Monsters?" was ousted from his position for opposing reform.

Since the 1980s, people from the Daxinganling area of Heilongjiang had beaten a path to my door to report on the rampant theft of public property and the general state of lawlessness in that area. Their pleas for help had caused me to think of Daxinganling as one of the darkest corners of the country. Throughout the years, my relations with the leaders of Heilongjiang Province had been far from cordial, and so I refrained from going to Daxinganling to report on the problems there, even though I had promised to do so. I knew I would not get any cooperation from the provincial Party Committee. But now that the former secretary had been removed and the Party rectification program was operating in full swing, I thought that the provincial authorities would perhaps change their attitude. Since people were coming in great numbers to Beijing to report on their local leaders, it seemed inevitable that the provincial leadership would have to take some action. I thought they might send an inspection team to Daxinganling and that I would be able to work with them.

But contrary to my expectations, the head of the Propaganda Department of the provincial Party Committee evaded me when I arrived. He was one of the two secretaries of Binxian County I had portrayed positively in "People or Monsters?" He had not had good relations with the previous provincial secretary, but he had now become the right-hand man of the new one. The fact that he refused to see me was thus a sign of disapproval from his new boss, so I decided to abandon my plan of reporting on Daxinganling.

I headed east and arrived at a city on the northeastern tip of the map. There, economic losses due to political corruption were quite startling. In more than one instance, tens of millions of kilos of grain had rotted due to mismanagement. I hoped to use this material to show that without political reform, any gains from economic reform would surely be lost.

On my way to that city, another subject caught my eye. It was the story of Fu Gui, a broad-shouldered peasant whose whole life clearly reflected how Mao's misguided policies had stifled all initiative on the part of ordinary people and led to general stagnation. Fu Gui had refused to join the cooperatives that Mao had forced on the peasants. He saw that that type of leveling would encourage laziness and create a sluggards' paradise. He left farming to be a worker, hoping for a chance to prove himself. That chance came when he was asked to become the leader of a production team. On the strength of Fu Gui's organizational ability, his knack for business, and the force of his personality, the production team doubled their income under his leadership. What followed this success, however, was a string of libel and criticism until Fu Gui was sent to prison for "economic crimes." After his release from prison, his luck improved, and he was made leader of a production brigade and began to manage things on a larger scale. Once again he proved his ability and helped several villages escape from bleak poverty. When I met him, however, he was still plagued by old enemies and remained in danger of arrest and imprisonment.

I liked Fu Gui's open nature and perseverance, and his life story made me start thinking about the potential of the masses of people who had been stifled for the last thirty years.

chapter thirteen

There's More to It Than Meets the Eye

On April 20, 1981, the *PLA Daily* (the official paper of the People's Liberation Army) suddenly published an unusually long article, "The Four Cardinal Principles Must Not Be Discarded." It was signed by "a specially invited guest commentator" and was basically an attack on Bai Hua's filmscript *Bitter Love*. The script was an exposé of the Cultural Revolution centered around the story of a patriotic artist. According to the article, Bai Hua's first error was to use the past mistakes of the Party as an excuse "to paint a black picture of a socialist state under the leadership of the Communist Party." This, the article contended, was "the equivalent of attacking one's motherland and flinging curses at her." Bai Hua was guilty of "placing the Gang of Four and the Party into the same category and castigating them in the same breath." The article pointed out that Bai Hua should not have hinted that Mao had become a deity, and it warned that one should never detract from the sayings and thoughts of Comrade Mao Zedong.

The day the article appeared, the Central Broadcasting Station broadcast the entire article six times, and all the local papers carried reprints. All the signs indicated that a new campaign was brewing.

Were we going to hunt for rightists again? Some of the older writers grew anxious. Even the farmers in the Beijing suburbs were outraged. "What! Another *Hai Rui?*" they said (the play *Hai Rui Dismissed from Office* had been attacked by the Maoists as a prelude to the Cultural Revolution). The atmosphere across the nation was tense. The leftist writers looked forward to cleaning up the cultural mess caused by the rightists; leftist politicians looked forward to Hu Yaobang's removal from office and foresaw a return to the good old times. It was the first time since the end of the Cultural Revolution that the two political camps were pitted openly against each other and were prepared to fight it out. Others kept silent, watching the moves of the leftists, but as soon as the tension relaxed, many expressed their reservations about the campaign altogether. Meanwhile, there were rumors that the army was planning to rely on its leftist core to make a clean sweep of any rightist elements. I thought it was highly probable.

Bitter Love was then released as a film for "internal" viewing. This practice dated back to the days before the Cultural Revolution, when a cultural attack was always preceded by "internal" viewing, presumably to mobilize an army of critics. The film was then still being revised at the Changchun Film Studio at the direction of Hu Yaobang, but under some pretext, a cultural official of the PLA obtained a copy of the original and gave a showing.

The attack on *Bitter Love* was a drama in itself. The attacking side never overtly used Mao's teachings and policies in their attack, which would have revealed their retrogressive program and personal ambitions. Instead, they prepared their ground by lambasting a work of art while stalking their real political prey.

Of course, one should not be misled by the slogans of the leftists; some of them were exclusively bent on power and had little belief in their own rhetoric. Bai Hua was not their main target. Their actual target was Zhou Yang, at the helm of cultural affairs at the time, and after him, Hu Yaobang.

From the very beginning, Hu Yaobang was against the campaign. As early as May, right after the first article, he spoke up and diverted the impending attacks. Later, Deng Xiaoping himself spoke. He directed the *Literary Gazette* to publish a substantial criticism of Bai Hua, but in an effort to keep publicity of the affair to a minimum, he decreed that apart from the *People's Daily,* no other paper or magazine would reprint the critique. Gradually, Deng himself seemed to lose interest in the campaign.

It was apparent that the Central Committee of the Party was divided over the issue of *Bitter Love.* Yet with few exceptions, writers and artists did not stand up to protest this first assault on "bourgeois liberalization." At meetings over this issue, the so-called leftist writers and theorists attacked the play, while those in Bai Hua's camp remained silent.

I had been warned that I would be the next target and that articles attacking me had already been written. I had to act with caution. Within the reporters' section at *People's Daily,* the leftists and the opportunists voiced their support of the attack on Bai Hua, while a few others and I kept our thoughts to ourselves. The meetings of the two Party cells to which we belonged presented an interesting contrast. The Party secretary personally chaired the meeting of our group. Her opening speech was a close approximation of the attack on Bai Hua published in the *PLA Daily*. But after she spoke, a veteran reporter spoke up. "I can't make sense of all this," he said. "Corruption within the Party has reached such an appalling state, why don't we do something about that? That is the real danger. Why disregard that and launch attacks on 'liberalization' and what not? Granted *Bitter Love* is not perfect, but so what? It's not even shown publicly!" Now that he had started on this track, I followed quite naturally, and after me the others all said what they really thought. Nobody supported the position of the *PLA Daily*. At the other group meeting, however, everybody followed on cue and supported the attacks on Bai Hua. I thought this was a perfect reflection of the conflicting attitudes within the Party as a whole.

Long after the Bai Hua affair was over, I learned that a highly placed official visiting West Germany that fall had warned a group of students studying abroad to be prepared for a repetition of the antirightist campaigns. These words certainly carried weight, and they were certainly not said merely on his own authority.

In July a high-level meeting was convened within the precincts of Zhongnanhai, a "Discussion of Issues on the Ideological Front." I wonder what it was meant to achieve anyway. All the heads of Propaganda Departments and Party secretaries in charge of ideology at provincial levels were present; all the secretaries at the Central Committee, all the leading cadres at the Propaganda Department of the Central Committee, and those at the Ministry of Culture, all the notable figures in art and cultural circles—all were present. If the purpose was not to launch something, then why was there mobilization on such a scale? Notes of all the individual group discussions were printed in leaflet form, but, contrary to practice, they were not distributed to the participants. Evidently, this was to keep each group from learning what was going on in other groups. Why this precaution? Copies of only one speech were distributed, and that was a speech by the novelist Yao Xueyin, in which he wantonly attacked *Bitter Love*.

The meeting lasted three days without any results. But all present unanimously concurred with the conclusion issued by the Central Committee, which stated that for the last couple of years, the Party had slackened its control over ideology, alluding to bourgeois liberalization. It could also be understood as a critique on Hu Yaobang, as well as a point-blank criticism of Zhou Yang, then in charge of cultural affairs.

A new antirightist campaign did not materialize, but the tone was set for striking out at theorists, writers, and reporters all over the country. Since 1949, the Chinese intelligentsia had always been timid about confronting authority. This flurry of activity made them even more cautious. Writers and artists, whose sense of mission had never been strong, had more reason than ever to turn away from reality. Some took refuge in the ivory tower, writing with an eye to the Nobel Prize, while others turned to commercialism as a way out.

But the campaign was not without results: after the attack on Bai Hua, contributions to literary magazines dropped to one-sixth their normal level; some journals ran out of material altogether.

China on its path to reform was seemingly being propelled by two contradictory forces—one was economic liberalization, the other political and ideological antiliberalization. The first force would push forward a certain distance and then the second would take its turn and push it backward, to show the world that China had not betrayed Mao Zedong and socialism.

Deng Xiaoping had first put forward the slogan "Uphold the Four Cardinal Principles and Oppose Bourgeois Liberalization" in March 1979. At the beginning of 1980, there was a nationwide campaign to publicize the Four Cardinal Principles. In some provinces like Shandong and Jiangsu, where the leftists and the holdovers of the Gang of Four were still in power, there was widespread jubilation, as if the line of reform adopted by the Party Congress in 1978 had been discarded. County after county, factory after factory vied with one another in an uproarious publicity campaign to celebrate the end of reform. Big-character posters attacked Deng Xiaoping and Hu Yaobang by name. The local Party Committee and Public Security officers just sat back and watched. By then, I thought, Deng Xiaoping must have surely realized that the Four Cardinal Principles were diametrically opposed to his reform program and to thought liberation. What took me by surprise was that one year later, the army used those very slogans to launch the attack on Bai Hua and *Bitter Love*.

The Four Cardinal Principles had puzzled people from the very beginning. How did they differ from the ideological clichés of the past, from the early days down to the turmoil of the Cultural Revolution itself, when countless such catchwords had been tossed about? No politician had been able to explain the difference, and yet the new principles had now been written into the constitution.

There can be only one explanation for the Four Cardinal Principles; that is, the leadership of the Party wanted to limit reform to the economic field and would not tolerate any tampering with the existing political order and the ideology.

As for the slogan "oppose bourgeois liberalization," that could be used any time the interested bodies or their ideology were threatened. Since 1981, there have been three such purges on a national scale. Writers, journalists, poets, educators, philosophers, economists, editors, political theorists—none had escaped unscathed.

The leadership was, in fact, conducting an experiment to permit a high degree of liberalization in the economy while holding on to the four immutable principles: socialism without democracy and freedom; an authoritarian leadership of the Party with no supervision; a dictatorship of the proletariat with no mass participation and no accountability to the masses; and a Maoist school of Marxism-Leninism.

The results of such an experiment rapidly became very clear. First, economic reform was obstructed right and left; many leaders of reform, managers of enterprises, and political activists were toppled. Second, corruption, bribery, embezzlement, theft, smuggling, and tax evasion flourished on a national scale, while the children of the Party leaders seized the opportunities offered by the reform to enrich themselves.

In the fall of 1983, I was in Harbin, and a friend warned me there was trouble ahead. At the Second Plenary session of the Central Committee, Deng Xiaoping had called for an all-out effort to combat spiritual pollution. I was totally confused. From my recent research, I knew that corruption within Party ranks was the outstanding problem on which the Party should concentrate its efforts. Why, then, this repeat of 1957 and this renewed attack on intellectuals? I made haste to return. I canceled a speaking engagement in Shenyang; under the circumstances, my host at the Shenyang Writers' Association might have had second thoughts about the invitation anyway.

The atmosphere in Beijing was threatening. In the courtyard of the *People's Daily* building, the expressions on people's faces matched the general atmosphere. Unlike the attack on Bai Hua two and a half years ago, this new campaign was initiated by Deng himself and was not to be taken lightly.

I met the head of a department and asked him what was happening.

He was afraid to commit himself, and he asked my opinion. I told him I was just back from the provinces, and that at worst, I supposed it would be a repeat of the antirightist campaign, but that it would not be as easy nowadays to label people with the rightist tag. When I asked him what he thought, he answered, to my surprise, that you never can tell. Then I met Wang Ruoshui, a leading philosopher and the deputy editor-in-chief of the *People's Daily;* he was depressed. I assured him that it would not be so easy to get another campaign going. He was the prime target this time and could not afford to be so optimistic. "It's hard to say," he said; "power is in their hands."

A few days later, I read Wang Zhen's two speeches in the papers. In both, Wang Zhen, a hard-liner and president of the CCP Advanced Training Center, emphasized that the teachers of political theory at the center had to be screened for anti-Party elements, that the teaching staff must not be allowed to pursue anti-Marxist, antisocialist studies under the cover of theoretical research. What he meant to say was that there were class enemies within the ranks of teachers and researchers, and that issues in theoretical research were not pure research, but could be considered "enemy" activities.

Soon after the publication of Wang Zhen's speeches, the basic thoughts of Hu Qiaomu's and Deng Liqun's speeches were relayed to us. They were the two leading conservative ideologues, and they went much further than Deng Xiaoping himself. Their main target was Zhou Yang and his speech on the centenary of the death of Marx, in which he touched on the problem of humanism and alienation. Wang Ruoshui had helped in the drafting of that speech, and was therefore placed on the bench of the accused along with Zhou. Hu Qiaomu said:

Spiritual pollution is a real political issue. Zhou Yang's sayings could be used by dissidents for their political program. According to his theory of alienation, there is no freedom in our country, and exploitation has not been abolished. He says that in our society, workers are not masters of their own products, that they are oppressed, and that compulsory division of labor makes creative work impossible, and so on. This is counterrevolutionary agitation, reversing right and wrong.

In his speech, Deng Liqun pointed to two then largely unknown articles in an academic journal on alienation published in Heilongjiang Province, and labeled them counterrevolutionary pamphlets disguised as discussions of alienation.

As for Wang Ruoshui, he attacked Mao Zedong as early as 1979; he suspected Mao of base motives in launching the Cultural Revolution; he questioned Mao's personal ethics, and recently, attacked Mao's saying about poverty being an advantage. . . . In any event, he used every opportunity to attack Mao. In addition, he was always making insinuations about public servants turning into lords and masters, seeking private gains, lording over the people, sons of the people who then turned against their parents, civil servants turning to rulers, evading supervision by the people, and so on. . . . The underground groups quote him to instigate a second Cultural Revolution.

To implicate Wang Ruoshui, Deng Liqun added that he was always making grand statements about man as the starting point of Marxism, while ignoring the historical context, and therefore providing the theoretical grounds for bourgeois liberalization.

Why this ban on discussing alienation in socialist society? The only reply given was that Marx had never mentioned alienation in connection with socialist society. But there were many things that Marx never mentioned: when Mao started his Cultural Revolution, did he stop to consult Marx and Engels?

The meetings for criticism of spiritual pollution were even more glum than the ones to criticize Bai Hua. Two years before, while opening fire on Bai Hua, the leftists had spoken out in the open and filled the gaps of silence during meetings. By doing so, they damaged their own image and had not reaped any benefits. So this time, they decided to lie low; they silently kept watch, in case this campaign sizzled out as the previous one had. If it didn't, they figured, there would be time to speak out later.

The present campaign encountered one stumbling block from the very beginning: the campaign was focused on the abstract term *alienation*. This term not only was unknown to the masses, but was unfamiliar even to educated people, as it had been avoided in orthodox Marxist discourse. Thus those who were against the campaign but didn't want to oppose it openly because Deng Xiaoping was behind it hid behind this abstract term. For instance, at the staff meeting of the *People's Daily*, one old reporter would invariably begin by saying, "Now what is this alienation about, anyway? I've never read of it. Suppose we ask someone who's knowledgeable about it to give us a talk. After that, we can begin our criticism." Some units did indeed invite scholars to lecture on the subject. At the time, the All-China Federation of Workers was holding a national convention; this convention, of course, had to make an official gesture in support of the current campaign and in repudiation of the concept of alienation. Since the delegates did not know anything about alienation, they had to begin by learning and listening to lectures. Contrary to the anticipated effect, people found in the concept of alienation some of the answers to questions that had long baffled them: How was it that a Communist Party that had started out well could produce a Lin Biao and a Gang of Four? How was it that Mao had deteriorated from a revolutionary leader to a national scourge? Why was there so much corruption within the Communist Party? People were asking these questions, and the concept of alienation gave them clues to what they were looking for.

As for the politicians and ideologues who were releasing volleys of attack against the concept of alienation, they did not have a word of explanation for the corruption that was going on all around them, but simply kept harping on alienation according to their own definition of the word.

In no previous campaign had the target been so loosely discribed. From the most abstract concepts, such as humanism and alienation, to the most concrete details of everyday life—anything that ran counter to Mao's long-upheld model of self-effacement, anything that overstepped the bounds of a rigid nationalism that rejects the slightest foreign influence—all these were listed as spiritual pollution. Can you imagine a notice posted on the gates of the imposing building of the Beijing Party Committee that says "No admittance to persons with hair too long, skirts too short, slacks too tight, or face powdered and rouged"? But there it was. So you can imagine what it was like in the provinces.

The Chinese leadership could no longer ignore reactions at the grass-roots level. Hu Yaobang and Zhao Ziyang advised Deng Xiaoping of the negative reaction to the campaign and of its possible adverse effect on economic reform. The reaction abroad also added weight to their arguments. Around November, word came down that the countryside would be exempt from the campaign. One week later, it was reported that the economy would also be exempt. Following that, science and technology were added to the privileged list. And so this short-lived campaign ended.

But the leftists in Beijing did gain something from the campaign against spiritual pollution after all: the leadership of the *People's Daily* changed hands. I still remember that Sunday morning of October 30, when a meeting of all Party members was called. Knowing beforehand what the meeting was about, I was punctual and took detailed notes. Hu Qiaomu and Deng Liqun came personally to announce the change.

Hu looked pale and emotionally tense—for him, it was a victory at long last. He announced the decision of the secretariat of the Central Committee—to accept the resignation of Hu Jiwei as head of the *People's Daily*, and to remove Wang Ruoshui from the post of deputy editor-in-chief. He announced at the same time that this occasion marked the beginning of rectification for all administrative units affiliated with the central government and the Central Committee. I could not help seeing the irony of it all. So this is how rectification started, by sticking the knife into the *People's Daily*, the paper that had promoted reform of the Party and the society most faithfully during the past few years.

Hu Qiaomu pointedly criticized one of Hu Jiwei's talks, saying that the latter had tried to put the position of the newspaper above the Party as representative of the people. Hu Jiwei had, in his talk, drawn lessons from the past, when the newspaper was just the mouthpiece of the Party, aggravating its mistakes, and he proposed that the newspaper should scrutinize the Party on behalf of the people. Hu Qiaomu denounced this stand as "reversing the role of the Party and the people." "The people are not infallible," he exclaimed; "suppose the people make mistakes, then what? This attitude reveals Hu Jiwei's distrust of the Party." Hu Qiaomu was high-strung; during this speech, he was twice on the verge of tears when he pointed out how Hu Jiwei and Wang Ruoshui had deprecated the Party, thus displaying his own devotion. After Hu Qiaomu's talk, some people clapped, which surprised me. I had a high opinion of my colleagues, but it seemed I had overestimated some of them. The weather that day was fine, but to me it was dark and bleak.

Deng Liqun, also present during Hu Qiaomu's talk, smiled throughout. Those two had reason to exult. Since 1978, the *People's Daily* had always been a sore in their eyes. Xinhua News Agency had always followed their lead, as had a few other papers in Beijing. But not the *People's Daily*. It remained independent and immutable.

Still, those two had counted their chickens too early. In that same speech, Hu Qiaomu had threatened, "Leadership in theoretical and art circles must be readjusted; many people will be affected." But in fact, they only had time to "readjust" the *People's Daily*. A few days later, the situation changed drastically, and their dreams of all-round readjustment had to be put aside. They had planned to remove Zhou Yang, but that fell through. They had also planned to disband the Research Institute of Marxism-Leninism of the Chinese Academy of Social Sciences, but that, too, failed to materialize.

chapter fourteen

I Tear

Apart the

Curtain

People were disgusted with the prevalent corruption within the Party and the society as a whole and placed their last hopes on the Party rectification program of 1984.

As for myself, I had good reason to distrust the campaign altogether. The campaign in 1978–79 to round up followers of the Gang of Four had in fact been the first stage of the current drive. But what I had seen in Shandong was a repeat of the persecution of their former victims by those who had grabbed power in 1967. In some areas, these persecutions were just as bad as they had been during the Cultural Revolution. In Liaoning, on the other hand, the reinstated veteran cadres had shielded the followers of the gang for their own reasons.

In 1980, the rules regulating Party members had been announced. The rules forbade special privileges for leading cadres, as well as all forms of seeking self-interest through power. During the next four years, however, things had gone from bad to worse.

In 1983, the Central Disciplinary Committee of the CCP had published an open letter to the Party, requesting Party cadres to give up their extra housing space, and later issued another special order requesting them to register any living space over and above their legitimate allotment. The whole thing turned into a joke. In Harbin, an old friend told me that veteran cadres were not only holding on to their extra housing, but snatching up more. He said, "To date, there has not been a single case of extra housing being retrieved." I asked why, and he said it was simple. The leading cadres did not dare pursue their subordinates because the latter would ask, "What about you?"

In my notes, in the more than ten thousand letters stored in my house and my office, there were countless examples of cases where cadres had encountered all sorts of difficulties while trying to combat corruption within the Party according to the new Party regulations.

But given my naïveté and innate optimism, I soon forgot all that, even forgot all the circumstances of my own life. In those few years, all the problems that I had written about were precisely those that the Party itself was trying to deal with; they were all targets of Party discipline. If this was so, why was I being pushed into a corner? Why was it that I never heard the voice of the Party in my support when I was attacked by the various provincial committees?

At the beginning of the year, Hu Yaobang sent down this directive:

The Party rectification program must settle down to the job in all seriousness. In the coming three years of the Party rectification program, the People's Daily *should publish ten thousand examples for emulation and expose three thousand for criticism.*

I made a rough calculation. This meant a thousand exposés a year, or roughly three a day, which was simply unprecedented. I rubbed my hands in anticipation.

Of course, I knew that holding up positive examples for emulation would be no problem—ten thousand, a hundred thousand, you name it. The problem was criticism and exposure. A few years prior, Hu Yaobang had also said that praise and criticism could share the pages of the *People's Daily* on a seven-three ratio. In fact, criticism never took up more than 3 percent of the paper's copy. But even this amount earned warnings from above. As with other aspects of the Party rectification program, there was no means of guaranteeing the quota for criticism and praise. Still, I believed that since the general secretary had given the word, it should be accepted. After all, I thought, times had changed; and what's more, we are in the midst of Party rectification.

That year, I made three visits to Xian, the capital of Shaanxi Province. In the process I came to understand how difficult rectification would be.

In 1964, Hu Yaobang had taken up his post as the first secretary of the Shaanxi provincial Party Committee and third secretary of the Northwest Bureau of the Communist Party. In 1964 and 1965, the whole countryside was embroiled in the Socialist Education Campaign. Mao had announced that most of the power in the countryside had fallen into alien hands; that is, the leadership positions were held by people who were Communists only in name. Armed with Mao's doctrine, the campaign was characterized by more ultra-leftist violence than previous ones. The barbarity in the Shaanxi countryside was the most extreme. Hu Yaobang made a tour of Changan County and discovered that local cadres had been incarcerated and made to confess under physical abuse, even torture. Shocked, he rushed through eight counties in a single week, issuing orders right and left to end the violence. As a result, he managed to offend the first secretary of the Northwest Bureau, and was himself under severe fire from the bureau. The attacks continued even after he left the area to recuperate from illness in Beidaihe.

In the twenty years since then, factional interests had prevailed, and the leaders who had wrongly attacked Hu were still in positions of power, while those who had sided with or sympathized with him had been left out in the cold.

I wondered whether the Cultural Revolution had subsequently changed the balance, and this was precisely the point on which I was enlightened. During the Cultural Revolution, the political forces in Xian, capital of Shaanxi Province, had in fact been divided into two factions, as they had everywhere else. But the faction that had gained the upper hand and benefited the most from the chaos was not the Red Guards and makers of revolution, but the political cadres who had been in favor before. The upright and kind-hearted people who were better educated and more open-minded lost out, while those who were adept at the political game and who were not above toadying found their path to officialdom was always smooth and easy.

In Shaanxi Province, known as the cradle of Chinese civilization, the ancient traditions of the Han people are passed on to the Communist Party through the members with peasant origins. North Shaanxi was the most important base of the Communist Party before it took over the mainland, and it produced a batch of veteran leaders who had been involved in the peasant uprisings since the twenties. Their cultural and theoretical training, however, was sadly out of keeping with the power they wielded. But position and power had invested them with blind self-confidence and absolute power in decision-making. These cadres of peasant origin were the first to wield power within the Communist Party, given their long experience of warfare, and the first to enjoy the privilege of power immune from any supervision. The sweet savor of power, the obedience of the peasants under them, and the cadres' habituation to cruelty through war made them absolutely unscrupulous in the struggle for power. In these struggles, they had to count absolutely on the loyalty of their friends and relatives; consequently, notions of loyalty and kinship through blood links or locality or work relationships were stronger here than anywhere else.

At first, I was not particularly interested in the case that now brought me to Xian. It was a timeworn case of a debt owed by the army to a peasant—a debt incurred forty years ago, during the war. Hardly a matter of any significance to present-day China, I thought, particularly when so many vital cases, affecting the lives and fates of thousands of people, filled my dossiers and notebooks, waiting to be written. I simply did not want to get involved in this particular case. But when the peasant, Guo Jianying, walked into my room with his son and sat down in front of me, I was struck by his appearance. Decades of hard work in the wind and sun of the desert plateau of the Northwest had turned Guo's face a deep brown. He sat before me, stoic and motionless, as his son recounted his story. His attitude seemed to me a silent accusation.

Guo came from a very poor area, so poor that when one family fried their vegetables in cooking oil, the whole village could smell it. Because Guo and his family could not make a living on farming alone, he supplemented his income by transporting household wares from Xian to his village for a local shopkeeper. Later, Guo set up his own store, selling straw sandals, wooden eating bowls, cigarettes, and other small items. The Kuomintang's ruinous taxation policies, however, had forced him out of business.

In the late summer of 1946, Li Xiannian's troops of the Communist Fourth Army broke through the encircling troops of Kuomintang general Hu Zongnan, and arrived at the southern part of Shaanxi Province. With the enemy at his heels, and with no provisions or reinforcements on the way, Li Xiannian had no choice but to look for help from the local people. Since Guo Jianying was considered rather well-to-do among the villagers, Li Xiannian's troops approached him for assistance. Out of resentment against the Kuomintang and pity for the shivering soldiers, Guo agreed to help. He even gave his own pair of lined trousers to a soldier.

That night, he traveled to the city of Xian, and on the basis of his honest reputation, borrowed money from several acquaintances. He hid the banknotes in a basket and made his way back on foot, not stopping until he had personally delivered the money—more than twice as much as many of the wealthier landlords had brought—to the Communist Fourth Army. Guo was given a handwritten IOU and told he could retrieve the money at any time from the chairman of the border government, Lin Buoqu. The Kuomintang army, however, soon caught wind of the affair. Guo was sought on charges of "aiding and abetting Communist bandits" and had to flee the area with his wife and son. They hid in the mountains for some time and eventually made their way to Xian, where they then settled. Guo returned to the retail business and began repaying the debts he had incurred on behalf of the Communists. He had to take out a large loan to do so, and for collateral, he used his brick house with a courtyard.

Following liberation in 1949, Guo hoped for reimbursement from the government. The Communists did in fact repay many of their debts from the war, so his hopes were not far-fetched. By this time, Guo had become a clerk at the state-run Lanzhou Transportation Company, and in filling out a form about his personal history, he had mentioned the debt. To his surprise he was fiercely reproved. "Do you mean to say that the Communist Party is in *your* debt?" he was asked.

Guo was, by nature, a timid man. By 1949 he had become a man of substance; he owned not only a house, but a share in a truck as well. Of course, the truck had long since been deeded to the state, since Guo was afraid of being labeled bourgeois. Following that initial reproof, he never mentioned the debt again and continued paying the installments on his loan.

At the height of the socialization program in 1958, Guo's house was appropriated by the state and then rented to him again. During the Cultural Revolution, conditions became even worse for Guo; he and his family were forced to leave their home with nothing but the clothes on their backs. Why? Because Guo had lent money to the Communists. And what was the reasoning behind this accusation? Before 1966 the reasoning was: If you had that much money to lend, then you were a capitalist; after the Cultural Revolution, the new reasoning was: If you were a capitalist, then how could you lend money to the Communists unless you were a political swindler?

Guo had six children and a monthly salary of only fifty yuan. After they were forced out of their home, they could barely survive. What was even more tragic, however, was the political legacy left to the children. As children of a capitalist swindler, they were discriminated against everywhere. Their chances for study, for employment, and for marriage were cut off.

In 1972, Guo's wife decided to try to help the family before it was too late. But what could she do without a formal education and wobbling on bound feet? Too poor to afford a bus, she wandered the streets, but her pleas fell on unsympathetic ears. She waited for hours outside of closed doors, only to be sent on to the next house to wait again. By 1983, Guo's wife had grown too weak and tired to walk, and Guo had developed a heart problem. The couple could die at any minute; they might never see a reversal of the unjust accusations against them. It was at this point that they decided to come to Beijing.

Guo Jianying wrote a letter to Li Xiannian, now president of China, who had signed the IOU for Guo in 1946. Li issued a directive to the municipal committee of Xian to ameliorate the situation of the Guo family. The Party secretary of the municipal committee, He Chenghua, however, paid no attention to the directive. Further official inquiries into the matter only resulted in further measures against Guo. The court ordered that Guo give up the piece of land he still owned for a public building. When Guo contested the court's ruling, he was manhandled and his daughter was detained. It was at that point that Guo and his son came to me.

I had already learned, and written, quite a bit about things in Xian. With the help of a young free-lance reporter, Yuan Chunqiang, I had unearthed a relic: there in a hospital in Xian, I discovered the political and social atmosphere of the Cultural Revolution preserved unchanged. The people who had come to power during the Cultural Revolution were still in charge, and the people who had been victimized were still oppressed, some of them forbidden to work at their original jobs. The living conditions of the intellectuals were atrocious. The piece that I published, "Dirt Under a Surgical Gown," described the situation of Shaanxi Province in a nut-shell. That the preposterous absurdities of the Cultural Revolution were still a way of life in Xian and Shaanxi was shocking beyond belief.

The same morning that my piece was published in the *People's Daily*, the Central Broadcasting Station broadcast excerpts, which created a sensation in Xian. People rushed to buy the day's copy of the *People's Daily*. As supply was limited, copies were resold at a profit; the price grew and grew until one copy cost two and a half yuan, more than thirty times the original price. People even made photocopies that sold at over eighty fen a piece. All this excitement was because my article was the first to expose the political situation in Xian in the thirty-five years since the founding of the People's Republic.

And a misunderstanding on the part of readers had inadvertently helped boost publicity. In that article, the phrase *north Shaanxi cronies* had twice cropped up. Coincidentally, the local high-ranking cadres who held the reins of power in the province and were at the root of all the backwardness and poverty in the area were called the "north Shaanxi gang." When I mentioned "north Shaanxi cronies" as the supporters and shielders of those people running the hospital, my readers incorrectly assumed I was giving a signal that the Central Committee was ready for an all-out attack on the "north Shaanxi gang"; thus the wave of excitement.

While Shaanxi is one of the poorest, most backward areas of China, far removed from the economically developed coastal cities, it was also the most important revolutionary base of the Communists after the Long March. Unfortunately, it also had many senior cadres, who were under-educated, narrow-minded, and conservative. One writer described them in the following terms:

They had lived in cave dwellings for generations, never having seen a house. One can imagine how they felt after the liberation, when they entered the city of Xian with its multistoried buildings and cars. They must have thought this was what Communism meant. They held all the reins of power and took their privileges for granted as a reward for their hard struggle. They had no use for culture or science, no use for intellectuals; in fact, they saw them as a threat to their own authority. Hence their dislike of and discrimination against intellectuals.

It was in this special world in Shaanxi, the cradle of our ancient civilization, that I came to a deeper understanding of the problems of China. This was possible because circumstances gave me access to new information. For previous six years, I had often conducted long interviews late into the night, my notebooks filling with virtually illegible notes scribbled down in a state of complete exhaustion. But all those interviews were nothing compared to what I learned in the days I spent in Xian. Workers, ordinary citizens, government cadres of all levels from section leaders to former provincial governors—all requested interviews. Often two or three people would be waiting as I interviewed, and I had to apologize for keeping them waiting. Stopping for meals was out of the question. We simply bought food and ate as we talked. When I left Xian, my throat was sore and swollen from all the talking I had done during that stay. But I felt enriched and rewarded.

One night in late January 1984, a man named Gu Laigen walked into my room. He was short, somewhat stout, and his rather homely appearance and a voice slightly hoarse from a cold gave him an air of credibility. Had I not known of him, I would have taken him for a good man.

But I knew his story: a native of Shanghai, an orphan from a poor, working-class background, who had come to Xian in the early fifties to work, first in a construction unit, then for the local youth organization, and now at the Land and Housing Bureau. He had twice played a major role in the case of Guo Jianying. In 1970, he illegally appropriated a piece of land belonging to Guo and built a house with a courtyard on it for a section leader. Some years later, this same house was demolished to make room for an apartment building. The Guos, of course, did not agree, and put up a makeshift dwelling on their own land. Gu Laigen had bribed a court official to evict the Guos. He called in the police and hired some rough-necks to use other methods of persuasion, causing an incident that shocked the city.

Gu Laigen affected the air of a worker; obviously, that status had brought him countless privileges over the years. He began by saying how busy he was and by recounting the problems he always had to overcome in demolishing and constructing buildings—all, of course, for the benefit of others.

I interrupted him. "It is said that you were a prominent figure during the Cultural Revolution, that you carried a gun and were protected by bodyguards."

"Nothing of the sort," he protested. He also denied having instigated an armed mass demonstration in front of the municipal building, during which people had been killed—an offense for which he had been arrested and convicted, but then acquitted, with the help of his gang. He denied everything, insisting he had been framed. I did not argue. I had read his files.

A few months later, after I had gathered more information, I came to realize that a man like Gu Laigen was a key to understanding the China of the last thirty-odd years. He was the typical product of the "socialism" that had been in effect years before the outbreak of the Cultural Revolution. Through the socialization program of the early fifties, the private houses of law-abiding citizens such as Guo Jiangying had been appropriated and made public property under the management of the Land and Housing Bureau. At the same time, over a period of more than twenty years, our special sort of socialism had encouraged population growth without the construction of new housing. This brought about an increase in the value of housing, and a comparable increase in the power and privileges of the Land and Housing Bureau. Had these houses been left in the hands of private owners, the most they could have earned from them was some rent. But as public property in the hands of cadres acting in the name of the public, people had to pay far more than rent. According to reliable sources, Gu Laigen and his gang had more than once exchanged the houses under their management for arms and ammunition for factional infighting. And not a few of those state-owned houses had been converted to prison cells and torture chambers during the Cultural Revolution. Gu Laigen had also used much of the 40,000 yuan of rent collected under his management to reward his supporters.

Thus, our special kind of socialism not only created a housing shortage, but also bred thugs such as Gu Laigen, who accumulated power and wealth under the guise of the Party line. Gu was masterful in flattering his superiors and absolutely ruthless in evicting people from houses to be demolished. More important, he controlled the houses taken from the evicted. The profits he made from handling these houses are incalculable. In Guo Jianying's case alone, judges, lawyers, officials of the public-security bureau, and witnesses had been bribed with housing. On the train, a local traveler told me that to insult a person in Xian, you might say, "You're as bad as the Kuomintang," but an even greater insult would be to say, "You're worse than the Bureau of Land and Housing."

I was shocked. While the perpetrators in this case were Communist Party members, not even the Party's deadliest enemies could have committed worse crimes.

The Party leadership was in fact divided over the question of Guo Jianying's claims. The team of investigators headed by Deputy Mayor Li Tingbi had reached the conclusion that the Communist Party was indebted to Guo Jianying and that confiscating his house had been a mistake. They recommended that his house be returned to him and that the debt be repaid. But the team of investigators headed by the general secretary of the municipal Party Committee, He Chenghua, had come to the opposite conclusion. Both Li Tingbi and He Chenghua were high-ranking Party leaders of over forty years' standing. They did not discuss the issue face to face, but I listened to both sides.

The investigators from the municipal Party Committee of course had to concede that Guo had lent a considerable sum of money to the Fifth

Division of the Fourth Route Army thirty-eight years ago, but they insisted that he had not done so voluntarily, that the troops had kidnapped him and extorted the money from him as an enemy sympathizer. What's more, they accused him of having betrayed a Communist cadre, who was later killed by the Kuomintang. And finally, in order to have grounds to hold on to his house, they made Guo out to be a capitalist. To this end, they tried to inflate the value of Guo's property by adding in his grandfather's property, as well as any other property he had owned in the past. Then, to inflate his rental income, they calculated as rental space all of the rooms occupied by his family and the rooms he lent his relatives free of charge.

I could not stop thinking about this poor man who had been forced to flee to the mountains for helping the Communists and whose eldest son had died during the flight. The Party should have been thankful to him, but for the past thirty years it had only returned evil for good, and now in Guo's sickness and old age its representatives wanted to deal the final blow so that his children would never see justice.

Of course, I am not saying that He Chenghua had intentionally worked hand in hand with the Kuomintang. But twenty years ago, He Chenghua accomplished something that neither the Kuomintang nor the other enemies of the Communist Party ever managed to do: he had exaggerated the size of the harvest in Gansu Province (where he was then working), and he had withheld information about several natural disasters that had destroyed the crops. As a result, one-tenth of the province's thirteen million inhabitants died of starvation.

I took a hard look at his hands as we talked. A friend of mine who is an artist told me that he had once met He Chenghua in the sixties, at the height of the famine. He had waited for the Party secretary in the lobby of the grandest hotel in the city of Lanzhou, while "his highness" was dancing. When the dance was over, He deigned to meet with my friend the painter, who could not help but notice the Party secretary's hands—plump, white, and delicate. My friend was burning with anger, for outside the hotel, hundreds of thousands of peasants were starving to death.

He Chenghua bore no personal grudge against Guo Jianying, any more than he did against the starving peasants of Gansu Province. And money to repay Guo's loan would certainly not come from his own pocket. But once Guo went to Beijing to petition for justice, he became He's personal enemy. Any accusation leveled against the city of Xian was a slap in the face to the Party secretary, even though he was not named in the accusation. To a Party leader, it is a matter of life and death always to be right. And so He Chenghua had to prove Guo wrong, which was not hard to do, considering he had so many people under him to help him either find or fabricate evidence against Guo. There were also plenty of volunteers from the public at large. The families who had been renting Guo's rooms since the state had appropriated them, for example, benefited more than a little from turning the "class struggle" against their landlord. A man by the name of Wei, a former soldier in the Kuomintang army who was now head of the neighborhood committee, had systematically used the bit of power in his hands to make things hard for the Guos. One of the Guo children, who was looking for a job, had to move his residence registration elsewhere, to escape Wei's petty malice. And then there were the Zhangs and the Yangs, who had profited from spying and reporting on the poor family. And Gu Laigen, officer in the Land and Housing Bureau, was of course a staunch supporter of Party Secretary He Chenghua.

In the case of Guo Jianying and other cases of the obstruction of justice, the perpetrators were perhaps motivated by abstract leftist ideology, but basically they were driven by personal interests or the interests of a group, as Gu evidently was. Leftist slogans were often just a camouflage for self-serving acts.

As I was about to leave Xian, I was struck by the fact that ever since Hu Yaobang has been attacked for rightist tendencies in this area during the sixties, leftist tendencies had been in ascendancy. Many ultra-leftists of an earlier era had passed through the Cultural Revolution unharmed and were now doing quite nicely for themselves. Those cadres within the Party, on the other hand, who were more humane in outlook, who strove for practical results in their work, who were better educated, had more of a conscience, and were more independent-minded were bound to lose favor sooner or later, and would either lose their positions or simply be pushed aside and forgotten. Why was this so? As to the so-called leftists, old hands at attacking the so-called rightist elements and victimizing innocent people, how many of them were motivated by their beliefs, and how many were just pursuing self-interest under leftist slogans?

Thinking along these lines, I realized that all the so-called struggles between the left and the right in Party history had to be reassessed. Especially once the Party had come to power in a particular area, it was a struggle not between different sets of political beliefs, but between those who were more humane and more devoted to public interests on the one hand, and political opportunists seeking personal or group interests on the other. Now if the second category had always been in the ascendancy in the Party, was it any surprise that the Party had been bogged down by mistakes and even diverted from its original goals?

Leaving Xian, I felt terrible heartache and frustration. Cases of injustice which had already shocked me in 1979 had not been righted, while new ones were piling up. The per capita productivity rate for Xian had dropped while production costs had risen. The situation continued as late as 1987, when another scandalous case of persecution, in which one of the provincial governors had had a hand, made headlines across the nation. The victim had made contributions to reform, but ended up a fugitive on the list of those wanted by the police.

My report on Guo Jianying's case, entitled "The Rights and Wrongs of Thirty-Eight Years," was completed in March. The leadership of the *People's Daily* knew that it would offend the Party leadership of Shaanxi Province and the city of Xian and decided to wait for a favorable opportunity to offer it to the public. They waited a full five months; the article was not published until August 1984. This piece, five thousand Chinese characters long, did not contain a word of reproach to the provincial Party Committee of Shaanxi or to the Central Committee of the CCP. The furthest it ventured was to criticize the Party secretary of Xian, He Chenghua, by name. To my complete surprise, however, it provoked the biggest storm in my years as a reporter.

In September, I was reporting in Chengdu, Sichuan Province, when a long-distance call from the head of the *People's Daily* suddenly ordered me back to Beijing. I guessed the reason, but on my way back I was very calm. My report was based on voluminous data from investigation teams, as well as on evidence given to me by fair-minded comrades from the Bureau of Land and Housing. I was confident.

The appearance of "The Rights and Wrongs of Thirty-Eight Years" rocked the city of Xian the day it appeared. It was an even greater shock than my earlier piece, "Dirt Under a Surgical Gown," had been. Readers from all levels of society were intrigued by the case of Guo Jianying. They also wondered also whether the Party leaderships of Xian and Shaanxi Province could be toppled, whether they would see some change. They speculated that I might possibly be sent down by Hu Yaobang on a special mission.

The first information that was hurled at me when I arrived in Beijing was that "The Rights and Wrongs of Thirty-Eight Years" had aroused such opposition from certain quarters that the normal work schedule of the Secretariat of the Party Central Committee had been disrupted for the last month. The one who bore the brunt of the attack was Hu Yaobang. The situation was so serious that Hu Yaobang could not avoid making a public gesture. At the meeting of the editorial staff of *People's Daily*, Hu's comments were made public: "Liu Binyan has not drawn a lesson from 1957. He had better give up reporting and keep to creative writing." My colleagues were shocked by the injustice of these remarks.

But of what was I guilty? Nobody could find any holes in the article itself. The only problem was an oversight in the process of seeking approval: for publishing criticism of heads of a provincial government, prior permission from the Central Committee was required. But I was a reporter, unconcerned with those rules. It was the editor-in-chief's business to seek approval for publication, and the deputy general editor had already acknowledged his own negligence. So where was my error? There was none. But they would not let me off. To calm the ruffled feelings of people at the Shaanxi provincial Party Committee, a member of the Politburo and member of the Secretariat produced a memorandum of a tripartite discussion between the Central Committee, the *People's Daily*, and the provincial Party Committee, stating that Liu Binyan was guilty of gross errors and should be punished.

It was a clear warning that a very big cloud was hanging over me. But I had no intention of backing down.

At first I thought that Hu Yaobang had not meant it when he said that I should give up reporting. I thought he had said it to appease my opponents. But later, a member of the Politburo talked to me and repeated the injunction that I give up reporting, so it seemed it was meant in earnest. Yet at almost the same time, the leadership of the *People's Daily* asked me to publish something to dispel rumors afloat in Shaanxi that I had left the *People's Daily*. So the October 3 issue of *People's Daily* carried a signed article of mine, and after that nobody from the Central Committee bothered me about giving up reporting.

The Fourth Congress of the Writers' Association convened in Beijing on New Year's Eve and ended during the first week of 1985. Before this meeting, Hu Qiaomu and Deng Liqun had already taken measures to limit freedom of creative writing with the intention of returning to what they felt were the good old days of 1958 to 1966. They also, of course, had moved to put their own people in leading positions in the Writers' Association. To this end, they called a meeting of writers in their own camp in September at the Jingxi Hotel. At the meeting, they publicly expressed their dissatisfaction with the situation in art and literature since the Third Congress of the Writers' Association, which had been held in 1979. Some even attacked Hu Yaobang by name. They were clearly collecting their energies for an attack during the coming congress.

Somehow Hu Yaobang got wind of this movement of the leftists before the congress, and he was on his guard. On the eve of the Fourth Congress of the Writers' Association, at a meeting of the Secretariat of the Central Committee of the CCP, he put forward a set of guidelines that were to be followed at the coming congress: (1) that freedom of creative writing should be endorsed and (2) that the leadership of the Writers' Association should be elected democratically. Politburo member Hu Qili gave his talk on the freedom of creative writing on behalf of the Central Committee, but of course he had Hu Yaobang's full backing. It was the first time ever that unconditional support for the freedom of creative writing had been publicly proclaimed in a socialist state under Communist rule. I rejoiced, as did the other delegates at the congress, although I was aware that there was still quite a distance between the proclamation and reality.

The idea of democratic elections for the leading body was also welcome, and several adjustments were made on the list of candidates put forward by the various provinces. The elections took place, and the number of votes for me was second only to the number of votes for the most respected writer in China—Ba Jin. I was taken by surprise, and my colleagues who had supported me were all happy on my account.

The *People's Daily* also took the unprecedented step of publishing the results of the election by listing the candidates according to the number of votes they got. Ever since the Eighth Party Congress, results of elections were invariably listed in order of the number of strokes in the calligraphy of the candidates' last names—the Chinese equivalent of alphabetical order. It was one way of concealing the true result of the elections and enabled the candidates to save face. In this election, many leftist writers and cadres in literary and art units, and some critics, had their names far down the list for the Council of the Writers' Association, while names of people like me led the list. This was of course deplorable to the leftists.

During the election of members of the Presidium and of the president and vice-president of the Writers' Association by the members of the council, there was much lobbying on behalf of a handful of candidates by the leaders of the congress. The members of the council were urged not to drop out, but all to no avail. They were outvoted and had to withdraw from the Presidium. My name was not on the list of candidates for the presidency and vice-presidency. Many of the delegations protested, and I was finally included on the list of candidates. It was the same in the case of the poet Shao Yanxiang. Only under mass pressure was he included on the list of candidates for the Presidium. One must remember that at the time, over two-thirds of the delegates were over fifty-five years old, which is to say that younger writers were in a minority, and still, the leftists were left out in the cold. Only in this light can one fully appreciate the signifi- cance of this election. It sent an unmistakable message both to the Central Committee and to the leftists—the writers of China have changed.

But the leftists did not want to acknowledge any change, and did not want to do any honest rethinking of the discredited campaign against spiritual pollution of the previous year. They simply wanted to move ahead along the old lines. Unfortunately, they enjoyed a special kind of liberty, something uniquely Chinese. And their attitude led directly to the two major setbacks of 1985 and 1987.

chapter fifteen

Treading

on

Thin Ice

On January 1, 1985, I received a greeting card. It was an ordinary picture postcard, but on it were no ordinary words of greeting for the New Year. It carried one sentence: "The great Qing dynasty is coming to an end!" My heart gave a thump. The phrase was borrowed from *Tea House*, the famous play by Lao She, one of China's foremost writers, who was driven to suicide during the Cultural Revolution. It was the first time that I had ever received such a message. "What foolhardiness," I thought, "to write such words openly on a greeting card." But I could not really believe that message: that the Communist system was now as doomed as the dynasties of old. It was probably the work of some hotheaded youth. According to prevalent concepts, these words were the sort of political blasphemy that might come from an enemy of the revolution. But I did not believe that. Behind these words, I could see a generation extremely angry at the incurable corruption and growing impatient with the Communist Party for putting off political reform again and again. It was a desperate cry brought on by repeated disappointments.

C., my elder in the world of journalism and a true friend, although a new acquaintance, strolled into my room. He had been a Communist Party member since the early days of the resistance against the Japanese and had spent many years as a reporter in the countryside and in the war zone. Long years within the Party had left little mark on his character; he had kept his integrity intact and spoke his mind unreservedly, sometimes with flashes of satire. In the fifties, many reporters close to him were labeled rightists. At Party meetings to expel them, he had had the courage to refrain from raising his hand like others, thus signifying his dissent. At the time he got off unscathed, but in 1959 he was labeled a "rightist opportunist." A few years ago, during the criticism of Bai Hua, he again voiced a different opinion. Many others followed his lead, and the meeting organized to criticize Bai Hua turned into the exact opposite of what had been intended.

When we met that day, we talked, as we invariably did, talked about the current situation. I remember that a year prior he had said, "Keep your head. Don't be afraid of those attacks. Now they are starting the Party rectification program, which proves that you are right. All your writings have helped Party rectification." That particular morning, when I showed him the card, he again said, "Keep your head," but he finished by saying, "China will not come to an end; if anything is coming to an end, it will be the Party!" C. was perhaps exaggerating, but he was certainly not joking. Indeed, the Party rectification program started the previous year had so far been an empty display, and a great disappointment for the masses. Nevertheless, I was shocked at the depth of his disillusionment.

The Party was diseased. It was a universal wish that the Party would cure itself. But with the failure of the Party rectification program, the last hope was a reform of political structure. But that hope too was frustrated in 1985.

At the beginning of January, the Fourth Writers' Congress had barely ended when Hu Yaobang's words were passed down: "Freedom of creative writing is not the same thing as freedom to publish." "Journalism cannot enjoy the same kind of liberty as creative writing."

The first sentence was like a bad joke; it basically meant that the writer had the liberty to write in his own diary. As for the second sentence, there had never been any expectation that the Party would give journalists the same kind of freedom as that for creative writing. The point was how much the restrictions would be loosened, and Hu Yaobang's words signaled that the situation for journalism was to remain as it was without any new dispensations of freedom. A month later, the papers published Hu Yaobang's February 8 speech in full. It was like a cold shower for journalists.

In the early 1980s, the *People's Daily*'s editor-in-chief, Hu Jiwei, had said that a newspaper should primarily be the voice of the people and should exercise supervision over the Party; he said that when the Party made mistakes, the papers had the right to their own viewpoints. Hu Qiaomu and Deng Liqun seized on these words to attack Hu Jiwei, repeatedly, and now Hu Yaobang was throwing his weight behind the hard-liners.

According to Party tradition, the words of a Party leader were equivalent to a Party pronouncement, so after Hu Yaobang's talk, there was no more room for discussion on issues of the press in China.

Under such circumstances, what was there for me to do? It was impossible for me to publish reports in the *People's Daily*, the job closest to my heart. From 1985 onward, no important criticism appeared in the papers. Still, I did not want to give up. Since it was impossible to publish anything worthwhile in the *People's Daily*, I decided to shift to literary reportage.

A university teacher from Harbin, a certain Chen Shizhong, attracted my interest. Judged by either old or new ethical standards, he was the very best of men, but he was also one of the most unfortunate. I had read his letter explaining his case before we met. He was a typical Chinese intellectual, slight of figure, with thick glasses, rather ordinary-looking on the whole. But his sincerity and earnestness gave him a special attraction. He was a good speaker; he spoke from his heart, with no high-flown rhetoric. One could say that he was at once loyal and disloyal to the Party—he supported it, but not at the expense of his own integrity. He was a dreamer, but also a down-to-earth practical fellow who worked like an ox. His specialty was in engineering, but he was as full of dreams as a poet.

Chen was an orphan, and but for the Communist Party, he would not have been able to to the Soviet Union to study. As a result, he was full of gratitude to the Party and to Mao. On graduation in 1960, he returned to a promising career in China. But he risked everything for his belief that the Chinese Communist Party should change its domestic and foreign policies and not cut off relations with the Communist Party of the Soviet Union. Holding to this outlook, he repeatedly wrote admonitory letters to Mao Zedong himself. When there were results, he wrote a letter to Khrushchev and tried to take it himself to the Soviet Embassy in Beijing. He was stopped by the Chinese guards outside, arrested, and given a prison sentence for being a traitor. And so his youth was over. His wife divorced him and took away his little daughter. He loved his family, but he did not hesitate to give up all that he loved, to risk death, in order to act out his beliefs. In prison, he wrote articles and letters, literally hundreds of thousands of words, of admonition to the Party and to Mao.

The second time we met, his first words were: "I'm here on behalf of someone else who has been unjustly convicted." And he showed me a written petition, "Blood Is Not Water: An Appeal to a Reporter's Conscience." The document described a case of murder in April 1970 in Heilongjiang on the Nenjiang labor-reform farm, which Chen Shizhong had witnessed with his own eyes:

On the farm where we served our sentences, there were over a hundred of us, working under the surveillance of Captain Li (a city youth sent to the country

who later stayed on) and three soldiers. We cut grass and dried it for burning,
and our quota was three hundred pounds a day. Li Zhirong, one of the inmates,
always worked hard. He had already surpassed his daily quota in the morning,
but continued working in the afternoon. Usually, when we were working, our
guards would set up four red flags to mark the a square of ground we were to
work on; we were not allowed to cross those borders. That morning, strangely,
apart from the four red flags marking the square, there was another flag a ways
inside one border. Li Zhirong was bent over cutting grass and did not notice
the new flag. He approached the new boundary set by the fifth flag without
noticing. One of the soldiers called out a warning, but Li was not aware he was
crossing bounds. The soldier called out to him to come over; he did and was
thus standing outside the new boundary made by the fifth flag. At that, another
soldier walked over to his comrade, and after whispering to each other, they
ordered Li Zhirong to turn around. You can guess what happened afterward.
One of the soldiers fired, and Li fell as he was hit. Then the soldier who fired
the first shot fired again into the air and announced to all the inmates present,
"The prisoner stepped outside of the restricted boundary; he ignored the warn-
ing and was shot."

Even to someone like me, accustomed to gruesome stories of murder,
the way Li Zhirong was killed was shocking. It sounded like a game. A man
had been killed for nothing. But had it really been done without a motive?
Of course not. Only a Chinese person who understood the vagaries of
Chinese political life could guess the motive: to put up a show of revolutionary vigilance. This was an important political quality, very useful for
getting into the Party, for getting a promotion or a citation of honor. It
was sure to be reported, and your name would undoubtedly be noticed by
leaders.

What was doubly unbearable to Chen Shizhong was that the man did
not die immediately. He struggled to a kneeling position after falling, as
if he wanted to explain that it was all a misunderstanding, and then he fell
back. The next day, when the authorities sent two soldiers to pick up his
corpse, it was still warm. The whole night through, there had been soldiers
on duty; they must have heard him groan. There would have been over
ten hours to save his life. Chen Shizhong named fourteen other people
who had witnessed the murder, in case I didn't believe him. How could
he have remembered all these names after all those years? He must have
had this case firmly in mind all these years.

The murdered man was neither a personal friend nor a relative of Chen. But since 1981 when he was released, he had spared no efforts in petitioning on the murdered man's behalf. During the last four years, he had written to the Standing Committee of the People's Congress of Heilongjiang Province, to all levels of the court in the province, to the district court of Nenjiang area, to the military tribunal of the People's Liberation Army, to the head of the Shenyang military zone, to the Jilin provincial military zone, trying to trace the murderer, but all his pleas fell upon deaf ears.

"Li Zhirong was a physical-education teacher," Chen told me. "He was arrested in 1957 as a counterrevolutionary; he would not confess to this, and his appeal only extended his sentence from years ten to fifteen. I am sure he was unjustly convicted. If he were alive today, he would surely be rehabilitated. But while serving his term, he was so hardworking, so well-behaved. He observed all the rules, and evidently hoped to have his sentence shortened so he could be reunited with his wife. Then they killed him. Isn't this a double injustice?

"Even more to be pitied is his wife, Hu Peilan. In 1971, she came to visit and stayed with him for a while. She gave birth to a son when she returned home and called the child Early, evidently hoping that his father would get an early release. The child must be twenty years old by now, and has never seen his father. Even now his wife and son believe that Li was executed for trying to escape."

Chen said he was going to find the mother and son and tell them the truth. As he finished his story, he gave a deep sigh. He said he would not give up. I looked around my study, lined with brown paper folders. Looking at those folders, I thought, "In these cases of injustice, the culprits have been identified and still nothing is done to them. How could you hope for justice when you don't even know the name of the murderer?"

Thirty-two years ago, I had looked for a special type of person, one who sees the world through his own heart and his own eyes and does not follow the herd, one who thinks with his own head, who stands up to injustice and doesn't just protect his own skin. I searched high and low, I encouraged the younger generation of reporters to seek them, but we had little success. And for the last twenty years, people who had such qualities were labeled "enemies of the people." Submission and slavishness were upheld as national virtues bred and encouraged by the system.

For a man like Chen Shizhong to have survived, and to have preserved his original qualities as a man while doing so, was rare indeed. Chen's caring for his dead fellow prisoner was doubly precious in that, since the Cultural Revolution, social behavior had so deteriorated that rape, robbery, and murder could be committed in broad daylight and passers-by would not offer to help or even step forward as witnesses; people simply wanted to wrap themselves up in their own security. And to think that Chen's own situation was so wretched. Although he had been released, he was still discriminated against, and exposing the authorities did not gain him any favors. Luckily, his work record was impeccable and they could not really do anything to him. But to think that in the midst of all his own problems, he would still occupy himself with a case of injustice that happened fifteen years ago to somebody who was nothing to him! The relentless struggles of the last thirty years had so hardened people's hearts that they had lost all capacity for pity. I wondered what had kept Chen Shizhong's heart vibrating with sympathy for his fellow men. I decided to write his story, using him as one of the protagonists in my report, "Another Kind of Loyalty." The newly launched magazine *Pioneer*, decided to publish it in their first issue in January 1985.

In my article, I quoted Chen's letter to Mao:

I believe that the Central Committee of the Chinese Communist Party is guilty of a series of grave mistakes; the most serious is that it is not conscious of its own mistakes. I must speak out, or I would not be faithful to the Party. The underlying reason for all this is the cult of Mao. You will not tolerate the slightest criticism, especially on matters of principle. You go back on your word and wreak havoc. If this continues, will there be anyone left to speak the truth? You expect people to take every sentence, every word you say, as an absolute truth; you do not tolerate any questioning. Why is it that the Communist Parties of Yugoslavia, the Soviet Union, Poland, Hungary, France, Italy, the United States, and India have all committed mistakes, while that of China is the only exception? You shut yourself up in an isolation ward, hoping to make yourself immune to mistakes. But isn't that an enormous mistake? You say that Marxism-Leninism is not afraid of criticism. Yet think of all the people who have offered criticism from 1957 onwards, not to mention earlier periods. How many of them have escaped an evil fate? Please hold your anger for a while. . . . Judging from the situation of recent years, I fear that sooner or later, all your comrades-in-arms—Liu Shaoqi, Zhu De, Chen Yun, Lin Biao, Deng Xiaoping, Chen Yi, and company—all those leaders of the Central Committee will sooner or later be labeled anti-Party, counterrevolutionary revisionists. That is because it will be impossible for them to follow you at every step. I wish that all my forebodings were unfounded. All the better this would be for our country and our people. As you finish this letter, your "dragon heart" will rise in fury, and my life will soon be ended. Even so, before my execution, I will say one last word: "Jupiter, you are angry, therefore you are wrong!"

To promote publicity, *Pioneer* magazine printed copies of the galleys and sent them off to several provinces, asking the local papers to publish excerpts with a notice that *Pioneer* was publishing the story in its entirety. This caused unexpected trouble. The first to interfere was the Shanghai Institute of Oceanography, the unit of another protagonist in the same piece, Ni Yuxian, of whom I will speak later. Representatives of the institute came up from Shanghai and called on the editor-in-chief of *Pioneer*, asking that "Another Kind of Loyalty" be removed from the first issue. They then went on to several departments of the Central Committee to put forward their case against me. At the same time, the leading body to which *Pioneer* was affiliated, the All-China Workers' Union, also stepped forward and ordered the magazine to stop distribution, but did not give reasons.

Finally, the views of the leadership filtered down. Some said it was depreciating the campaign to learn from Lei Feng; some said it touched on sensitive issues between the two Communist Parties of China and the Soviet Union; some said Chen Shizhong's letter to Mao was disrespectful. All shied away from mentioning the basic theme of the piece, the two kinds of loyalty. But I suspect it was the main cause of their disapproval. My article ended:

There are different kinds of loyalty, as there are different kinds of beauty. One kind of loyalty stresses meekness, modesty, submissiveness, deference; an individual might have to make some personal sacrifices to maintain this kind of loyalty, but he is safe, his path will be smooth, disaster will not strike him. And because of the approval of his superiors, he usually makes his way upwards.

The second kind of loyalty, the kind exhibited by Chen Shizhong and Ni Yuxian, does not invite approval. Even until recently, the followers of the second kind of loyalty have often had to pay the price of freedom, happiness, or even life itself for their kind of loyalty.

For the past years, the first kind of loyalty has been carefully fostered, and has brought forth abundant fruit; in the fields of our political life, by contrast, the second kind of loyalty struggles on the poorest soil; the fact that it has survived at all is a miracle. . . .

But the most dangerous is a third kind of loyalty, an extension of the first.

According to this kind of loyalty, obeying orders, even wrong orders, comes
before everything else. Believers in this loyalty pretend modesty and do not
commit themselves and seek to put the responsibility elsewhere. The general
rule guiding their behavior is to be on the watch for changes of wind and to
always be ready to shift allegiance. This kind of loyalty is even more attractive
than the first kind of blind obedience, but the fruit it bears is bitter, sometimes
even poisonous. . . .

The issues I raised were not new ones. Throughout the last forty years,
the majority of Chinese have come to the same conclusion. That is why,
although *Pioneer* was ordered to stop sales, and other papers were not
allowed to publish excerpts, the demand was nevertheless so great that
more than a dozen magazines and newspapers across the country published
excerpts. One newspaper in Shaanxi, which published the entire article in
two issues, ran one million copies.

The accusation that I was deprecating the campaign to learn from Lei
Feng was true. That campaign was a political expedient of the early sixties.
The Great Leap Forward had brought failure and famine, and the people,
especially the educated young, began to question the infallible wisdom of
the great leader and the Party. That was the background for the emergence
of people like Chen Shizhong. There was a crying need to restore morale,
political stability, and belief in Mao. Thus was launched the campaign to
learn from Lei Feng, a self-sacrificing soldier of the army who had died
in an accident. And the campaign worked. Through the fanfare of the
campaign, Mao's prestige was restored, thus paving the way for the Cultural Revolution.

Nearly thirty years had passed since 1958 publication of an article
written under the direction of Liu Shaoqi, "Communist Party Members
Must Be Pliant Tools of the Party." The campaign to learn from Lei Feng
had also been underway for over twenty years. During this whole period,
the Communist Party had made many mistakes and had also made resolutions to correct its mistakes. But in light of its unchanging attitude toward
Lei Feng's kind of loyalty and to Chen Shizhong's kind of loyalty, it was
clear that in matters of ideology it did not propose to change. The Party
still believed that as long as the Chinese people unreservedly placed their
absolute trust and obedience in the hands of the "great, glorious, and
correct" Communist Party of China, all of its problems could be solved.
It did not see that the masses of the people had long rejected the blind

subservience of Lei Feng, that the Communist Party itself had changed, and that reiterating the tiresome exhortation to learn from Lei Feng would only alienate the people. And they also failed to see that suppressing criticism would only make the evil fester until it was beyond cure. On the surface, this attitude seemed to reflect confidence, but beneath the surface, it betrayed a lack of confidence, the fear that once the people were allowed to think for themselves, they would break out of control.

I gradually realized that what infuriated the Party leaders, and what at the same time elicited such a wide response far and wide, was the fact that I had depicted an independent-minded person such as Chen Shizhong. In China, independence of mind was equivalent to insurrection.

I myself was not aware of this sensitive issue at the beginning. I just felt that Chen had many precious qualities in his character. In a wilderness of conformity, fostered by thirty years of indoctrination, Chen Shizhong's individuality stood out like an oasis in a desert.

The clash over "Another Kind of Loyalty" made me think hard about what set me and the Party apart from each other. It had expelled me, then corrected its mistake and rehabilitated me. But from the day of my return to its ranks, it had always eyed me with distrust. Why?

There were too many people in the Party who were alien to me. They had been shaped by the last three decades. But even earlier, I had begun to have doubts about some of the Party traditions. Since arriving at the liberated base area in 1944, I had often heard the term *modesty and circumspection* linked with *loyalty and submission* as the highest moral standards to strive after. When I saw with my own eyes what kind of behavior these standards added up to in practice, I was revolted.

In keeping with the Party's iron discipline and caste system, modesty and circumspection had become wariness and slavish obedience to one's superiors. As for the evaluation of one's work, one's hopes for promotion and general well-being all hung on the lips of your superiors, and as a result the so-called modesty and circumspection were both linked to self-interest.

In the summer of 1979, a middle-aged cadre of intellectual background whom I met in Harbin said to me: "Summing up my twenty years of experience, I would say that if you want to survive in China, the first thing you must remember is not to differ with your superior. Second, and more important, you must remember not to be smarter than your superior." These words sent a chill into my heart. At the time, I had only looked at the problem from the angle of the need to keep informed. I thought, "How can China not remain static, or slide backwards, if her decision-makers never hear of things from the grass-roots level and never hear a different opinion?"

China seemed like a monstrous mill, continually rolling, crushing all individuality out of the Chinese character. Every one of your words and deeds, every aspect of your life, had to conform to the norm. Your "relations with the masses" formed an important standard of political assessment, a requirement that had to be met by all applicants for Party membership; you must never offend, not even people who needed to be spoken to in clear terms.

This unseen mill ground on relentlessly, silently, trying to wear out all edges and create a mass of people with the same set, ingratiating expression when facing their rulers.

The net result was to make a virtue of hypocrisy. Between superiors and subordinates, in relationships with one's own peers, a superficial atmosphere of good fellowship prevailed, while plots and intrigues went on behind your back. But some people, once installed in power, showed their fangs.

Still, the majority were not political climbers, nor necessarily mean plotters; the majority merely sank into mediocrity. Individuality was crushed, conscience was stifled, and people followed the rule "better safe than brilliant."

With time, a segment of the population in China deteriorated into a set type, with a smirk on their faces, rote words on their lips, a noncommittal stance on issues for which they have responsibility. They simply carried out their daily work according to routine, choosing their words carefully, leaving no loopholes, and taking every precaution to ensure their own political safety.

Thus, mediocrity was turned into a virtue, incompetence ensured promotion. When you saw waves and waves of the talented, the brave, and the upright destroyed by successive campaigns for this and against that, how could you blame those others who sacrificed their identities in order to save their skins?

But you certainly couldn't admire them. They had lost the qualities of the really human. They had to train themselves not to be angered at injustice, not to be moved by suffering, not to be roused by crisis, not to see that their country was in peril, and not to feel responsible. In a word, they learned not to be concerned with anything except their own official position, while still maintaining a clear and unruffled conscience.

To ensure this peace of mind, another set of people had to cooperate; millions of Chinese had to remain ignorant and docile, and put their fates into the hands of such officials.

On another front, encouraged by the opposition I was encountering from high quarters in Beijing, the Shanghai Institute of Oceanography—where the other protagonist of my reportage, Ni Yuxian, worked—stepped up its attack on me. I was perplexed by their attitude. Ni was but a low-ranking member of their library staff. He was not a threat to the Party Committee. I had concentrated on the story of his victimization during the Cultural Revolution, which did not implicate the Party Committee now in office. Why was their resentment even more violent than some of the people that I had named by name in other exposés? Was it possible that they themselves had something to hide, and feared that my report would draw attention to them?

The main accusation that the Institute of Oceanography brought against me was that I was misleading readers by making a hero of a scoundrel. I decided to conduct an on-site investigation.

I arrived in Shanghai in April 1985 with two young assistants. In light of the nature of our work, the best place to stay would have been the institute itself. But we soon discovered that this was impossible. The fact was, the Party Committee of the institute had already set the stage. They had sent out directives through various branches that Ni Yuxian was a bad element, that Liu Binyan had gotten the facts confused, and that the Central Committee of the Party would punish Liu and the leadership of *Pioneer* magazine. They had also sent out people to probe Ni's doings over the last twenty years to prepare for an even bigger assault.

Under the circumstances, we stayed at a hotel across the Huangpu River and asked the people at the institute to come over for interviews. Our investigations confirmed my writings on Ni Yuxian on every point, but also brought new results. The first to arrive, and the one who met with us most often, was Ni Yuxian himself. We started from scratch and went over the facts which had been denied by the institute. For several nights, my assistants and I pored over the case of Ni, weighing the validity of his version. Both Chen Shizhong and Ni Yuxian were natives of Shanghai. But apart from their basic quality which I wrote of in my report—the courage to speak the truth and brave consequences—their personalities were quite different.

Ni was smart and well-spoken, qualities which Chen shared. But in contrast to Chen, who was brought up under the orthodox political indoctrination of the fifties, Ni was a bit too volatile. Ni had written letters to members of the Gang of Four in the past. The institute held this up as proof that Ni was a political swindler, only pretending to have opposed the gang during the Cultural Revolution. As they construed the facts, the evidence against him seemed overwhelming. But on further probing, we found that all these letters had been written under special circumstances.

First, in 1971, Ni was expelled by the institute and had no means of living. In order to interest the Shanghai Party Committee in giving him a job, he wrote them a letter against his own convictions. Then again, in 1975, he dared to write a criticism of Zhang Chunqiao, a leading figure of the Cultural Revolution (and later one of the Gang of Four), refuting his theory as put forward in "The All-Rounded Dictatorship of the Proletariat," and sent one copy to Mao and another to Red Flag, the official journal of the Central Committee of the Party. He soon found his own security threatened. His diary was surreptitiously taken from him and he was followed. Some fellow workers advised him for his own safety to make some kind of political gesture of conformity, such as writing a letter to the Shanghai authorities. He refused at first. Later, a well-meaning person drafted a letter for him, which he signed and sent. During those years, many high-ranking cadres wrote letters to the Gang of Four, offering allegiance in order to climb the political ladder. But Ni was not even a member of the Communist Party and wrote only under duress, desperate for a means of living and for personal safety. Just how was he guilty?

The institute had another handle on Ni, which was that he had been an activist during the Cultural Revolution, a leader of a group. I did not conceal this in my writing. Ni had always been deeply interested in politics. The minute the Cultural Revolution started, he sided with a leading cadre, pitted against the majority. That was the first time he turned his hand to politics. For his resourcefulness, his ready tongue, and his strong convictions, he was elected deputy of the Provisional Revolutionary Committee. But he was not guilty of violence to students and teachers, and when he saw that the violence was getting out of control, he quit and went roaming across the countryside to study the society.

But the strategy of the Institute of Oceanography was to discredit Ni and preserve on record all that he had been accused of, while discrediting any exonerating evidence. In 1962, for instance, Ni had written a letter to Mao reporting on the famine in the countryside, suggesting that he stop the leftist policies raging at the time. Well, the institute wanted this fact overturned. They interviewed people concerned and the "consensus" was that Ni had never written such a letter, or in any event, that the people concerned could not remember. We also made inquiries, and the majority of people interviewed answered that, yes, they remembered the letter. One even recalled, "He borrowed the money from me to pay for the postage." Ni's enemies were so intent on discrediting him that they had even sent people to Beijing to search the files for a record of letters sent to Mao in 1963. They could find no trace of Ni's letter and came back jubilant. Perhaps it was my fault, because I had mistakenly put down the year of the letter as 1963 in my report, while it was 1962. A few months later, the general office of the Party Central Committee notified its counterpart in Shanghai that the letter had been traced and requested them to send this information to the Shanghai institute. And thus the affair of the letter was closed once and for all.

Two reasons were given for expelling Ni from the institute. One was political—that he had compiled and printed at his own expense a booklet of quotations from Lenin with "antileftist" leanings. Now that being an antileftist was not so damning anymore, they claimed that the other charge, of sexual offenses, had been solidly verified. How could they still cling to confessions extorted during the Cultural Revolution? But they did, most emphatically.

And because the Chinese still think sexual behavior is a valid criterion for judging people, we had to take it seriously and do some investigating. But an investigation of this nature really left us baffled. Did or did not Ni Yuxian take a woman behind his bike one night fourteen years ago, bring her home, and later have sexual relations with her on several occasions? The girl denied it, but on further probing acknowledged it. They had gone through it many times before; which version were we to believe? Ni's second sexual offense had been sleeping with a woman who was not his wife. To whom should we turn to investigate this? To the woman herself, who was now a mother? Whether the accusations were true or not, neither episode was a case of rape. Even if the above had been true, the most one could have accused him of in the second case was adultery, and that was no longer a crime; and in the first, he could be accused of premarital sex.

But what did this say about Ni's politics? Or even his ethics? If these things were so important, why was there never an exposé of the sexual offenses of the Gang of Four?

We learned that Ni was not the only one who suffered at the Institute of Oceanography. One afternoon, a middle-aged couple crossed the Huangpu River and came to our rooms for an interview. The man, Shen Renjie, was an English teacher at the institute; his wife, Huang Jingru, was a middle-school teacher. That whole afternoon, Huang did most of the talking; her husband seemed to be suffering from delayed shock, and was still dazed. Disaster had struck their family in May of the preceding year. It seemed preposterous—considering that Shanghai had been opened up to the outside world a hundred years ago—but the fact was, their daughter Huang Lan had fallen in love and was planning to marry a foreign student, and the Shanghai Institute of Oceanography had opposed the marriage violently; they did not come out into the open, but worked on the father, who was on their staff and a newly admitted member of the Party. They put so much pressure on the poor man that it nearly killed him.

The upholder of morals at the institute tried to prevent the marriage until the very last moment, but when they couldn't stop the young couple from registering for marriage, they used the Party rectification program to continue their criticism of Sheng, the father, by saying: "It is beyond understanding that a comrade who has worked under the leadership of the Communist Party for so many years fails to draw a line between capitalism and socialism. Of course, that foreigner might be harmless, but on the other hand, he might be a bad one, and probably is a bad one!" And these words were spoken by someone who worked in an institution of higher learning and had control over intellectuals! But why did Sheng Renjie not protest? After all, he not only was a professor of English (although nominally just a lecturer), but had been honored as a model worker of Shanghai; he was a man of position. But in fact, he was helpless against these pressures of ignorance and prejudice, and suffered in silence. He lost more than fifteen pounds in half a month; he was in a mental daze and even attempted suicide. The oppressors were strong, while the victims were weak and timid. This was precisely the kind of relationship that subsisted between the Party Committee and the teachers in the Institute of Oceanography as well as in many other parts of China.

In the weeks we were there, many teachers at the institute called on me; some were older than Shen Renjie, some younger. Each of them had a particular story of grievances. Since the early fifties, they had been victims of one or the other of those campaigns. They kept the school going, turning out batches of graduates year by year. By all rights they should have been the directors of the institute, but in fact, like institutions of higher learning all over China, they, the teachers, were among the lowest of the low. Their fates were all in the hands of the political and administrative cadres, who decided on their promotion, academic titles, salaries, housing allotments, permission to go abroad, even permission to attend academic meetings and to publish.

As I studied the political history of this institute, I came across an interesting phenomenon: the Cultural Revolution was a power struggle between different factions of political cadres, and between students who were repressed and those political cadres who did the repressing through their tools among the students. The teachers were there, as they had been over the years, only as objects of suspicion and political attack; otherwise, they were completely segregated from the political functions of the institute. Just as I had seen in Xian a year earlier, those who emerged as victors from these ten years were the same ones who had been in power before. The leftists always had the upper hand.

It was only by proving themselves right that these cadres could expect to hold on to power. And to do this, they could never acknowledge a fault; they could not apologize to people they had wronged, and could not make any reparations. History had to be written according to their ideas of right and wrong. But suddenly the figure of Ni Yuxian confronted them; he claimed that he was in the right, that he had been victimized, that the Institute of Oceanography was still pursuing an ultra-leftist policy, counter to the current line of the Party. Of course a person like Ni could not be tolerated!

One of the things that Ni did do, which his hostile investigators could not deny, was the fact that on January 8, 1977, he had put up a big-character poster on the iron gates of the Donghu Guest House. They could not deny this, because it was precisely for this act that Ni had been sentenced to jail, and when this sentence was reversed, Ni returned to his job at the institute's library.

The gist of the poem on Ni's poster was something like this: "After three ups and downs without coming under the imperial knife, Deng

Xiaoping's achievements are clear to all the world. His lack of wile makes him vulnerable to slander, while his forthrightness makes him incompatible with intrigue. . . . The masses will not be satisfied until Deng is restored to his position."

At the time of the poem, the Gang of Four had been overthrown only a few months earlier. China was still dragging along on its old track; there were still some fifty-odd people in jail awaiting the death sentence for opposing the Gang of Four during the Cultural Revolution, and even at that late hour, they (the cream of the Chinese population) were all executed. Long after the gang was overthrown, no one was allowed to deny the merits of the Cultural Revolution or to question the reactionary nature of the crackdown in the Tiananmen Square incident in 1976, much less to debate the rights and wrongs of Mao's career.

As far as I knew, Ni's poem was the first of its kind to express dissatisfaction with the situation at the time. Under the circumstances, it took a great deal of courage, for Hua Guofeng, Mao's appointed successor, opposed Deng. But Ni went even further. On the night of March 30, he posted another long poem on the walls of the International Hotel, demanding the reversal of the verdict on the Tiananmen Square incident. The title was "I Will Not Believe It: On the Anniversary of the Tiananmen Square Massacre." The first secretary of the Shanghai Party Committee signed orders for Ni's arrest; he was then jailed for nearly two years. By sheer luck, he escaped execution and was cleared and released in January 1979.

The investigators from the Institute of Oceanography could in no way prove that Ni Yuxian's acts had been reactionary or toadying to the Gang of Four. Nevertheless, they still tried to depreciate the whole affair by saying that Ni had put up the first poster but not the second; they admitted that the Shanghai Party Committee had indeed had him arrested, but that they did not sentence him to death. We located a person who had helped Ni put up his second poem at the International Hotel. Moreover, a former leading cadre of the institute also verified that during a speech made by a leading member of the Shanghai Party Committee, the speaker had mentioned that Ni Yuxian was on the death list along with Wang Shengyou (a student at East China Teachers' University, who was executed). I did not acknowledge any "factual errors" as alleged by the Shanghai Institute of Oceanography. On the contrary, I used the material gathered during the investigation to write a sequel to "Another Kind of Loyalty."

I returned from Shanghai on May 17, went to a secluded spot, and started working on the sequel to "Another Kind of Loyalty," which I entitled "An Unfinished Burial."

Then, on May 22 I went back to Beijing to prepare for a projected trip to West Germany. To my dismay, the head of the Foreign Affairs Bureau of the *People's Daily* came to my home with a message: "The editor-in-chief informs you that your West German trip is canceled."

So instead of sailing on the Rhine, I arrived on the banks of the Yangtse River.

The Hubei branch of the Chinese Writers' Association had invited me to their congress for the reelection of the leading body. I was just about to leave when I received a phone call from the Party leader of the Chinese Writers' Association, not forbidding me to go, but hinting that it would be best for me not to go. What did it mean, that I, a validly elected vice-president of the Writers' Association, should not accept an invitation from a branch association? I replied on the spot, "I assure you, I am going." Then they took another step, evidently after much deliberation. They sent the deputy editor-in-chief of *People's Literature* to go with me and entrusted him with the letter of congratulation to be read out at the meeting. Why all this petty scheming? It was the same kind of meanness that had led to the blocking of my West German trip. Evidently, a high-ranking official had spoken out against me, and the Party core organization at the Writers' Association made haste to distance themselves from me.

After the meeting in Hubei, I sailed down the Yangtse River and arrived in Nanchang, the capital of Jiangxi Province. The provincial Party Congress was being held right in the hotel where I was staying. During the meeting, violent crimes were reported every day.

Now why was that? During that year, wherever I went, people came to see me. I would ask: "Since the Party rectification program of 1984, how would you evaluate ethics and behavior within the Party ranks, better or worse?" The answer invariably was "Worse!" When I was in Jiangxi Province, incidentally, editors-in-chief of twenty-eight weekly magazines on legal matters were holding a meeting on Lushan Mountain. Fourteen of them visited me, and I asked them the same question. All gave the same reply: "Worse."

I wondered about the increase in violent crime, and the growing corruption within the Party. Was there a connection between the two? It made me think of the New Year's card I had received: "The great Qing dynasty is coming to an end!"

Still I did not think the political situation in China was beyond cure. I planned to write about the Party secretary for Jiangxi Province, Wan Shaofen. Through the story of her career, I wanted to explore the social crisis, as well as point out a path of hope for China. So I proceeded to interview Wan Shaofen and study the situation in Jiangxi, its positive aspects as well as its problems.

Meanwhile, in Beijing, a conference was being held in June to hear reports on the progress on the Party rectification program in six provinces. At that June meeting, a certain high-ranking official in charge of Party rectification on the national level tossed a remark into the discussion: "People say this Liu Binyan dares to speak out. Yes, he does; but what does he say? It's a pile of rubbish!" Evidently he was singling me out as an enemy of Party rectification. That person went on to say, "He stirs up trouble wherever he goes, disrupting unity and stability. Liu Binyan and Wang Ruowang are both representative figures of bourgeois liberalization."

I did not hear of this attack until I returned to Beijing. Although the speaker was a high-ranking official, I did not let his words bother me. The only problem was that these comments, like others whether true or untrue, were passed on to the county level, causing my friends to worry and my enemies to gloat.

Three years earlier, friends had repeatedly warned me to give up reporting. "It earns you so many enemies. Keep to fiction," they advised. Others were even more specific: "Hu Qiaomu and Deng Liqun have their own ideas about you! You must take them seriously!"

"Of course I take them seriously," I would say. "When they give specific orders for me to stop writing, then I will."

People also asked me, "After all that you have suffered for so many years, why do you have to pitch into a subject like 'People or Monsters?' the minute you start writing again? Don't you think of your family?"

When first asked the question, I had said, "At the time, I had never imagined that a piece of work like that would be considered dangerous." Later on, of course, this answer was not adequate, as I had already been attacked but had continued writing. I couldn't find a satisfactory answer.

The writer Zhang Jie found one for me. She said, "Liu Binyan is a slow wit. He truly is 'Old Liu the Simpleton.'" This was an allusion alluding to the prize-winning short story "Old Wang the Simpleton," about the trials of an old peasant during the Cultural Revolution. The film based on it was banned.

In observing my grandson Liu Dongdong, I found another answer. Dongdong was smart, but he was also quite slow in other ways. Other children sometimes took advantage of him, and he didn't even seem to notice. His mother would say, "Our Dongdong is a slow wit." Suddenly I saw myself in him. Yes, I, too, was slow-witted in some cases, and to certain situations I react very slowly.

Later, I found a fuller answer. When I first resumed writing in 1979, I was not aware of the dangers lurking. A year later, the threat materialized. I had incurred the displeasure of three "ducal lords"—provincial Party secretaries—who attacked me from their respective dominions. But by that time I felt a growing force pushing me forward, and that force came from my readers, readers from all levels of Chinese society. I could feel their breath on my back. By then, I could not stop, I was defiant.

Another reason for my intrepidity was that I did not share some of the values generally held by intellectuals. I did not hope for favors from those in power. Honorific titles, such as delegate to the National People's Congress or member of the People's Consultative Conference and the like, were beyond me. I also thought it was strange that these were not responsibilities but honors. Many writers have been so honored, but I did not envy them, though I do have my own share of vanities and worldly ambitions. Perhaps, never having known the sweet taste of these honors and the advantages they bring with them, I had no fear of losing them. At most, what I lost were many opportunities to go abroad and access to better housing.

Nonetheless, the state of the country, the mood of the people, and my own situation combined to push me toward a decision: to relax for a while. I accepted a longstanding invitation from a former student and went to a seaside resort in Liaoning Province.

I had finished the draft of the sequel to "Another Kind of Loyalty" and was about to send it off when I received a wire from the editor-in-chief of the *People's Daily:* "The Shanghai Institute of Oceanography announces that its students and staff will march on Beijing to protest if the sequel is published. Stop publication or take sole responsibility." They had actually succumbed to a handful of people at that institute! "Sole responsibility"! I had never tried to shift my responsibility to others! I decided to publish all the same.

A phone call followed, relaying a message from a member of the political bureau of the Party Central, who was also a secretary of the Secretariat, urging me not to publish. And as a consequence, publication was withheld.

The report on the Party secretary of Jiangxi Province was also withheld from publication, though for other reasons than purely to spite me. Later, however, a member of the Politburo and a member of the Secretariat went to Jiangxi on a tour of inspection and inquired, "Who invited Liu Binyan to Jiangxi? What were his motives for coming here? Why was he seated in the Presidium of the provincial Party Congress?" By the way they talked, I had practically been relegated to "illegal-migrant" status, just as I had been treated by the leadership when I intended to visit Hubei.

Of course I was depressed. At a routine work meeting at the *People's Daily*, I said, "It's getting harder and harder to write literary reportage. It seems as if I should call a stop." My words were passed on, but completely out of context. The September issue of the Hong Kong *Mirror* published my photograph with the caption, "Liu announces his retirement from writing," which of course helped spread the false news of my intention to stop writing. Other overseas newspapers also carried reports, commenting on my situation. Several publishing houses vied with each other to publish my collected works; the rumors lasted for several months.

Although there was no basis for the report, this whirl of news and comment did, to a certain extent, reflect a dual situation. First, at the time I was indeed plunged into my worst plight since 1979. But second, the overseas press began to gauge the shifting political climate in China through my personal situation.

While the report of my retirement from writing was being circulated, my own situation took a turn for the worse. The inspection team of the Central Disciplinary Committee descended upon the *People's Daily;* their mission, as stated in their letter of reference, was "to investigate the problems related to Comrade Liu Binyan and others." I was the main target, along with Wang Ruoshui and possibly also the editor-in-chief, Qin Chuan.

Ironically, while a team from the Central Disciplinary Committee was sitting in the office of the *People's Daily* to investigate me, I myself was sitting in the office of the Central Disciplinary Committee helping, through my own words and deeds, to right a case of injustice of twenty-four years' standing.

Jiang Huaiyu was a primary-school teacher in Wendeng County, Shandong Province. During the 1960 famine, he discovered that the Party secretary of the production brigade had lined his own pockets by dealing in the collective's grain, while over fifty people in the village had died of hunger. Jiang Huaiyu exposed the theft, and from then on, a string of misfortunes befell him and his family. The Party secretary, Dong, had backing from the county Party Committee as well as support from a certain Zhang, a "model worker" of the province who had risen in the ranks during the Cultural Revolution. Dong repeatedly had Jiang Huaiyu jailed and tortured. The whole family was harassed beyond endurance; some died, some became fugitives, the children became vagrants, often beaten up, with no chance to go to school; the family's ration of wheat and kindling wood was held back; their house was destroyed. In order to survive, they had to buy grain with cash. Jiang's daughter Jiang Shanhua began to accompany her father on trips to petition for justice from the time she was seventeen years old.

The officer who received them at the Public Complaints Section of the General Office of the Central Committee also worked hand in hand with the "lordlings" of the county and the prefecture in Shandong. They faked evidence to reverse right and wrong. Jiang Huaiyu contested their verdict, of course, and looked me up. Two young reporters from the *People's Daily* helped me do an on-site investigation in Wendeng County, and we sent the results to Hu Yaobang. On the recommendation of the Central Committee, the Disciplinary Committee of the CCP ordered a new investigation. The second investigation team reached the same results as we had.

To our surprise, the representatives of the provincial, the prefectural, and the county Party committees from Shandong who were sent to Beijing to help resolve the case held to their position. They insisted that Jiang was a bad element and had no business making accusations.

The veteran cadre in charge of conducting the new investigation, Li Zhilian—himself a member of the Standing Committee of the Party's Disciplinary Committee—was a just and upright man who sympathized deeply with the oppressed. The group from Shandong angered him so that at one point he banged on the table and rebuked them roundly. We three reporters from the *People's Daily* joined our voices with his and argued with the group from Shandong in meeting after meeting.

The Disciplinary Committee finally made a relatively just ruling. But according to the well-worn practice, they did not pursue the wrongdoers. They merely proclaimed that Jiang Huaiyu had been a victim of injustice and decided that 1,000 yuan was to be awarded to each member of his family.

But the Shandong Party Committee refused to accept this decision. They accused Li Zhilian of protecting Jiang Huaiyu. And so the case dragged on.

Later, when the Disciplinary Committee handled other types of cases, they were quick to act indeed. Its handling of two famous cases in 1985 amply proved that the committee had totally betrayed its trust, and was working hand-in-glove with the enemies of reform.

The first case was the "fake-medicine case of Jinjiang Prefecture," which was used in 1985 to topple Xiang Nan, the Party secretary of Fujian Province. Of all provincial Party secretaries, Xiang Nan was a man of rare vision and insight who was totally committed to reform. In the second case, the victim was Lei Yu, Party secretary of the region of Hainan, another reformer with outstanding achievements to his credit. The first case involved a village pharmacy that was selling "health strengtheners" as real medicine. The second case involved car smuggling and violations of the government's car-import regulations that allowed Hainan to conduct a car-import business to finance the island's backward economy.

And so on the one hand, we had leading cadres and their sons using their special power to monopolize import and export business and reap unlawful gains from foreign companies by sacrificing national interests, who were let off scot free. While on the other hand, the most outstanding and dedicated reformers were victimized by the investigators. The actions of the Disciplinary Committee thoroughly discredited the committee in the eyes of the Chinese people.

November brought another piece of bad news. A memorandum for the meeting of the Secretariat of the Central Committee of the Party belittled the *People's Daily* while singing the praises of the conservative Xinhua News Agency. It also added, "Some people endeavor to use the media in their control to sway the Party's policies. This is dangerous." These words of warning were evidently not directed at the mouthpiece of the hardliners. It was clearly directed at the *People's Daily* and its two successive

editors-in-chief, who had led an unremitting fight against the conservatives. It may also have been directed at me and Wang Ruoshui, who had
just left his post at the *People's Daily.*

What I could not understand was how Hu Yaobang, who was perfectly
aware of the struggle that the journalists had to conduct to support the
reform, could condone such a chilling memorandum.

The memorandum made me disappointed with the Central Committee, but I was not intimidated by its implied warning. I had always felt that
journalists had never truly fulfilled their duty to influence the Party
throughout the past thirty years when it committed one colossal mistake
after another. Now I felt it imperative for journalists to influence the
Party's decision-making. Hadn't the Party continued to make strategic
errors even after 1979? Wasn't the November meeting of the Secretariat
in itself a colossal mistake?

That fall, students in Beijing and other areas demonstrated on September 18, the national day of humiliation, the anniversary of the day the
Japanese had invaded northeast China in 1931. They were protesting the
Japanese economic incursion, although they were actually using this as a
pretext to demonstrate against the political situation. The authorities
concentrated their energies in breaking up the student movement. Even
some veteran cadres who had led anti-Kuomintang movements in the old
days were stunned by the methods used, calling them as bad as the
Kuomintang.

The news from over a dozen provinces disquieted me. I felt that China
was in the midst of a crisis, that the tensions were tearing the country
apart. Unfortunately, there was no way for me to exert any influence.
Reports on the most pressing issues could not appear in the *People's Daily.*
I did write three pieces from material gathered in Shaanxi, but had to
change the names and locality before they could be published in a literary
magazine. Consequently, they ceased to be reports in the true sense of the
word.

But I would not be silenced. What could I do? I had to find a way out.

My old friend Mei Duo, editor-in-chief of *Encounter Monthly,* invited
me to write a special column for his magazine. Like me, Mei Duo had been
labeled a rightist, but had suffered an even worse fate than mine. Now he
was devoted to making *Encounter Monthly* one of the best literary magazines in China.

I accepted his offer immediately. During the past two years, I had accumulated a lot of material that I had no way of getting published. I wanted to speak out for those people who had poured out their grievances to me. Of course, not all the material was appropriate for reportage, and I also could not do on-site investigations of every case. Instead, I decided to use the letters and information I got every day and publish them in diary form. The wording could be simple and completely objective, thereby forestalling accusations of "factual error." Beginning in February 1985, "My Diary" appeared in the pages of *Encounter Monthly.*

And it worked exactly as I had planned. My vistors and the letters coming in every day provided me with a wealth of material, and I wrote about countless cases.

A lawyer in Taian County, Liaoning Province, had offended many people through his outspokenness. He was arrested on some pretext, and was then bound and paraded in the streets before being thrown into jail.

A young student in Nanjing fell in love with her teacher, thirty years her senior, an ex-rightist; they were forcibly separated, and she lost her job on account of the love affair.

The Party secretary of Siping, Liaoning Province, Huang Xunzhang, made enemies while relentlessly pursuing the remnants of the Cultural Revolution and while pushing for reform; he was slandered and expelled from the Party.

A technician and a member of the Standing Committee of the People's Congress of Sichuan Province, Liu Yongjiang, was arrested and jailed for consistently opposing the nomination of unqualified people to official positions.

A cadre of Shanghai Normal University, Zhao Xinhua, who had been a victim of the Cultural Revolution, joined the struggle against remnants of the Cultural Revolution and ended up without a job.

These are just a few examples, but my diary spoke up on behalf of many people. I can't say that it changed the fate of every one of them, but it did serve to promote "openness" and help quite a few victims.

I was not particularly elated by the publication of the diary. The fact was, the more serious the case, the less I could focus on it. And then, to preempt any accusations of "painting China a uniform black," I had to insert slices of "glory and light." In June of the same year, I ended the diary.

In November 1985, six months after I had been prohibited from traveling abroad, I suddenly received a notice that I and two others were to leave on a two-week visit to West Germany for a tour of six cities. Although I wondered what I could gain from such a short trip, I was resolved not to come back empty-handed. During all of 1985, I had not published a single worthwhile piece of reportage in the pages of the *People's Daily*. On this trip, perhaps I would be able to find a suitable topic to communicate with my countrymen, to give them some information, or start them thinking. I hoped to repeat the experience of 1983, in other words, to exert an influence on China's affairs indirectly by speaking on a foreign subject. Although this seemed rather pitiful to me at first, I decided it would be a challenge and a pleasure to speak to Beijing from the streets of Frankfurt. As long as I could break through the obstacles set by the conservatives, as long as I could cut through the ignorant, ossified layers of their existence, it was reward enough for me.

I began looking for a topic to start out from, something that Germany and China had in common. Our first stop was Frankfurt, and the first place we visited was Goethe's residence. Thanks to inspiration from Goethe perhaps, it suddenly occurred to me that this was the fortieth anniversary of the end of the Nazi regime, and that the next year, 1986, would be the twentieth anniversary of the Cultural Revolution. We had long been warned not to dwell too much on the Cultural Revolution, and a directive to that effect had been issued in 1981, basically implying that it was preferable to forget about it altogether. What was the point of shedding more tears over what was past and gone? The Germans, however, seemed to think otherwise. The German constitution passed in 1949 had been a revision of the Weimar Republic's constitution in the light of the disaster of the Hitler regime. China by contrast had preserved the political set-up of thirty years ago without a change! At that point I realized that I had found my point of departure.

I decided that during the two-week visit, no matter where I was or to whom I was talking, I would concentrate on this one topic of interest to both Germans and Chinese: How did Germans look at the 1933–45 period in their history? What changes had been made in their political system following the disaster of the Nazi regime?

About a third of the items on our schedule provided me with opportunities to look for answers to these questions, and about one out of every three answers was useful to me. While pulling my notes together on my way back, I found that I did have enough material for my article. I gave it the title "They Will Not Forget." My wife advised me not to mention China outright, since the message was clear. She was right, and sure enough, everyone who read the article assured me that it was obvious what I was aiming at: "You didn't once mention China by name, but the whole article made me think of China's problems."

I described for my countrymen how the people in this part of Germany had shaken themselves free from the negative aspects of their national heritage, how they had woken from a nightmare. I believed that Chinese readers could be startled out of their own tradition. I described for them how the Germans eliminated the systems of highly concentrated power and set up the Federal Republic, not by chanting slogans and waving flags, not by covering up contradictions, but by reforming the political system to achieve unity and stability. My countrymen understood me perfectly and liked the piece of "tourist literature." As always, their appreciation encouraged me and dispelled the troubles of the year.

Meanwhile, in early 1986 a meeting of eight thousand leading cadres was convened in Beijing in a renewal of efforts to continue Party rectification, to deal publicly with some of the more serious cases. Hu Yaobang first used the word *corruption* in his speech to this meeting. The first case to be discussed was that of a veteran writer and high-ranking cultural official. He had been expelled from the Party for "violating discipline" and for visiting the Peace Shrine on a visit to Japan. Meanwhile, in Shanghai, two sons of leading cadres, who had raped many women, were shot. The new cases were widely publicized, aimed at displaying the Party's sincerity in enforcing discipline.

I, however, did not put much confidence in the new efforts. The meeting itself was very sudden, and no steps were taken to enforce rectification on a national scale. In addition, although the "serious cases" were widely publicized, they were under the direct control of the Xinhua News Agency; none of the national or local papers were allowed to seek interviews with those involved. The *People's Daily*'s could only publish comments. There was not much for me to do in Beijing, so I left for Sichuan.

chapter sixteen

Cloudy to Clear, and Cloudy Again

The political climate of China shifts back and forth, cloudy one moment, sunny the next. Starting in April 1986, the weather once again began to improve.

At the time, I was living in "retirement" in Sichuan Province, and I learned from the papers that the Party was advocating a spirit of "relaxation and harmony" for intellectuals. I noticed that the head of the Propaganda Department of the Central Committee, Zhu Houze, a figure much respected by intellectuals, had spoken in public again. He was former Party secretary of Guizhou Province and had been chosen by Hu Yaobang to come to work in the capital in 1985. But since taking up his post at the Propaganda Department, he had kept out of the public eye, due to the adverse political climate. I felt that Zhu's public appearance and the call for a spirit of relaxation and a reduction of tension for intellectuals were signs of a change for the better.

My guess was right. Deng Xiaoping's talk on reform of the political structure followed soon thereafter. There was nothing new in what he said; in fact, the word *democracy* was not even mentioned. But still, the speech confirmed that reform of the political structure was on the agenda. As I passed through Jiangsu and Anhui provinces on my way home, I could feel the warming effects of the thaw in my contact with intellectuals. I myself was encouraged by the benign atmosphere and decided to write the story of Zhao Yunpeng, a thwarted reformer of Hefei, Anhui Province. I did not finish the report, but I did interview the Party secretary of Hefei and succeeded in getting Zhao reinstated to his managerial post after he had been unjustly suspended from his job while awaiting investigation.

In July, Wan Li, member of the Politburo and vice-minister of the State Council, gave a long speech at a conference on the soft sciences, signaling a democratization in political life.

Long before Wan Li's speech appeared in the papers, some of its contents were leaked out and circulated among intellectuals. I myself heard of it from friends who rushed to give me the good news. We were particularly struck by his remark: "The people should also have a say in making political decisions." These words were striking when one remembered the fate of Guo Luoji—a professor of philosophy at Beijing University—for his article published in *People's Daily* calling for free discussion of political issues. He was publicly attacked and banned from publishing. Now, Wan Li himself was talking about the right of the people not only to participate in discussions of political matters but to offer different opinions as well.

At one point, Wan Li strayed from his prepared remarks and talked about my case. He said, "I hadn't read Liu Binyan's 'Another Kind of Loyalty' when it was first attacked. But then I looked it up and read it. I think it's a fine piece of work. Another kind of loyalty is exactly what we need." These words of his were of course passed on to me by friends as especially good news.

A few days later, Wan Li made an appointment to meet with me. I went to his residence in Zhongnanhai. Wan Li's wife, his son, and Wu Xiang, a noted agronomist and adviser on agricultural affairs, were also present.

It was the first time I had a private conversation with Wan Li. Previously, two things stood out in my impression of him. The first was an occurrence in 1965, when Mao called on leading cadres to revolutionize their lifestyles. Wan Li was then Party secretary for Beijing, and he took the lead in answering the call. He joined up with the model worker Shi Chuanxiang and went collecting night soil with him in the streets of Beijing. The affair was widely publicized, with Wan Li's picture in the papers. I hadn't liked it at all. At the time, there was a propaganda drive for "shouldering the burden" and the praises of latrine cleaners had been sung. I had thought such kinds of service should be abolished, the less said about them the better.

My next impression of Wan Li was from ten years later, when he emerged from the shadows to head the Ministry of Railways. At the time, Deng Xiaoping at the Central Committee had just begun his monumental adjustment of the chaos that China had sunk to following the horrendous ten years since 1966. In the spring of 1975, Wan Li achieved the impossible. At the time, the two vital railway lines, Xuzhou to the east and Zhengzhou to the west, were paralyzed by strikes and factional fighting. Daily supplies for the population of Beijing, never bountiful, dwindled to a dangerous low. Wan Li rushed to these centers of discord, arrested the ringleaders, gave a rousing speech to the workers, telling them where their interests lay, and set the trains running again. It was a real tour de force, injecting new life into a hopeless situation.

After the downfall of the Gang of Four in 1976, Wan Li threw himself with equal fervor into implementing the "responsibility system" in the rural area in Anhui, which allowed the peasants to dispose of their own surpluses after the tax on grain was paid, in spite of the campaign against the "restoration of capitalism," which was moving in on him from the surrounding provinces. He succeeded so spectacularly in healing the wounds of poverty and hunger that people often said, "Look to Wan Li to fill your rice bowl." During the past few years, he had steadfastly supported Hu Yaobang on the ideological front. During the winter of 1983, it was he and Hu who effectively stalled the campaign against spiritual pollution. I remember hearing his talk on agricultural affairs, in which he slipped a warning to the hard-liners between the lines. At the time, it was not yet possible to oppose the campaign against spiritual pollution outright. Shortly thereafter, at a meeting on higher education, when the prevailing mood was depressingly conservative, Wan Li attended the last session and made a speech that overturned the entire program that had been laid out.

Wan Li's first words of greeting to me were, "What we need is precisely the second kind of loyalty you wrote of." He then added, "A party is doomed if it doesn't tolerate differing views. Communists, Kuomintang, Socialists, Christian Democrats . . . no matter which, if you can't tolerate criticism, your days are numbered." He continued, "In this land of ours, there are just too many clever ones, and too many slavish ones. And too few of the single-minded types, the 'fools.' So few have the courage to speak up." He went on to quote from Lu Xun's famous article, "Of Wits, Fools, and Slaves." He had read a lot of Lu Xun as a student in a teacher's college in Shandong and had wanted to be a writer; in fact, he had read Lu Xun's articles when they first appeared. Later, when he was incarcerated during the Cultural Revolution, he had read through the *Complete Works of Lu Xun* twice. "Men with such a cultural background are few and far between in the leading body of the Chinese Communist Party," I thought. The Party placed such importance on ideology; yet in the sixty years since its founding, it had not been able to find a secretary who was cultivated in the true sense of the word.

Wan Li suggested that I write something on Wu Han and Deng Tuo.

He could not overcome his outrage over the way Mao had victimized these two men, the one a historian and deputy mayor of Beijing and the other the head of the *People's Daily,* who had been persecuted to death during the Cultural Revolution. If there were time and opportunity, I told Wan Li, I would like to write their stories.

I then took the occasion to raise a question that had been weighing on my own mind and on that of my colleagues in cultural circles: "Ever since 1979, the political climate of China has been so uncertain, sunshine one day, rain the next. At one time, people thought the conservatives were gone for good, when their two great exponents, Hu Qiaomu and Deng Liqun, stopped showing their faces in public. But the situation never lasts; it doesn't take long for the next storm to brew. Right now, it's clear again, but how long will it last? Perhaps sometime these two will appear again in public. What do you think?" Wan Li laughed; he seemed full of confidence. He said not to worry, and since I had always been somewhat of an optimist myself, I now felt doubly reassured.

I then mentioned his talk at the conference on soft sciences and told him how well received it had been by the intellectuals. When I asked whether it could be published in whole, he showed me the polished version and said it had been sent to Deng Xiaoping and Hu Yaobang for approval. He assumed there wouldn't be any changes and gave me a copy for the *People's Daily,* suggesting that some articles on the same topic be published along with his talk, to reinforce the theme. News of Wan Li's talk with me and his words on "Another Kind of Loyalty" spread far and wide. Some local papers printed the news. This, and the appearance of Wan Li's speech in the pages of the *People's Daily,* were taken as sure signs of good weather and the intellectuals gained heart.

But bad news followed soon thereafter. At a meeting in Beidaihe of the Central Committee and the Central Consultative Committee of the Communist Party to discuss a document on "spiritual build-up" of the country, the former head of the Propaganda Department from pre–Cultural Revolution days stood and suggested that the term *bourgeois liberalization* be struck from the document. Wan Li seconded his proposal, but Deng Xiaoping insisted that the term be preserved in the document. I was not alarmed. When my friends pointed out these omens of an impending reversal, I reassured them that it was only a word. What's in a word, I argued. Deng wanted it in the text to conciliate the conservatives. After the fiasco of the campaign against spiritual pollution, I couldn't believe that Deng Xiaoping would consider starting another movement against so-called "bourgeois liberalization."

Later, the political situation in China did go through another reversal, and both Wan Li and I were proved wrong. But that was four months later. Meanwhile, throughout the summer, and up to the end of the year, there was uninterrupted good weather. The shock of the campaign against spiritual pollution had been dispelled. Now, I thought, was the time for me to go north to Heilongjiang Province to help release Wang Fumian.

For more than two years, the image of Wang Fumian had haunted me. We had met only a few times, but of all the victims of persecution, he was the one for whom I felt the most.

Wang Fumian was a worker in his forties from Yichun, Heilongjiang Province. On the afternoon of March 14, 1984, he was sitting with me in my apartment, and that same night he was suddenly arrested. Early the next morning, his wife Li Huasheng rushed over to me with the news. I was thunderstruck. It was as if he had been snatched away before my own eyes. We had not finished our conversation from the day before and had made an appointment to go to the Disciplinary Committee of the CCP, where he was to present his exposure of the former Party secretary of Yichun, Wang Fei. It was the security men of Yichun, a thousand miles to the north, who had come to take Wan Fumian away in their police cars. Wang had struggled, but was told, "You'd better behave yourself! We have a long way to go. We won't kill you, but you might end up raving mad."

I knew the kind of thugs these people were. I was extremely alarmed. If Wang's mind was destroyed, then his case would never see the light of day. I made haste to call the security police of Beijing as well as the local police. I thought that the man was locked up somewhere in Beijing and vowed to get him out by hook or by crook. Frantically, I kept dialing the security police, and when I finally got through I was told that these matters could be discussed only on the security's internal line! At the same time, my wife was taken ill and I had to take her to the hospital. I was certainly not the excitable type and rarely got worked up over anything, but that day, I was in an utter state of anger and anxiety. The same afternoon, news came back that Wang Fumian had already been taken away to Yichun, that very night. I had underestimated the efficiency of these thugs.

I had never been so crestfallen. The fates of dozens of men I had known flitted across my mind, but my thoughts returned again and again to Wang Fumian. Such a giant of a man, and to be caught and whisked away like a timid child. China had been liberated for more than thirty years, yet her citizens could be seized at a moment's notice without any regard for civil liberties. And I stood by and could do nothing. That night, I wrote in my diary, "Today is the darkest day in my whole life!"

I worried about what would happen to Wang on the way. Anything could happen on that thousand-mile ride. The next day was a Sunday; there was nobody to answer the phone when I called long distance to the Party Committee in Yichun. Realizing such efforts were futile, I decided to call Wang Fumian's adversary himself, Wang Fei, at his home in Harbin, where he now headed the Organization Department for the provincial Party Committee. I gave my name and said: "Wang Fumian of Yichun has just been seized and taken away by force. The warrant for his arrest says he is accused of libel. As far as I know, he was in Beijing to expose you, so I assume that you are the person he is supposed to have libeled."

Wang Fei of course knew who I was. He sounded a bit tense and began to justify himself: "I myself was a victim until 1970, when I was sent to work in Yichun." He stressed that he carried no private grudge against Wang Fumian.

I then asked him what they had against Wang Fumian anyway.

"The man really suffered a lot during the Cultural Revolution," Wang Fei said. "But later he was rehabilitated and his salary was paid back to him, four thousand yuan altogether. He also received special health services, since he had been injured on duty. But the fact is that at present, the situation in the city is very complicated. Some people are attacking the leadership of the Party Committee. Wang Fumian may have been used as a tool by certain old cadres."

Hearing him say this, I knew for certain that Wang Fumian was no crook at all. Still, I did not understand what Wang Fei meant by his last words until three years later.

Wang Fumian's case was more complicated because it was directly linked to high-ranking officials in the provincial capital. Since the head of the Organization Department was in charge of promotion and demotion, he ranked second only to the Party secretary himself. The fact that Wang Fei got this job was proof that he had backing in the provincial Party leadership and that his appointment had also been approved by the Central Committee. He would not be easily removed. I realized I would have to wait my chance.

And that chance came in the 1986 thaw.

At a meeting at the *People's Daily,* with the editor-in-chief and his deputies present, I laid out the basic facts of Wang Fumian's case and pointed out the negative role that the *People's Daily* had played in the affair. The fact was that after Wang was seized on March 14 1984, his enemies had waited three months without further action. Then, *People's Daily* had published a report that had been submitted by the Heilongjiang provincial Party Committee. Taking this as a signal, the local court started their interrogations. The *People's Daily* not only had published that biased report but had used a term in association with the man, naming him as one of "the three categories," which pinned him down as a creature of the Gang of Four. The report submitted by Heilongjiang had described Wang Fumian and his activities during the Cultural Revolution as common gangsterism, but had refrained from using the official label. Their chance came when the *People's Daily* used that critical term. They reprinted that particular issue of the *People's Daily* in the provincial and municipal papers, creating the impression that the Central Committee of the CCP itself had indicted him. My argument therefore was that the *People's Daily* should undo the wrong it had done.

Since the editor-in-chief was a new arrival and very cautious, I feared that he would refuse to get involved. I stressed that it was a clear case of private revenge sought by public means. The warrant for Wang's arrest listed his offense as "libel"; during the trial, he was accused of "disorderly behavior" in public. But finally, they simply withdrew all the previous accusations and locked him up in an asylum for the mentally ill! And all the while they had gone to such great lengths to get him convicted. They had set up special investigation teams and coerced people to give evidence. If Wang Fumian was indeed a criminal as they avowed, why was there a conspiracy to concoct evidence? And why, after collecting so much incriminating evidence, did they retract their accusations and turn it into an insanity case?

I finally was able to convince my audience. The head of the paper decided then and there to send a team to Heilongjiang Province. I was picked for the job, and two other reporters were to join me.

I arrived in Harbin full of confidence. Wang Fumian's case was straightforward. The political climate was favorable. Above all, his enemies' case against him did not hold any water at all.

The man who received me at the provincial Party headquarters was

Zhou Wenhua, standing member of the Secretariat. We had met in 1983 in the city of Jiamusi, and our working relations had been cordial. Besides, he had been a student at the Young Cadres' Training Center in Harbin, where I had once taught, and so in a sense, we stood in a teacher-pupil relationship. He was his same old self, soft-spoken and mild-mannered. But his overcautious attitude was not to my liking. It was the trademark of a successful political climber. Still, it was better than doing business with a complete stranger, and I treated him with courtesy.

I handed him my letter of introduction from *People's Daily* and put forward our request for the files on Wang Fumian's case and for an interview with the people handling his case in the provincial high court. We also wanted to see Wang Fumian in the asylum. Zhou Wenhua listened to us politely and promised to help.

Three days passed without a word from him. When we met again, Zhou said that there was a new regulation regarding access to files and that he now had to get permission from the Central Committee in Beijing. As for seeing Wang Fumian, he told me they would have to find out which asylum he was in. And regarding the interview with the people of the high court, well, he told me, they were on a business trip.

It seems incredible that at the time I did not suspect these were just flimsy pretexts to put me off. I had many old acquaintances to look up and was making new friends, so I had plenty to occupy myself with while I was waiting.

Another three days passed. We inquired by phone and the answer was that they were still waiting for permission. Eight days later, the people from the high court finally turned up. Two of them talked to us while the other took notes. I glanced at one fellow and noticed he was taking down everything I said. Now I knew where we stood. I realized they were sending out feelers.

We phoned our own paper in Beijing and asked them to find out straight from the Supreme Court what requirements needed to be filled for access to those files. Their reply was that we simply needed permission from the provincial Party Committee. So that's how it was! On the telephone I unleashed my anger at Zhou Wenhua: "Look here, we are not asking to see those files out of curiosity. We are on an assignment to right a wrong which our paper may have done to this man. Reading his files is imperative. This case does not involve any state secret, the man has already been declared insane, his criminal case is closed, likewise his files. Why this secrecy? What do you have to hide?" I was extremely agitated, but no matter what I said, Zhou Wenhua kept his temper and went on saying polite nothings.

We waited for fourteen days to get permission to interview Wang; the subject of the files was dropped altogether. They thought they had scored one over us by keeping back the files, but actually it just went to prove that they had something to hide. Such a thing would not prevent us from getting at the truth; we decided to go straight to Yichun to do an on-site investigation.

As it turned out, they had so much to hide that they kept betraying themselves. The deputy editor-in-chief of *Heilongjiang Daily* volunteered to send a young man on his staff to help me, and the young man was more than willing, but they were overruled. Another editor of the same paper planned to use his holiday to go with me to Yichun, but even that was forbidden. His boss more or less gave away the secret when he said, "If you had asked earlier, I would have said yes, but now, my answer is no. You don't even need to ask why not. You can guess." The efforts to obstruct me became downright farcical. A young reporter from the provincial TV station was waiting to join me at the Harbin railway station with camera gear ready to go—and his boss pursued him to the station and dragged him away.

Still, in spite of all this buffoonery, we set off in a group, the three of us from the *People's Daily,* along with three reporters—from the provincial, the municipal, and the railroad papers—and a young woman poet. A worker from Yichun, a self-taught, part-time lawyer, had set out before us. These people were well aware that the investigation was frowned upon by the higher authorities, but they simply ignored that and went ahead notwithstanding.

The night before we left for Yichun, the two reporters and I finally got permission to visit Wang Fumian. He was interned at the psychiatric ward of the provincial Security Bureau.

As we walked into the ward, a dozen or so inmates all dressed in blue uniform stood up at attention. I could hardly recognize Wang Fumian among them, until one of them smiled at me. There he was, clean-shaven and looking younger than before.

Neither the head of the ward nor the two doctors in charge could detect signs of mental illness in him. We talked to him and taped the conversation. He sounded sane, even logical. We saw no signs of illness.

Before that, I had talked to three doctors who had diagnosed Wang Fumian's condition as "mania." They had interviewed Wang for an hour in prison. The two more qualified ones decided that it was a case of "obstruction of personality," while the third, a veterinarian who had become a psychiatrist, insisted that it was a case of "mania." The two doctors then apparently had accepted the judgment of the third doctor, which I found very strange indeed.

And what were the symptoms of "mania"? I looked up the "Criteria for Diagnosing Mental Diseases" drawn up by the provincial Security Bureau during the Cultural Revolution. It read:

> . . . *a rare kind of mental disease. Symptoms are overconfidence, extreme wilfulness, found mostly in people of advanced cultural background. They are biased and tend to distort facts, although their delusions are not wholly divorced from reality. Taken for normal at an early age, the patient gradually asserts his (her) will power more and more forcibly, he (she) rushes about offering petitions, writing endless letters of accusation. A few are deluded into thinking they are making exceptional contributions to humanity. . . .*

My hair stood on end and my blood curdled as I read these words. The definition seemed specifically phrased to match Wang Fumian's case! It could equally be applied to myself! "Overconfidence," "biased," "delusions of grandeur" . . . those were exactly the words Party leaders used to denote intellectuals with any independent thinking. "Rushing about to offer petitions" and "writing endless letters of accusation" could be used to describe any one of the thousands of vagrants roaming the streets of Beijing. And yet these criteria had been drafted by one of the authorities on mental diseases in Heilongjiang, a man who had himself been a victim of political persecution.

The doctors in charge of applying these criteria were neither overeducated nor overscrupulous. Few, if any, had ever heard of Freud, particularly since Freud was not introduced on the mainland until the mid-1980s.

I searched my memory for signs of abnormal behavior on Wang Fumian's part when he had talked to me. Well, he was certainly unusual; his writing was as impassioned as if he were making out impeachments of treacherous ministers in the classical style, with many flourishes and turns of phrases. In conversation, he would jump to his feet and walk about excitedly, as if he were addressing a crowd. But if there had been nothing out of the ordinary in him, then he would not have been what he was, the only man who dared to take on a single-handed fight against the evil forces behind the PLA propaganda team and its factions—a man who was arrested, tortured, but undaunted to the end.

But now, he had been pronounced a "maniac" and was locked up in a psychiatric ward. This kind of disease had no cure; it was life imprisonment, worse than if he had been sentenced to twenty years on criminal charges. What did Wang Fei have against the man to do this to him?

The municipal Party Committee of Yichun treated us with the same affable courtesy as Zhou Wenhua of the provincial Party Committee. A deputy chief of the Propaganda Department was in charge of receiving us and treated us to three full meals a day. Very nice indeed. The third day after our arrival, we mentioned to our host that people were being kept from seeing us. The deputy chief said, "That's nonsense. Haven't you received thirty-one persons in the last two days?" I wondered how he knew that we had met with thirty-one persons. We hadn't asked him to calculate the number of our guests. His slip made it clear that we were being watched.

Later we found out that the secretary of the municipal Party Committee had issued a warning that we were not to have access to files or documents relating to Wang Fumian's case. Detailed directions had been given about ways and means to balk us; the plan of action had been discussed at the two guest houses for several days running. Once we arrived, we had asked to see the secretary and head of the Organization Department in charge of Wang's case. But suddenly they were all taken ill and were in a hospital. Of course this was all part of a plot to keep us from digging up the case.

In all the years I had been a reporter for the *People's Daily,* rarely had I come across such a reign of terror as I encountered in Yichun.

A local writer had been talking to me in my room and quite off-handedly I put his phone number and address on the tag of the cassette lying on the table. He fidgeted nervously when he saw me do that and ended by saying, "Would you mind erasing that?" I erased the phone number. He still eyed the cassette uneasily and said, "And the address too?" Actually it wasn't an address at all, only the name of the district where he lived.

The news had gone around the previous spring that I was due to arrive in Yichun. While the people in power were alarmed, many of the local people had hoped I would come. In June, the leaders of Yichun, who hated me for meddling in the Wang Fumian affair, had heard that the member of the Central Committee in charge of the Party rectification program had condemned me and they rejoiced at the news. This piece of good news was passed down to the grass-roots level so that every man, woman, and child would know that Liu Binyan was in disgrace, so they would have second thoughts about looking me up and getting entangled in the mess. Even so, a steady stream of people came to talk to us about the injustices that had taken place in that city. At night we visited people who were too frightened to come to us but who still wanted to talk.

The question remained: Why was Wang Fei so vengeful toward Wang Fumian? Wang Fumian simply could not tolerate the fact that over a hundred people of the opposite faction who had persecuted him and his faction during the Cultural Revolution should be elevated to high positions by Wang Fei. He repeatedly raised the point and wrote his appeals, but all to no avail. And so after years of waiting, he decided to seek justice in Beijing.

But why, after all, should Wang Fei shield people who were involved with the Gang of Four during the Cultural Revolution? The man couldn't help himself. The fact was that he carried the same stigma himself. During the Cultural Revolution, when he was ruling it over the city, he had outdone himself in calling meetings to repudiate the capitalist-roaders, to study the theory of the proletarian dictatorship, and to condemn Deng Xiaoping. In fact, Wang Fei had done such a thorough job that he had been cited for good performance by vice-premier Sun Jian, who was serving under the Gang of Four. Wang Fei then printed Sun Jian's words in praise of himself and distributed them far and wide. Now if Wang Fei were to expose people who had been involved with the Gang of Four, as Wang Fumian called for, where would it lead to but his own door?

Fortunately for Wang Fei, he could decide whom to attack and whom to protect. As Party head, he managed to worm his way through the general investigation untouched, although he himself had attacked Deng Xiaoping. At the same time, he gave orders to incarcerate another leader, Huang Ruiwu, who had opposed the drive to criticize Deng Xiaoping. Actually it was Wang Fei himself who had been responsible for putting up the big-character poster that said "Down with the small Deng Xiaoping, Huang Ruiwu!"

Under Wang Fei, the Four Cardinal Principles were implemented as follows: The Party represented the dictatorship of the proletariat, and so the Party secretary could decide whom to put under the dictatorship and could justify his actions later. Since Wang Fei had very little evidence to work with, he decided that Huang Ruiwu, as a Party leader, must surely be guilty of putting trust in enemy elements. Therefore he had to look for one of these elements among the people who were close to Huang, and he found an old doctor, Zi Shengwen. This old man had been suspected of everything under the sun since liberation in 1949—he had been accused of being "a colonel in the Kuomintang army," "a refugee landlord," "a drug dealer with blood on his hands," and so on, but nothing had ever been proven in spite of thirty years of unrelenting probing. But they could not let the old doctor off so easily. Instead, they found another Zi from the same village, who had been labeled "a bad element," and they replaced Dr. Zi's file with the other man's file. So there he was, with a label tagged to him out of the blue, while his own file disappeared without a trace! In addition to the label, Dr. Zi was vulnerable in another aspect. He had examined patients, among them women, and he had done acupuncture for them. "Didn't he handle you?" the patients were asked. Of course the patients denied that he had. "Well, he touched you, didn't he?" "Well, yes," they replied, "but only to do acupuncture." "Anyway, touching is touching." And so Dr. Zi was clapped into jail for three years for obscenity. And by the same exquisite logic, Huang Ruiwu, Wang Fei's political opponent, was found guilty of trusting a man who was in prison for obscene behavior.

Seven years later, the iron hand of the dictatorship of the proletariat was felt by Wang Fumian. An investigation team was set up. The next step was the arrest, although the indictment and the evidence were still in the making. The Party Committee knew that it had little to work with. But Wang Fumian had quarreled with the leaders of the Party Committee, so his first offense was "wreaking havoc at the Party headquarters"!

During the Cultural Revolution the members of Wang Fei's faction had all been elevated to important positions, and for appearance's sake, Wang Fumian and his faction had been consulted about suitable positions for themselves. Wang Fumian's group felt that he had always been outspoken in defending the weak and suggested that he be appointed vice-mayor in charge of legal matters. And now, this was being held up as incriminating evidence, as evidence that he had blackmailed the Party for office and position! Wang Fumian had also helped victims of persecution write big-character posters accusing the district court of injustice, which was now regarded as libel.

All this seemed pretty slim evidence to convict a man. But there was a way out. Everybody who had had dealings with Wang Fumian was ordered by the Party secretary of his or her unit to be suspended from the job and confess any dealings they had had with Wang Fumian. So suddenly there was an abundance of "evidence"!

Still, there were a handful of diehards who joined Wang Fumian to oppose the Party Committee, but they were locked up. Although there was no evidence to convict them by law, the dictatorship of the proletariat had a way around that. They simply assigned them to "education through labor," an administrative punishment that was meant for those who were not convicted criminals, but who repudiated the leadership of the Party. "Education through labor" was not a criminal sentence, but was enough to take away your liberty.

The problem Wang Fei now faced was that the good old days of the Cultural Revolution were over, and there had to be some gesture to legality. The "dictatorship of the proletariat" no longer came in quite so handy. A warrant for arrest had to be procured and the words *slander and libel* put in. Only after putting Wang into jail did they discover that *slander and libel* meant something that had been committed in public, and they could not muster up enough people willing to give false witness. Consequently, Wang Fumian languished in jail for four months without a trial. They finally managed to give him four years for disrupting public order, but when Wang appealed, the members of the provincial court again found themselves in a dilemma. After investigating the facts, they found that the verdict of "disrupting public order" had not been based on facts, and so they could not repudiate his appeal off hand. On the other hand, they did not dare to set a retrial, because Wang Fumian might have been able to slip off to Beijing in the interim. Apparently necessity was the mother of invention. They looked up three psychiatric doctors and had him pronounced mentally ill. It met the legal requirements, and satisfied the dictatorship of the proletariat.

In the hands of Wang Fei and his like, the dictatorship of the proletariat could be a supple tool indeed. They searched the living quarters of Wang Fumian and his associates whenever they liked. When Wang's wife took their child to Beijing for medical help, plainclothesmen broke into her hotel rooms and took away a letter of introduction I had written for her.

One result of making short work of Wang Fumian and his associates was the effective silencing of the inhabitants of Yichun. The message was clear. Want to try your hand at exposing Wang Fei? Want to pit yourself against Wang Fei? See what happened to Wang Fumian the notorious diehard. He's locked away for life in a mental asylum. Just remember that before you try anything funny.

We had already gathered enough evidence to reverse the verdict on Wang Fumian before we even set off for Harbin. And once we had arrived, we discovered a kingdom of evil such as we seldom saw anywhere else.

The forest resources of Xiaoxinganling (the mountains where Yichun is located) were being exhausted. At this rate, it would be laid waste within six or seven years. Under the reign of Wang Fei, every family, every school, every unit, was equipped with saws and other lumbering equipment. Many officials ran an illegal business in lumber export, drawing huge profits. At least two bureaus of forestry had set up private workshops for making furniture, specializing in luxury furniture for leading officials at the provincial or even state levels, in exchange for special favors.

This was a cursed land where all values had been reversed. Wang Fei's son Wang Xiaosan drove a truck to the State Fruit Company to steal fruit. He was caught red-handed by the security guard Guo Hongkui, and a fight ensued. The matter was taken to court—but Wang Xiaosan, the thief, was the accuser while the guard became defendant. Guo ran away and was a fugitive for three years on the list of those wanted by the police.

Prices and values also underwent a change. Official positions within the Party leadership and the dictatorship could be bought and sold. There was a saying that "two thousand yuan could buy the position of head of department," while "getting into the shoes of the head of a bureau was worth five thousand." Official positions could be calculated in terms of yuan precisely, because they brought with them substantial material benefits.

Payments for the following were listed on the expense account of a chief of the Bureau of Cultural Affairs: "down coat, beaver hat, electric cooker, leather shoes, medicine"—all listed as "office equipment." A half-million-yuan loan from the bank for the manufacture of "cultural supplies" was frittered away to pay for such luxury items. It was said that the officials at the Population Control Office were so addicted to eating and drinking at public expense that they had paid for banquets with the money earmarked to buy contraceptive devices for the women of the district.

The people had no outlet for their pent-up resentments, but nature took revenge for them. In that one year, first a high wind swept the area, and then human error added its toll in two devastating fires. In Yichun, every house had wood stacked in front of it all year round, so the danger of fire was ever-present. In the past, those fires had affected twenty, thirty, or perhaps fifty families at most. But the two recent fires each destroyed two thousand households. The government's preventive measures did not work, and efforts to quench the fire were ineffective. But in the aftermath, there was no serious investigation into the cause, nobody to bear responsibility.

There was a flood that year as well, but it was no natural disaster; it was purely a result of the misuse of power on the part of the municipal government and the Party Committee. They had decided to build a highway around the city area and had to destroy a dam in the process. As a result, the city was flooded.

Some officials, however, benefited even from the disasters. Some factories that had been running at a loss were compensated through insurance and made a "profit." Thus, some officials were inspired to fabricate a loss by starting a fire. A deputy head of the Central District of the forestry area, Liu Dewei, did precisely that. When his action was uncovered, he committed suicide.

On our return to Beijing, the two reporters and I wrote a joint report on the rigged case of Wang Fumian and the blatant abuses of power by Wang Fei. We sent it to Hu Yaobang and Hu Qili, and proposed that an investigation team with greater authority be sent to tackle the problems there.

That was in November. Two months later, Hu Yaobang had lost his position, while I was kicked out of the Party. There was little hope then of restoring justice to Wang Fumian.

While I had been struggling to help free Wang Fumian, my enemies had been gathering their strength to deal me a final blow. All the people that I had offended during the last couple of years, while exercising my own freedom of speech, had banded together to realize their long-cherished plot against me. At the time, I did not know the facts, but I had some premonitions and decided to step up the pace of my work. In 1986, I traveled extensively in the provinces of Hunan, Sichuan, Jiangsu, Heilongjiang, and Fujian as well as Shanghai. In May, I began a second round of lectures, giving over a dozen talks in five cities.

I was two generations removed from the current student population, but as always, I felt very much at home talking to them, and they did not treat me as their senior either. Sometimes I was surprised at myself. Why did I still feel that I was in my thirties? Had the progress of my life stopped with those momentous events in 1957?

It was said that the present crop of college students could not compare with the classes that had gone through the Cultural Revolution. This batch had gone straight to college from middle school, and they were said to be immature and politically apathetic.

Thus I had been astonished by the scene before me when I stood up to talk in the auditorium of Nanjing University a year earlier in April 1985. The hall was packed; every available space was filled, including the aisles. When my talk was over, I had to borrow a bag to hold all the slips of paper with questions that were passed to me. The enthusiasm was greater than at any of the universities I had visited since 1979.

On November 27, 1986, I gave my last public talk to date in China, at Nankai University in Tianjin, and the response surpassed that of Nanjing University. The hall was simply overflowing, so I asked the chairperson if we could move some of the audience up to the stage. As soon as the words left my lips, a wave of people surged upward and took over the stage, sitting right next to my feet.

I was very touched. I wanted to tell the students how much I loved them, for I believed they carried the hope of China. It was a pity that Mao's mistake had deprived China of millions more like them. I was elated. These young people were not apathetic toward politics. They knew there were no films and no acrobatics following my talk, but they came all the same. It was purely their concern for the future of China that brought them there. At the same time, I was saddened by the thought that this precious spark within, this yearning for truth, this readiness to sacrifice themselves for truth—none were valued. On the contrary, there were those whose main goal was to suppress such feelings and ideas.

I was also sad because I could not speak openly, as I had forty years earlier in Harbin—and had roused my audience. For now, I was considered a dangerous element.

I did, however, call for an expansion of the freedom of speech. I also pointed out that economic reform was seriously hampered by the obsolete political structure and by a decadent ideology, and that it was imperative to conduct reform simultaneously along all three lines. I pointed out that one of the strategic errors of the last thirty years had been the view that capitalism and socialism were two entirely separate entities, and that not a trace of capitalism should be allowed to linger on under socialism. I went on to point out the bias against the achievements of the historical period of capitalism, including all the rational elements of the political system. I exhorted my young audience not to be disheartened by the fiasco of the Party-rectification program and the general corruption, but to look forward to the pace of progress of the reform as a whole. History always worked in unexpected ways, I reminded them. Who would have imagined the eruption of the Tiananmen Square incident? The people who went to Tiananmen Square to offer wreaths and write poetry and make speeches in April 1976—who among them would have known at that time that they were making history? I said that in any society of any historical period, students were always at the forefront of the movement to shake up the old order of things. I said that the hope of China lies with its youth.

I called on young writers not to retire into their ivory tower, but to concern themselves with the fate of their people. "If literature alienates itself from the people, the people will turn away from literature." I said that in a country where the basics of living and the basics of civic freedom were not ensured, the writer could not afford to ignore the people.

At the end of the year, I was sent on my last assignment, to the Wuyi Mountains in Fujian Province. There, I was deeply moved by the story of the talented young artist Chen Jianlin's struggle to protect that scenic spot against the indiscriminate felling of timber and the persecutions he suffered as a result of his actions.

The secretary of the provincial Party Committee, Chen Guangyi, listened to my report on the crisis of forest preservation in the Wuyi Mountain area and the sufferings of Chen Jianlin, and he decided to send a high-level inspection team into the area. Chen Jianlin was also invited to join the team, and I was elated and confident that the problem would be solved.

Then on December 10, 1986, I received an urgent call from the People's Daily, asking me to return immediately. At the airport, someone told me that according to the Voice of America, the students of the Science and Technology University were demonstrating in the streets of Hefei. I was not completely surprised. The petering-out of the Party-rectification program and the protraction of the promised reform of the political structure had apparently worn out their patience, and they decided to take a stand. "It's not a bad thing," I thought, never dreaming for a moment that the student demonstrations could affect my own fate.

On the eve of the New Year's Festival, the Chinese Writers' Association held a special gala, with the theme "Writers and Readers, You and Me." It should have been an occasion for celebration, but under the circumstances, it had become quite a thorn in the side of the authorities. The fact was that the students' demonstrations were at their height and the students of Beijing University were ready to break out of the closed gates of the campus at any moment. Since the Capital Auditorium, where the gala was being held, was close to the university area, there was the possibility of students mixing with the audience to wave banners and shout antigovernment slogans. It was too late to cancel the program or to cancel my appearance. The director of the program, Zhang Xinxin, would not have heard of it anyway. One veteran writer had declined to participate when she learned that I was to appear on the program.

The night of the gala, I was tormented by mixed feelings. Sales at the ticket office were strictly controlled to keep out possible troublemakers among the students. Still the hall was quite packed, with many plain-clothesmen and students from the College of Public Security filling up the seats. The performance was being recorded for TV, but we already knew that it would not be shown. Why this fear of the people?

I sat in the audience and listened to the young poet Yang Lian recite his poem. He appeared very casual as the lights focused on him. I did not catch every word, but the refrain, "So many people! So many people!" sent a thrill through me. My thoughts went to all my countrymen outside the walls of the auditorium and to the thousands of students behind the walls of many campuses.

I was scheduled to read near the end of the program. Before I made my appearance, all the lights were turned off and the music played a low drumbeat, like the ticking of a clock. The director Zhang Xinxin told me to restrain myself. Then suddenly all the lights went on, and focused on me and followed me as I walked to the center of the setting. The audience applauded loud and long. The officials of the Writers' Association probably had their hearts in their mouths; anything could happen if the situation continued for too long. I covered the sound of applause with my own voice as I began my reading.

It was a piece picked by Zhang Xinxin after much deliberation. It was the story of Wu Tianming, the director of the Xian Film Studio, a man who had given heart and soul to reform. It was one of my less controversial pieces.

The audience's reaction was generous and warm. At the end, many of them came to the foot of the platform to greet me. As I acknowledged the applause, I thought, "Farewell, my readers. This may be our last meeting."

chapter seventeen

Hu Yaobang
and I

It is rare for two persons as far apart as Hu Yaobang and I to be joined by the same fate, rare indeed.

I was impressed by Hu Yaobang's personality from the early fifties, when he was heading the All-China Youth League. He had qualities rarely seen in people of his status. He was eager to learn, ready to think, full of initiative—in a word, he was a humane man. He commanded our respect through his personal characteristics and not through his position and seniority.

He was older than I by ten years, and although I basically had no personal dealings with him during the thirty-odd years of my career, he always intervened at critical moments. In the end, we were both dealt our political deathblows at the same time. The two items of news published on January 16 and 24, 1987, respectively, announcing our fates, had shocked the world. Had the campaign against "bourgeois liberalization" not picked us as their main targets, it might not have caused such widespread disappointment and disillusion, nor so damaged the image of the Party.

Hu Yaobang went to work as general secretary for the Youth League in 1953, bringing with him a new spirit. Hu's personal temperament and style—impetuous, dashing, unconventional—influenced the atmosphere at the league's central headquarters. The solemnity and rigidity adopted during the years of war and class struggle were abandoned and new forms of activities were born. The Youth League became more concerned with the problems of young people in their lives and their studies; it organized cultural activities and entertainment, and placed less emphasis on calls to follow the Party or to increase production.

Since the founding of the Youth League's paper, *China Youth News,* I had been a fervent advocate of public criticism in the press, but had met with little support. In 1956, Hu Yaobang set the guidelines for "loud praise and loud criticism," and my own ideas finally had a valid basis. With the support of Hu Yaobang, *China Youth News* launched its *Hot Pepper* supplement; it was the first time that satire had appeared in a Communist paper, and the supplement was welcomed all over the country.

But Hu Yaobang was no match for the whole apparatus of the Party structure and its traditions; he could not avoid compromises with certain demands from the Central Committee and the provinces. *Hot Pepper* was frequently attacked; as a result the satires became less sharp, until they were perfectly mild. One reader sent us a cartoon picturing a shopper asking for peppers that weren't hot. He was told he could get them at *China Youth News*! Hu Yaobang's support kept *Hot Pepper* running, but he could not keep it hot.

In 1956, I went to Hunan and wrote a report on the grand building of the provincial Party Committee, which was published in our paper for internal circulation. In the report, I pointed out that their building was getting bigger and bigger, while the information about conditions at the grass-roots level was getting more and more meager. To my surprise, my report was severely criticized by Hu. But I soon realized that his reaction was the result of pressure from Hunan.

Hu's own tastes were also limited by his war experiences. Shortly after he arrived at the Youth League Central, *China Youth News* published a song lyric that I had translated from Russian. It was the song of a soldier posted in Europe, far away from home. Later, I was surprised to hear that Hu Yaobang had criticized the song as containing "tones of depravity," a phrase he used to denounce similar songs on other occasions. It seemed that he could not appreciate any music except marching songs.

It was in 1957, during the antirightist campaign, however, that Hu Yaobang showed his true colors. When the campaign started, he was away in Europe at the World Youth Festival. As soon as he was back in China, he phoned the secretary of the Youth League in charge during a stopover in Xinjiang and asked how many people in the Youth League offices had been labeled. Secretary Luo said that over a hundred had been labeled. Hu was shocked and immediately ordered the campaign to stop until he came back.

In early June of the same year, I had just returned from Shanghai when Hu came to *China Youth* to listen for himself to criticism and suggestions from our staff. It was very hot, the meeting room was full, and people were standing in the doorway. The antirightist campaign had already begun, but with the exception of the top leaders, nobody on the staff knew of Mao's plot in the "hundred flowers" campaign to "lure the vipers out of their hiding holes," and so people still spoke their minds. Some of the criticism was quite sharp.

I was squeezed in the crowd. I wondered whether I should speak up or not. I was undecided. Intuitively I felt that the situation was delicate, but my neighbors encouraged me and I couldn't hold myself back. I stood up and spoke. I spoke from my own first-hand knowledge of a privileged stratum mushrooming within the Party, of growing bureaucratism and complaints from the masses. I also spoke of the new turn that the campaign had taken: "Earlier on, the campaign was proceeding normally: people were not afraid to speak up; they felt less repressed. My own feeling is that the Central Committee has exaggerated the adverse side of the criticism and underrated the harm that bureaucratism and special privileges are doing to alienate the Party from the masses. I fear that the creativity of the masses will be stifled."

The people in the crowded room held their breath and listened. They had all been my colleagues for years, and I knew that they agreed with my views. I felt that my words buoyed them up, and although no one clapped, I could feel their approval. I got carried away and criticized Hu Yaobang point-blank: "You don't know the masses, Comrade Hu Yaobang. You live in the inner court a of big house; how can you know the allowance of cooking oil for the man in the street? Of course you can't. And you don't know us either; you are always afraid that the intellectuals are up to no good; but how can we turn things back? If China starts a Hungarian-style uprising, I will not go out into the streets to attack the Communist Party. But I will also not blindly shout, 'Long live the Communist Party of China!' " I added the last sentence out of revulsion for recent propaganda in the papers. Since the *People's Daily* had published the editorial "The Workers Speak Up," a barrage of letters, purportedly by workers swearing loyalty to the Communist Party and threatening retaliation against the anti-Communist rightists, had appeared in the papers. I knew it had all been arranged to put pressure on intellectuals.

When I had finished talking, I looked closely at Hu and saw that he had a dark expression on his face. I had offended him, but I did not regret having spoken out.

The next time we met was February 1958. My fate had already been decided for me. I was about to be sent to the countryside for reform through labor. Hu interviewed some rightists of the Youth League Central who were Party veterans, and I was one of the group. He met us in the old manner, as if nothing had happened, and addressed us as "comrade" at a time when nobody dared call us comrades anymore. That was a point of great concern to us. Hu said that as long as we reformed ourselves, we would still have bright futures; he encouraged us not to be despondent. He made us feel that he did not regard us as anti-Communists. Finally, he pointed out the root of our mistakes and pointed to me as an example: "Take Liu Binyan; his problem is pride. He is so stuck-up."

At the time, I acknowledged that I had committed an error, but I could not see myself as an enemy of the Party. Hu Yaobang's words showed me that he did not regard me as an enemy, and that was balm to my heart.

After that interview, I did not see him until nine years later. But I do know that during the antirightist campaign, he did his utmost to minimize the number of people labeled. *China Youth News* had labeled seventeen—15 percent of the editorial staff. This was a lower percentage than at many other units, especially the provincial newspaper and broadcasting units, where the percentage ran as high as 30 percent. We all believed that had Hu Yaobang not intervened, the number of people labeled rightists at *China Youth News* would have been double.

A couple of people owed him their political safety. One was the head of our paper, Zhang Liqun. His temperament resembled Hu's, and his way of thinking was very liberal. In fact, he did a lot for the liberalization of our paper. During the "speaking-out" sessions, he gave a notable speech at a meeting of journalists, in which he deplored the existing state of the newspapers that were but trumpets of the Party. His criticism was sharp and was reported in various papers. This speech alone was enough to have him labeled a rightist, but Hu Yaobang personally appealed to Deng Xiaoping on his behalf, and he got off.

Then, one of the members of the Secretariat of the Youth League, Xiang Nan, together with the deputy editor-in-chief of *China Youth News,* Zhong Peizhang, advocated learning from the Yugoslav model and making the Youth League a more independent body concerned with young people's affairs. But since the Central Committee of the CCP was denouncing the Yugoslav Party as revisionist, many young people who were caught saying a word in Yugoslavia's favor were labeled rightists. Hu Yaobang did his utmost, and a year later, Xiang Nan was labeled a "right opportunist," and not a rightist. He kept his Party membership although he was disciplined; he was placed on two years' probation and demoted. For an entire year, Hu succeeded in keeping Zhong Peizhang from being labeled a rightist, but in 1958 at the National Conference of the Youth League, several secretaries of provincial Youth League committees clamored for his punishment, and Zhong was finally labeled.

After the outbreak of the Cultural Revolution, one winter day in 1966, I met Hu Yaobang again, and under less than pleasant circumstances. The Red Guards had ordered him over to the courtyard of *China Youth News*, and then dragged me down from the editorial office upstairs. They made both of us stand in the courtyard facing the gates. For one reason or another, they did not use the placards that were usually hung round the necks of those who were to be struggled against; instead, they took out two long strips of paper on which we were ordered to write out our crimes and hold them aloft. I would not comply, and so somebody else wrote out "my crime" for me. I think it said something to the effect that I was "a rightist who refused to reform." Throughout the struggle session, I did not once look at Hu Yaobang. I thought it was equally embarrassing for both of us. Consequently, I never knew what crimes were written on his strip of paper.

The theme of the struggle session was to denounce the crimes of Hu Yaobang in protecting the arch-rightist Liu Binyan in 1957. The evidence of his crime was that Chairman Mao had written a verdict on Liu Binyan that he was "interested not in solving problems, but in stirring up confusion." The issue was, Why had Hu Yaobang not made this decree of the chairman public? When I was ordered to confess, I protested that I had been sorely punished and that I had never been protected by Hu. I even mentioned an incident that I can no longer remember as an example of Hu's severity toward me. Because of all the confusion, I could not hear what Hu said in self-defense.

From 1969 onward, both Hu Yaobang and I were in the same May Seventh Cadre School in Henan Province, both working under political surveillance. Our paths crossed twice, and we looked at each other without speaking; at the time, we did not dare to greet each other.

He returned to Beijing first. It was said that many people who had worked under him, both in Beijing and in the provinces, went to visit, but I never did. Still, I was concerned about him. At the time, many victims of unjust verdicts went to Beijing to petition for justice, and some went straight to Hu Yaobang. At first, Hu's guards would keep them from entering, but when Hu was informed, he forbade the guards to stop them, and the petitioners were allowed to pass. It was also said that he enjoyed being with young people; when his eldest son's friends called, he would often sit and listen to them talk, and laugh as loud as any at a good joke.

In 1979, fate again linked me with Hu Yaobang. Early that year, my "rightist" label was removed. Undoubtedly, it was on Hu Yaobang's directive to *China Youth News* that this had been effected. At the end of the year, at the banquet closing the Fourth Congress of the Federation of Art and Literature, many people went forward to toast Hu Yaobang, and I did so as well. When our glasses clinked, I asked him whether he had received the book I had sent him. He said he had, but he was very cautious. The situation at the time was still uncertain. My article "People or Monsters?" and my recent speech at the congress had all roused protests from certain quarters. Evidently, Hu did not want to leave the impression that he was close to me. The book that I sent him was a collection of philosophical essays from Yugoslavia, which I had compiled and a third of which I had translated from the Russian. I had profited a great deal from those essays, and I thought Hu Yaobang would like them too.

The later developments in the political situation set the pattern for my relations with Hu: I was increasingly resented by people in high places, considered a "liberalist" element, while Hu Yaobang's position also became increasingly precarious. I therefore avoided all personal contact with him. During the spring of 1985, a member of the Politburo, who knew I had been offered a Nieman fellowship at Harvard told me frankly, "I suggest that you not accept the Nieman invitation. The stay is too long. You cannot avoid speaking, and once your words get into the papers and twisted out of context, the people here will use them against Hu Yaobang. Whatever you do, it will be held against him. They consider Hu the protective screen for all 'liberalist' elements."

As early as the spring of 1979, the movement against Hu Yaobang was already underway. As far as I know, the first chance that his enemies had to oppose him was over the case of Lin Xiling. Lin had graduated from the law department of People's University in 1957; at the time, she attracted a lot of attention by speaking out in public against the dogmatism of the Chinese Communist Party. The summer of that year, Hu Yaobang invited her to his house, and they talked for over six hours. Hu introduced her to his secretary, and the two fell in love. But before they were able to get married, both had been labeled rightists. Lin was jailed for fifteen years. Then, Mao happened to inquire after her, and she was released. Otherwise, she might still be languishing in jail. She was in her forties when she was released and was sent to her home town in Zhejiang to work.

In 1979, she came to Beijing to petition for a reversal of her case. By that time, she was married (not very happily), and the mother of two. She wrote a long letter to Hu Yaobang, very rude and unfriendly. Personally, I felt she should not have done that since Hu had never hurt her. But contrary to my expectations, Hu Yaobang did not seem to mind, and he wrote out a directive that it was advisable to reverse her case. He issued three such directives, pushing for Lin's rehabilitation.

But officials hostile to Hu Yaobang in particular and to the rehabilitation program in general were dead set against it. The more Hu advocated the rehabilitation of Lin, the more hotly they opposed it. It was apparent that the Party Committee of People's University (the very people who had labeled Lin and who were still in power) were not in a position to oppose Hu so flagrantly on their own authority.

Also, the deputy head of the Organization Department of the Central Committee, who had slandered me in front of Hu Yaobang in early 1980 and then spread rumors about me to the head of the *People's Daily*, actually bore no personal grudge against me. The attacks, ostensibly aimed at me, were all part of a move to embarrass Hu Yaobang as the supporter of the program to rehabilitate rightists.

At a meeting in 1982, the Party secretary of the Liaoning provincial committee, Guo Feng, handed a copy of my article "Good People, Why Are You So Weak?" to Hu Yaobang and said for all those present to hear, "A lot of factual mistakes in here." At the same time, the provincial Party secretary of Heilongjiang, Yang Yicheng, also stood up and said, "It is the same with his 'People or Monsters?'—no basis in fact!" Pressed by these two "ducal lords" (and not for the first time), Hu Yaobang could not afford to ignore my problem. He had to make some kind of statement in response. At the same time, from his own knowledge of my life and work, he could not totally condemn me.

The directive that he finally issued evidently cost him a lot of thought; it was incorporated into a letter dated July 6 and addressed to two deputy heads of the Department of Propaganda of the Central Committee of the Party, the president of the Federation of Art and Literature, Zhou Yang, and the head of the *People's Daily*, Hu Jiwei. It read as follows:

Comrade Guo Feng of Liaoning Province personally handed me a copy of the said work "Good People, Why Are You So Weak?" and announced in front of all present that there are factual errors in Liu's examples. Guo added that the provincial Party Committee also does not agree with Liu's comments on their work.

Comrade Yang Yichen of Heilongjian Province added that Liu's "People or Monsters?" also contained many factual errors and that the provincial Party Committee could not understand how such a piece could be awarded a prize. Because of their objections, I went over this work of Liu's published in January.

First of all, I felt that the work under discussion is not a literary work, but rather a feature report criticizing the political life within a province. Does or does not a writer have the right to comment on the dark side of political life? Of course, he has such a right. But then, the question arises, To whom should this kind of writing be distributed? The Party Committee concerned, the people concerned, or the media? This depends on which is best able to solve the problem. Is a newspaper or magazine authorized to publish exposures or critical comments? One can't say that it is not, but then one must adopt a responsible attitude; one must check the facts with the local Party Committee and the local people, so that one's work, when published, can bear scrutiny for factual veracity.

The issue at hand is that neither of the above two considerations have been taken into account. Let me reiterate that we are steadfast in our policy of righting the wrongs of the Cultural Revolution. In this respect, nobody can outdo the Central Committee. But it all depends on how you go about it. One cannot afford to be careless. I feel that some of our comrades have not grasped all sides of the issue, or frankly, are overconfident.

Comrade Liu Binyan has been wronged in the past. Many people sympathize with him, and this is perfectly commendable. We respect and cherish him, also perfectly commendable. But not a few comrades feel that he overreacts. I feel that we should listen to his comments and exchange views with him in a comradely fashion.

I perfectly understood Hu Yaobang's difficult position at the time and did not try to refute his saying that I was "overconfident." But I did want to clarify my position on the question of "overreacting." This was an accusation often flung at former rightist writers and reporters by the conservatives, who argued, "See, they are only interested in exposing the Party; they do not forget past wrongs. They overreact, nursing a grudge against the Party, looking for revenge." In my letter to Hu Yaobang, I said:

I do not hold any grievance against the antirightist campaign of 1957. It was an inevitable tragedy; if not Mao Zedong, somebody else would have done it. I do not hold any grudge, either against Mao or against the people who were in direct charge of labeling me. But don't I nurse grievances of some kind? Yes, but of a totally different kind. When I hear cases of Party cadres violating the law, pursuing their private interests and hurting innocent people in the process, I cannot contain myself; I want to lay them bare before the public. At those times, I may overreact, or get carried away by emotion; my work style and my method may be somewhat careless. That is where my problem lies.

Hu Yaobang was evidently satisfied with my letter and wanted to give me some encouragement. He did not write to me directly, but wrote to Zhou Yang and He Jingzhi of the Propaganda Department, and they showed me his letter. It wasn't as if Hu Yaobang never wrote personal letters to writers; he had written to the poet Zang Kejia and to the philosopher Guo Luoji. That he took extra precautions in my case goes to show that many officials thought I was a dangerous element. It also showed that Hu himself was in a very precarious position and did not want to provide any ammunition that could be used against him. Meanwhile, I was told that I was on a list of dissidents at the Propaganda Department of the Central Committee of the Party. Piecing things together, one could infer that as early as 1981, during the campaign against "bourgeois liberalization," such a list was already in existence.

The fall of 1981, during the first wave of the campaign against "bourgeois liberalization," which had the writer Bai Hua as the main target, must have been a trying time for Hu Yaobang.

On September 25, a meeting to commemorate the hundredth anniversary of the birth of Lu Xun was held in the Great Hall of the People. I was sitting thirty feet away from where Hu Yaobang was giving a speech. I could see many people in the front row, including my friend Leo Oufan Lee and other Lu Xun experts from abroad. For a moment, my attention wandered, and I did not hear what Hu was saying. Suddenly, the expression on the faces of those in the front row became very tense, and so I quickly located the passage in his printed speech that he had just read. I was astounded to read:

And there is another kind of people, who have a hatred for the new China, for socialism, for the Party that has long been ingrained in them; they are precisely the kind of people that Lu Xun has written of. . . . They disguise themselves and stick a knife in your back when you are unaware. . . . This sort of counterrev-olutionary crime must be punished by law.

I was taken aback. Were there such people in artistic and literary circles? How could Hu Yaobang speak in such a way? Had he forgotten that this was a meeting in commemoration of Lu Xun? How could he use this platform to attack and threaten writers and artists? When the meeting ended, I saw Zhou Yang and He Jingzhi leaving in haste with troubled expressions. Evidently, they had not expected Hu Yaobang to speak in such a way either. They could not help but take this as a sign that art and literature were going to feel the knife again.

Predictably, the response among the visitors from abroad was also very negative. They were already unhappy that after having come so far to commemorate Lu Xun, they had been excluded from the various seminars. And now this speech on top of everything else! While the commemoration program was being planned, Zhou Yang had decided to invite many scholars from abroad. But by the time the meeting took place, the political climate had changed, and things didn't work out as planned.

Hu Yaobang must have realized that his speech was a blunder; that same afternoon he met with a group of leading artists and writers in the Great Hall of the People, and explained: the draft of his speech had been revised by members of the Central Committee of the Party and did not reflect his personal views.

That same year, Deng Xiaoping mentioned a few people by name in his criticism of Bai Hua's *Bitter Love*, three of them experts on theory. All of them had made remarkable contributions in rationalizing Deng's new policy since the Third Plenary Session of the Twelfth Party Congress, and in refuting the dogmatism of the conservative leftists. The young philosopher Guo Luoji had corresponded with Hu Yaobang, and Hu admired his writings; and it was even said that Hu touched them up now and then. But during the last few years, Guo's ideas had fallen out of favor with the leftists. After 1981, he could not publish anymore, and Deng Xiaoping decided that he must leave Beijing. He did not go; but two years later, the order was repeated, and he had to leave for a teaching job at Nanjing University. Why was it imperative that he leave Beijing? There was only one reason: to cut off his ties with Hu Yaobang, so that his "liberalizing" ideas would not influence Hu.

Rarely could Hu protect any of the people that he should have protected. After Guo Luoji, it was Ruan Ming's turn. Ruan Ming at one time had been an assistant to Hu Yaobang. Ruan Ming's fate was even worse: he was expelled from the Party, and an official order banned him from publication. Hu Yaobang had proposed to set up an investigation team to review Ruan Ming's case, but before the team could be set up, an order came down: immediate expulsion from the Party. Hu Yaobang was absolutely helpless. During the campaign against spiritual pollution, the head of the *People's Daily,* Hu Jiwei, and the deputy editor-in-chief, Wang Ruoshui, both lost their positions. The well-known theorist Li Honglin, head of the Bureau of Theory at the Propaganda Department of the Central Committee, also lost his position and was silenced for a long time. These men were all associated with Hu.

In the fall of 1984, I had written about a case of injustice in Shaanxi Province that caused a huge storm of protest. So strong was the outcry, in fact, that Hu Yaobang was forced to criticize me publicly, advising me to stick to creative writing. When this pronouncement was made known to the staff of the *People's Daily,* people were shocked. They asked, "Now, whose turn is it to learn a lesson? Isn't it the Central Committee's? By what right do you expect people who have been victimized by an unjust campaign to learn a lesson from their unfair treatment?" Later, perhaps because Hu's position was strengthened, there was no more talk of my leaving the *People's Daily.* A year later, the proposal was raised again, but nothing came of it.

In February 1985, Hu Yaobang ignored advice and spoke on journalism. I was bitterly disappointed by the speech. I met his son Hu Deping and said, "This speech is clearly against his own long-held beliefs. Why did he give it?" But Hu Deping did not answer. My guess was that Hu Yaobang was in trouble again. The Fourth Congress of the Writers' Association, which had been convened in the early part of the year with the theme "freedom of creative writing," had probably provoked anger, and Hu Yaobang had rushed to appease it. But this speech was going to far. My friends and I understood Hu's precarious position and his various compromises.

But beginning in 1985, his position steadily weakened, until it was finally decided that he must step down after the Thirteenth Party Congress. He gave in meekly. That was going too far. Perhaps I did not sufficiently appreciate all the attacks, the threats, and the forces that were holding him back, but even so, the accumulated weakness of his own character was instrumental in his downfall.

In November 1986, Hu Yaobang was on a tour of inspection, his last, in Shanghai, when he made another comment on me. I had just published my report "An Unfinished Burial," about the remnants of the leftists in Shanghai institutions of higher learning, and the leaders of the Shanghai Party Committee had complained to him. Hu remarked, "I read everything that Liu Binyan publishes. It is said that three of his reports have factual mistakes. The recent one about Heilongjiang Province has also been accused of factual error. I sent somebody to inquire, and he has determined that there are errors." But where did this somebody conduct his inquiries? Probably at the Party Disciplinary Committee of Heilongjiang Province. And my piece was exposing the provincial Party secretary's son! Or did he make the inquiries down at the Central Committee's Disciplinary Committee? They had already given credence to the secretary's accusations against me and complained to the *People's Daily* about my "factual mistakes."

In January 1987, when Hu's resignation was made public, and I was expelled from the Party, many people spoke up on Hu's behalf. At the time, I told my friends, "Just wait and see; they will publicize Hu's self-criticism to condemn him." I figured out that he would make erratic statements, which would eventually hurt his own prestige.

About six months later, the Central Committee distributed a circular to all Party members, containing Hu Yaobang's self-criticism. In it, the passage about me read as follows: "Liu Binyan had worked at the Youth League Central. He has written several letters to me, but I did not see him. He has never moved from his 'rightist' position. I have on several occasions suggested to the *People's Daily* that he is not suitable as a reporter." These remarks, when made public in China and abroad, reflected badly on Hu. My belief was that he had been forced to make a statement under great duress. I could understand.

Just as I expected, a few months later, a friend of mine and a relative of Hu's both relayed a message to me that Hu had made the statement in 1987 while he was being forced to retire, that he had no intention of harming me, and that he himself regretted it later. I was told that in October 1987, at a meeting of the Presidium of the Party's Thirteenth Congress, Hu had directly confronted Deng Liqun; he told Deng that in preparing the copy of his self-criticism for public release, he had personally deleted the passage about Liu Binyan. Why, then, Hu asked, was it restored against the writer's expressed wishes? Deng did not answer. At the time, Hu had already stepped down, and I was expelled from the Party, but some people still used every opportunity to defame us, such was their vindictive malice. But Deng Liqun soon got his due: during the election to the various committees at the Party's Thirteenth Congress, he was outvoted twice. Part of the reason he lost so many votes was because of his underhandedness in publishing Hu Yaobang's self-criticism.

From the passage in Hu's self-criticism relating to me, it is evident that one of the factors that led to his downfall was his support and sympathy for me. Otherwise, why would there have been a passage about me, in such strong language? This verified the assertion of that Politburo member in 1985 that Hu's enemies (mine, too) regarded Hu as my boss behind the scenes, and that all the offenses heaped on my head were also held against him. It was true that I had written him a couple of letters, but they were mostly about cases of injustice, with my own report enclosed, and he had read them carefully and made comments. I had not asked for a personal interview, but if I had, I would have had no difficulty getting one. As for the suggestion that I give up reporting, he had made it, but mainly because my reports were stirring up trouble for him. Perhaps he had also thought that I might take the warning and stop offending people in high places, which inevitably harmed me. But he certainly did not suggest I give up reporting because of my so-called inflexible rightist position.

People still cherish the memory of Hu Yaobang. He made lasting contributions to cleaning up Mao's legacy and in leading China onto the path of reform. His personal obliteration could be seen as the price that the Chinese have had to pay in the fight for a better future.

In the last forty years in the history of the Chinese people, there is hardly a high-ranking leader who was more closely attached to the people than was Hu. There was hardly another like Hu, who, in spite of a demanding work schedule, found time to read over two thousand letters in three years' time from people petitioning for justice. He left his mark all over China: many isolated areas that were never remembered by other cadres at the Central Committee were visited by Hu Yaobang.

It was early in the morning of April 15, 1989, and I had just gotten up in my hotel room in New York, when Du Nianzhong, the New York correspondent for the *China Times*, rushed into my room saying, "Hu Yaobang has passed away."

I was dumbstruck. Although I had read of his illness the day before in the *Overseas Chinese Daily,* I never imagined that it was so serious, and I never thought that he would die so soon.

The symposium convened by the *China Times* to commemorate the seventieth anniversary of the May Fourth movement was scheduled to open in half an hour. Du Nianzhong invited Wang Ruoshui, Ruan Ming, and me to his room to exchange views on the momentous news. All three of us had been expelled from the Communist Party for offending hardliners by calling for thorough reform. And Hu Yaobang had not been able to protect us. The forces behind him had been too weak within the Party.

The next afternoon, after the symposium, a few of us were chatting, and I raised the question of whether the students in Beijing would seize the occasion of mourning for Hu Yaobang to demonstrate for freedom and democracy. Most thought it likely but also assumed that the authorities would use every means in their power to obstruct it. I did not argue with them, but privately I felt that if the authorities tried any tricks, it would only unleash a greater outburst. I did not think the authorities were ready for a confrontation. In my opinion, another mass demonstration like the one in 1976, which ostensibly had taken place to commemorate the death of Zhou Enlai but was actually staged in opposition to the Gang of Four, could not be ruled out.

Ten days later, in San Francisco, on the occasion of another symposium commemorating the May Fourth movement, many Chinese and American Sinologists were gathered in front of the TV. It was a tense moment. Hadn't Deng Xiaoping expressed his resolve the day before to put down the students at all costs, not stopping at bloodshed? Would not the demonstrations set for April 27 end in a bloodbath?

According to a practice well-established within the Chinese bureaucracy, every official acts according to orders handed down by his superior; the more important the issue, the less likely he is to act on his own or refuse to obey orders. And this would certainly be the case here, in which the highest dictator had ruled that the current movement was a counterrevolutionary upheaval manipulated by a handful of conspirators, which he was determined to put down regardless of consequences.

Yet, to the surprise of all gathered there, the demonstration on April 27 was unprecedented in scale and met with the least resistance. I was greatly buoyed by the way things had turned out, and not only because bloodshed had been prevented. It was the first time since the Democracy Wall movement of 1979—after which there had been three successive waves of crackdowns—that the iron will of the hard-liners had been bent and broken, at least for the time being. One could list many reasons for the failure, but it was interesting to note that the ruling clique found itself divided over how to deal with the democracy movement, and up against insurmountable resistance. It could perhaps afford to ignore the anger of the masses, but when Deng's talk was relayed to journalists and Party and government units, there was an eruption of outrage.

I felt that the price Hu Yaobang paid two years earlier for not putting down the student demonstrations and the prestige he enjoyed for promoting the liberal line had all, in some way, kept the axe from falling on the students. He was gone, but when the people who had pursued him to an untimely death found themselves at odds with each other and were undecided about how to act in this emergency, his ghost must have risen before them in silent warning.

A friend who had just arrived from Beijing for the symposium told me that two weeks before his death, in one last long conversation with an old friend, Hu Yaobang had again mentioned my name and had expressed regret for the unfavorable mention he had made of me in his 1987 self-criticism. This was the fifth time I had gotten this message. In China, an old colleague of mine and a relative of Hu's had brought it, as I mentioned above. Later in the U.S. when I was giving a talk at a university, two young men had called on me and my wife. They were relatives of Hu Yaobang and, knowing Hu's wishes, had undertaken to express his regret to me over the affair, hoping for my understanding.

In Beijing, he had said: "In my whole life, I have injured three persons. The first two date from the Yanan period; the third is Liu Binyan."

Now in the most recent message, in his last conversation, he had again mentioned Xiang Nan and regretted that he had not been able to protect Xiang from misfortune in 1957. But actually he had; because of Hu's intervention, Xiang had not been labeled a rightist and had not been expelled from the Party; he had only been disciplined.

Rarely had I come across high-level Communist Party leaders who repented their mistakes—not even if these mistakes had plunged thousands or even millions of people into suffering and ruin. They were above regret. This was another point on which Hu Yaobang differed from his peers. One thinks of those for whom he had spent so much energy restoring them to positions of power. Where were they when Hu Yaobang was driven into a corner? They stabbed him in the back, and to this day, they have not shown one whit of repentance.

I never imagined that Hu Yaobang would so take to heart his few words about me, nor had I imagined that he would die so early. Had I known, I would have written a letter to him before leaving China. Or perhaps I would have called on him and talked to him, told him that I understood perfectly. I would have offered him my gratitude. It would also have been the gratitude of my readers. Without his protection, my pen would have been stopped long ago.

chapter eighteen

"The Best-Laid Schemes of Mice and Men..."

We had an exceptionally cold winter in 1986–87. The third, and heaviest, snowstorm descended on Beijing on New Year's Day, the day that nearly ten thousand students from Beijing University and other universities as well as residents of the city demonstrated for democracy and against a corrupt bureaucracy in Tiananmen Square. I walked home from a friend's wedding, my boots crunching in the snow. I was deeply moved by the students. As I walked through the night, I dedicated a poem to them, condemning the savage repression.

On December 10, 1986, I had been in Fujian on what turned out to be my last assignment as a reporter, when I received an urgent telegram from the editor-in-chief of the *People's Daily*, calling me back to Beijing. Upon my return I was requested to clear up a few accusations against me. The most serious among them was whether I had or had not called on the students to rise up and fight for freedom and democracy when I was in Shanghai that year. I had indeed given a talk in Shanghai, but in April of the previous year. Moreover, my topic had been "My Reports," and I had talked about my own work and the obstacles I had encountered. There had been no reflections on current politics. I wondered how any misunderstanding could have arisen, since the meeting at which I had given my talk had been chaired by the permanent staff of the *People's Daily* based in Shanghai. But at the time, rumors about me were rife, and so I was not terribly surprised.

In Beijing, the atmosphere was tense, because of the students. I closely followed the movements in other parts of the country. Students started to take to the streets—in Wuhan, Lanzhou, Jinan, Shanghai, Hanzhou, Chongqing, Nanjing, Tianjin, and, finally, my own home town of Harbin. Every new wave of student protest filled me with exhilaration, for the hope of China rested in them. Strangely enough, I didn't feel the generation gap. I felt as though I were one of them. I was taken back to 1945, when I was a middle-school teacher, and demonstrated with students my own age, shouting slogans against the Kuomintang. Now, the students were

demonstrating against the Communist Party, the adept organizer of student movements in days gone by. But the passing years had proven that
it was only when pushed by the masses that the Party leadership would
inch its way forward.

At the time, the Central Committee of the Party had professed to be
committed to reform of the political structure. But at the same time, there
was much talk of the "four little dragons" of Asia—Singapore, Hong Kong,
Taiwan, and South Korea—which weren't dabbling in democracy, but
whose economies were booming.

By December, I kept hearing that names were being named at high-
level meetings, and that fingers were being pointed at intellectuals, foremost among them the so-called dissidents. I, of course, was always among
those honorably mentioned. What were they up to? Were they posed to
strike? Friends concerned for my safety advised me to sort out my papers,
in case of a raid.

I decided not to join in the student movement for the time being, so
as not to give my enemies ammunition that could later be used against me.
I wanted to retain my right to speak. So I asked the deputy editor-in-chief
for a brief holiday on Hainan Island.

On New Year's Day, the police arrested dozens of students, but released
them later. At the time, I was not aware that the Party was holding an
emergency meeting near Tiananmen Square at which there was a difference of opinion on the student issue; some were ready to spill blood. I was
also not aware that my own political fate was sealed at that same meeting.
I left Beijing, nevertheless, with a heavy heart, and in a state of mind
similar to that in 1957 at the beginning of the antirightist campaign.

I had had many chances to visit China's tourist attractions, chances that
I had never taken advantage of. But this time I decided to relax. I arrived
with my wife Zhu Hong at Sanya, a little city at the southernmost tip of
Hainan Island in the South China Sea. There we saw a pair of huge rocks
carved with the words "boundary of the heavens" and "edge of the sea,"
and I realized that this is where Su Dongpuo, the poet of the Song dynasty,
had spent the last of his years in exile.

By a lucky or unlucky coincidence on January 5 1987, the very day that
we had boarded the plane on our southbound flight, the Secretariat of the
Central Committee had decided to expel me from the Party. The *People's
Daily* took measures to recall me. But it was not until January 10 that I
got the message from the Writers' Association of Hainan Island, in the

city of Haikou: "The *People's Daily* called last night; please call back immediately."

I called, but the deputy editor-in-chief was not at home. I asked the operator to connect me to a friend at the reporters' section. He told me that the situation was very, very serious. "Haven't you heard about the No. 1 internal document?" he asked me. "Fang Lizhi and Wang Ruowang are to be expelled from the Party, and your turn is not far off. Come back quickly."

What did he mean, that my turn was not far off? There were two explanations: either I was already expelled, or the decision was still to be made.

The next day, the phone at my house rang; my daughter Xiaoyan answered the call and relayed the message to me: the secretary of the Party's Disciplinary Committee, Wang Heshou, had notified the *People's Daily* of the Secretariat's decision to expel me from the Party. In the days that followed, calls of condolence and support poured in. Foreign journalists asked for interviews, and strangers even stopped by to offer my daughter their goodwill.

My wife was concerned about how I would take the blow and tried to comfort me. Expulsion from the Party was a serious matter, and a deep injury to me. But I was already prepared for disaster and remained calm and collected.

Since 1982, I had learned to expect trouble. There had been countless examples before me. First, there had been the philosopher Guo Luoji, then the writer Bai Hua, and the poet Ye Wenfu, and later, the philosopher Wang Ruoshui, Li Honglin, the critic Ruan Ming, and others. All had been deprived of the right to publish and stripped of their positions, and some of them had been expelled from the Party.

I had once discussed our strange fates with Wang Ruoshui. I had said, "It's strange; we fully support the line laid down by the Third Plenary Session of the Eleventh Party Congress, we fully support reform, and yet we must always be on the watch for a stab in the back by those we try to help."

Wang Ruoshui had felt the same. As I had feared, he was stripped of his position as deputy editor-in-chief of the *People's Daily* one year later. Even before that event, his right to publish, to speak in public, and to go on visits abroad were restricted again and again.

I guessed my fate would be much like theirs: notice given to all the papers and magazines not to publish my writings; disappearance from public; my readers would think that I was too timid to write. I would lose my readers, and then I would not be able to tell them it was a forced silence.

But public expulsion from the Party was more to my advantage than a silent disappearance. No matter what the Central Committee said, I could be confident that my readers would understand the real reason behind my expulsion.

I had only three days to return to Beijing. I told Zhu Hong: "Let's enjoy the time we have here!"

We were at one of the most beautiful bathing beaches in the world. Miles and miles of white coral beach, sparkling on the edge of a pure azure sea. Even if you swam far out, you could still see the bottom.

I could not believe that this would be the end of me. I did not believe that this adversity would last as long as had the preceding one of thirty years ago. I felt sure that I would be back here swimming again in the not too distant future.

On my way back, I was calm and collected, not much different from returning from an ordinary job assignment. As the plane descended over Beijing airport, it suddenly occurred to me that I did not know what kind of people would be waiting for me at the terminal. Anything could happen. But then I thought, let it come, whatever it is.

Waiting for me on the other side of the glass partition were, not the military police, but two old-time colleagues from the *People's Daily*, the new Party secretary, Xu Zhongying, and the secretary of the General Office, Wang Gengnan. They had taken a minibus and had brought over my children. This was absolutely unprecedented; it was as if I were a conquering hero.

Three planes had landed at the same time, and the baggage-claim area was crowded. A handsome, well-dressed man walked over to me and addressed himself to me: "Excuse me, you must be Mr. Liu Binyan. I am embassy staff back for a vacation." He held my hand and said, "We have great respect for you at the embassy," and repeated the word *respect* several times. I thought that he must not know that I was already a political outcast. I asked him, "Do you know about the No. 1 document?" "Yes, I do," he replied, which somewhat surprised me. How could a diplomat pay me such a compliment, especially under such circumstances? Before leaving, he added, even less officially, "Hope you get the Nobel Prize!"

The Party Committee secretary and the Party cell secretary saw me home. I told them on my own initiative that I was aware of what had happened so as not to embarrass them. We made an appointment to be at the office the next day to read over the documents concerned.

That night, lying in bed, I went over some of my recent correspondence. A young friend, the philosopher Z., had written in a letter dated January 9:

In my last letter, I mentioned your naïveté, and events have repeatedly proved me right in my forebodings. Tigers will devour people, no matter which species of tiger they are. But, when all is said and done, history does not side with tigers. At present the situation is pretty grim, but I hold fast to the belief in the upward movement of history. A political party that expels its finest members from its ranks is draining its own life blood. Why should we distress ourselves? Buddha has said, "Who but I should descend to the infernal regions?" It is only in such a state of otherworldliness that one joins the ranks of the elect.

And now here is your turn, old fellow! My friend X. spent ten years in prison during the Cultural Revolution. And for what? Because he loved books! The day he walked out of prison, he composed the first half of a couplet as he contemplated its forbidding doors: "Never repenting, although the sea of bitterness is spread before me." But he has not yet been able to complete the couplet; his fate is still unclear. One day, he asked me, "Who do you think can complete the couplet?" I said, "Your humble servant here," and right away I recited, " 'Being released, three thousand epiphanies is not excessive.' And the intervening line is, 'I act according to my own rules.' " X. was overwhelmed.

Enough of that, old fellow. The times have forced on you the role of the all-merciful, all-daring, and all-knowing Buddha. Is there anything under heaven that cannot be tolerated? It is beneath us to feel resentment. The evil that has befallen our country has not played itself out yet; there's nothing we can do except stand by helplessly. The virus must work its cycle; meanwhile, no cure, Chinese or Western, can help. . . . Y. sent you a book, by Nietzsche. It will bear you up through this dark period. May the spirit of Zarathustra be with you. . . .

I love you dearly; thus, all the greater my sorrow. But living, a man must bear his burden. You are cut out for that fate. To suffer. But don't forget, the whole nation is suffering with you. Jesus cried before he gave up his spirit, "My people, you know not what you do!" A downtrodden people never knows what it is doing. You, the chosen, must suffer for them. . . .

How my wife and I wish we could be with you, to share your burden of
suffering, with you and your wife and children. I know that across the nation,
many, many people want to share your suffering if only they could!

Tears ran down my face as I read the letter. Thank you, my friend; you
have made my burden more bearable.

On the morning of January 15, I went to the meeting room to read over
the documents concerned. A man was there fiddling with a tape recorder.
Then the two Party secretaries appeared, and showed me the resolution
of the Secretariat of the Central Committee. There was only one sentence:
"On January 5, 1987, the Secretariat of the Central Committee has
decided to expel Liu Binyan from the Communist Party; the decision will
be carried out by the Party organization of the *People's Daily.*" The
secretary of our Party Committee then said that I was entitled to speak
my mind. I was not prepared, and so I said that I would speak at the
meeting of the Party cell and that I would need to speak at length. They
did not press me. I settled down to read the No. 1 document of the Central
Committee. But as I read on, I had second thoughts. It occurred to me
that this might be a chance to speak up. These people here were not
antagonistic toward me. Although I was unprepared, that was not really
a problem. I placed myself before the recorder and began my speech to
some key figures on the Central Committee, picking my words carefully
as I spoke into the machine.

First of all, I pointed out that since the beginning of 1979 when my
"rightist" label was removed, I had been a target of libel and slander from
within the Party. This meant that there was a power group within the
Party that was opposed to the decision of the Third Plenary Session to
rehabilitate the rightists, and that was also opposed to our returning to
membership in the Party. We who had been wronged, however, had
consistently upheld the decision of the Third Plenary Session. Our words
and deeds were testimony. As for myself, all my writings were about the
problems that the Party itself was seeking to tackle. I pointed out forcefully
that expelling me from the Party without giving reasons was not a responsible act. And I asked why there was such a rush to expel me. I asked why
I should be kicked out without so much as an explanation. How was I to
defend myself if I wasn't given any reasons?

Later, I was told that they made four copies of my forty-five-minute talk
that same night and sent them to the Central Committee, the Disciplinary

Committee, and the General Office of the Central Committee. I was assured that my voice would be heard by the highest in the land.

Starting in December, people had been put on the job of collecting all the tapes of my speeches. A team had been at work night and day to transcribe the recorded talks. So urgent was the need that they were being sent in by special messenger. My expulsion had been conducted along the familiar lines of the era of protracted class struggle—conviction first and presentation of evidence afterward.

Interestingly, a movement was going on at the same time within the *People's Daily* building to overturn the decision to expel me. Following my recorded talk of the January 15, the representatives of the Party Committee and the Disciplinary Committee at the *People's Daily* again asked me to speak in my own defense. I was better prepared and talked for two hours. I demanded an explanation for the second time. Later on, the ritual was repeated. Copies of my talk were made and sent off.

Finally, following the pattern of announcing one expulsion every five days, mine was scheduled for January 24. That evening, the Central Broadcasting Station would announce the news of my expulsion from the Party.

Meanwhile, news trickled in that the decision to expel me might be reversed. On the eve of the announcement, when I was already in bed, the writer Zhang Jie phoned to give me the good news: "I heard that the decision has been changed to a serious warning." I put down the phone and lay awake in bed, lost in thought. Until that moment, all my friends and I had hoped against hope that I might not be expelled. But after hearing from Zhang Jie, I began to have second thoughts about the matter: "Which is better? To be expelled, or to be kept in the Party?"

At nine on the morning of January 24, four representatives of the Party and the Disciplinary Committee showed me the written order for my expulsion. I wrote in the blank space: "The procedure of my expulsion is a violation of the Party constitution, and the decision has no basis in fact. I reserve the right to appeal." Even then, the Party secretary gave me a chance to make a last defense. He promised to make one last effort to have the decision overturned, since there had not even been a Party meeting held to lend some pretense of legitimacy to my expulsion. It wasn't that nobody was interested. But over 90 percent of the members in my cell had objected to my expulsion, and no persuasion would make them change their minds. So the people in charge just had to skip the meeting and risk violating the Party constitution. They had also sounded out the Party organization of the Writers' Association, whose reaction had been equally negative. Three leading members of the Party core had said that they thought the move unacceptable. Then, the secretary of the Beijing Party Committee, Xu Weicheng, had questioned six writers in Beijing; three had spoken out against my expulsion, while the remaining three had not wanted to commit themselves.

By this time, news of my expulsion, although not formally announced, was already widely known. On January 24, between three and ten in the evening, twenty-seven people called at my house to offer their support.

Eight years ago, on that very day, I had ended twenty-two years of political exile and had returned to the Party ranks. And twice, the reason for my expulsion had been simply that I had criticized abuses within the Party. During my life, I had been alternately heaped with insults and praised to the skies. But now I was going through both at the same time, an experience that was absolutely unique. For instance, I had met a worker in the yard of our building one day. He had said, "Congratulations! They have made it possible for you to be a full man." Another person had written me a letter, which said, "You have realized yourself." Strangely, I had never felt that way about myself before. It seemed that my influence had grown in direct proportion to the intensity of my enemies' attack.

At seven on the evening of that memorable day, the central TV station was scheduled to announce the news of my expulsion. They had already announced Wang Ruoshui's expulsion ten days before and Fang Lizhi's five days before, and now my turn had come. A young friend, Wang, whose acquaintance I had made recently, appeared. He had come specifically to keep me company during the broadcast. He was afraid that I could not bear the same kind of blow for a second time.

My wife Zhu Hong sat to my right and Wang sat to my left while we watched the broadcast. As the announcer spoke, the words were also flashed on the screen: "The Disciplinary Committee of the *People's Daily* has decided to expel Liu Binyan from the Communist Party." I could not help but smile at this piece of subterfuge. The Disciplinary Committee of the CCP and the corresponding committee at our paper had passed the ball between them, each trying to shove the responsibility for my expulsion onto each other. And so, I said to myself, the paper had been made to bear the burden after all. The announcer was completely expressionless. Not a hint of righteous outrage in his voice.

I myself was calm in the face of this insult delivered in front of one billion people.

I was later told that throughout the length and breadth of the land, at that very moment, many people had cried for me. Not for my personal fate, but for the lost hope of the Communist Party and our country. Some had voiced their anger; others had drowned their sorrow in wine. Not a few had decided to withdraw their applications to join the Party. Some had decided to put aside their pens, while others had decided to leave the country.

The official announcement of my expulsion carried the wording "libel and slander" in connection with my reportage. My own paper, the *People's Daily,* had stepped in and asked for the removal of those words, but the answer was that everything else was negotiable except those few words, which were essential.

More than one person passed on to me the news that one member of the Central Committee had issued a directive to the courts at the provincial and municipal levels that all cases brought against Liu Binyan must be accepted and inquired into.

My family took the news of my expulsion quietly. But we were on our guard against the arm of the law. We knew that in China, the police and the courts were there to serve the whim of the Party, and I took note of the fact that the highest penalty for libel and slander was a three-year sentence with the suspension of political rights for one year. Supposing all the people from all the provinces and municipalities I had offended decided to make a collective accusation against me? Some friends offered their services for my defense; others looked up lawyers. In a word, I had to prepare myself for a concerted attack by all the enemies I had made in seven provinces during the last eight years.

I continued to receive letters, telegrams, and phone calls. They brought messages of encouragement for me, condemnation for my enemies, and expressions of concern over the way the country was going. Innumerable visitors, from all parts of China—workers, students, peasants, soldiers, intellectuals of all kinds, most of them previously unknown to me—turned up. Gifts also poured in—food, medicine, a fitness apparatus, souvenirs of all kinds. Also checks, which we mailed back. A group of workers from Chongqing assumed that I was in prison and offered me a monthly allowance of fifty yuan and promised support for my wife and children as well. I received invitations from both the northern and the southern provinces to take my family and settle in those parts for good. Some high-ranking municipal officials and some senior officers in the army invited me for a vacation at their facilities. Businessmen in Hongkong and elderly overseas Chinese in Australia offered me financial aid. A scientist offered me a substantial sum out of the money that he had received from the sale of a patent—100,000 yuan. Over two-thirds of the letters were signed with the writers' real names and addresses, although they were aware that these letters could get them into trouble.

There were also a few letters from young people who believed the papers and who wrote to condemn me or to warn me that I was wasting my talents. These letters were useful in helping me to maintain a balanced view of things. Some of my old friends also wrote to remonstrate, saying that I exaggerated the dark side of things and was blind to others. But coming from them, this was not surprising, since they were all elders in comfortable retirement.

Extracts from statements Wang Ruowang, Fang Lizhi, and I had made were officially printed and distributed as a guideline for the general attack on us. They were printed in limited numbers and read at mass meetings at various work units. Nor surprisingly, their effect was basically the opposite of the intended effect. On one occasion, when the quotations were being read out, one latecomer, who had not caught the beginning, exclaimed, "How true! What document is that?" The higher-ups retrieved the "document," as it did not work the way they planned, but the damage was done. The document was duplicated and circulated widely; in some cases, it sold for as high as forty yuan a copy.

As for the official articles refuting me, even Hu Qiaomu, the man who had engineered the whole show, had to admit that they were dismal failures. Goebbels's lies had worked; so had the rhetoric of the Cultural Revolution, but only against a specific background. Those tricks could not be repeated under the present circumstances. Not all the literary flourishes of Hu's pen-pushers could save them from the well-worn clichés of the Cultural Revolution. Deng Liqun resorted to a material incentive to set the wheel rolling, offering ninety yuan per thousand words for denunciatory articles—four-and-a-half times higher than the normal rate—plus fifteen yuan per day living allowance. Thus he managed to muster a group of scribblers who racked their brains day and night, but still failed to write an acceptable article. Earlier, Hu Qiaomu had demanded that writers sign their own names to these articles instead of hiding behind pseudonyms—an added blow for the writers. These people were no fools. They knew very well that once their names were linked to these denunciatory articles, their reputations would be ruined. Nine times ninety yuan per thousand words could not make up the damage. With all this hanging over their heads, it was no wonder that their inspiration failed them.

"Of the three, Liu Binyan's influence is the widest and the hardest to refute"—so they said, placing the emphasis of this critical campaign against me. But even so, the meeting planned to repudiate me had to be delayed. Deng Liqun and his associates had ordered a dry run of the meeting and were dissatisfied with the results. "Why can't these people whip up their hatred for Liu?" he demanded, and ordered all the denunciatory speeches to be revised and "upgraded." The *Wenhui Daily* of Shanghai was ordered to send a delegate to participate in the attack on me. Understandably, nobody wanted to stick his neck out, and so they sent a young staff reporter. The young person arrived, and, sensing the atmosphere in Beijing, handed in his script and sneaked back to Shanghai. He preferred to face the music there for not doing his job rather than be involved in this business in Beijing.

Two weeks later, the meeting was finally called after much tidying up and upgrading. But it was a listless affair. The *People's Daily* had been obliged to send a delegate. Orders were orders, and the deputy editor-in-chief shouldered the burden. He did his job and read an upgraded speech at the meeting, which duly appeared in the *People's Daily* according to schedule. The poor man was roundly abused for his actions. One letter that was sent to him later ran: "Liu Binyan may not achieve immortality, but you will certainly go down in history as a skunk." How could the letter-writer know all the pressures that had been brought to bear on him?

Some friends who knew the inner workings of our country followed the "abstention" principle: abstain from writing, from phoning, and from calling. It was for everybody's safety, and I understood. Were my letters being intercepted? I could not say. But letters to me had been lost. And a stack of letters addressed to me had been seen on a desk in the office of a certain provincial Party Committee. Was my phone bugged? I could not say that either. But what sometimes happened was that the voice at the other end of the line suddenly got very faint in the middle of a conversation, as if it were coming from a long distance. As for the question of whether it was safe to talk at home, that will always remain unanswered. During those tense days in January, my guests and I used to carry on our conversations on paper, as if we were deaf-mutes. But it was too much of a strain, and so we changed tactics and simply played music as we talked. Later, I learned that this was futile because modern technology could erase the music and pick out the conversation. So we finally decided to drop all precautions. Whatever was said within those walls was being spoken by Chinese people all over the country. What was there to fear? Was I being followed? I was often asked. This question shouldn't be put to me, I would say. I hoped I wasn't. But I knew there were no scruples about sacrificing personal freedom for the sake of "national security."

Still, many people braved the danger and entered my house. I had thought that the events of January would give me three years' time to retire and do some reading. But a whole year did passed, and I still did not find seclusion, much less time to read.

Why did I say "three years"? Since the campaign against "bourgeois liberalization," the question uppermost in people's minds has been: What is happening in China? This is what we talk about incessantly. This time, the offensive of the conservatives has been much more sweeping than the two previous ones in 1981 and 1983. They have even managed to drag down Hu Yaobang, the standard bearer of reform. And I, too, have been caught in the net. Thus many people have turned pessimistic: it will take eight to ten years to see a change for the better. Some even felt that a Chinese age of Brezhnev is on the rise, and Brezhnev's reign lasted eighteen years! I thought differently. I predicted that we would see a minor shift in half a year, and big changes in three. But few believed me.

I had some reasons for optimism. Since 1985, I had ceased to read the signs of change in China by looking at personnel changes at the highest levels; I looked down and read the pace of Chinese history from the masses. My friends who were not deterred from visiting me kept me informed about what was happening in China.

I should thank my lucky stars that this twist in fate has brought me many trusted friends. A poet and a reporter both came to me the night of the broadcast. Since then, they have often brought me news, and we have discussed the situation in China. Thirty years before, when I had received my first political blow, which took me twenty-two years to recover from, only a few had dared to approach me. But now, the same Communist Party had dealt me the same kind of blow, but my house was full of friends and well-wishers. This was my reason for believing that a change would come about within a few years.

A majority of the people had opposed the campaign against "bourgeois liberalization." Some spoke against it openly. In addition, many people had been conducting private enterprises for the last few years, and were set against any political campaigns that might jeopardize their economic interests. They, too, were against the campaigns. They didn't have any confidence in the durability of the Communist Party's policies toward private enterprise to begin with. The campaign against spiritual pollution had confirmed their worst fears. Predictably, they refused to invest in expanded production. Some converted the proceeds from the sale of their enterprises into gold, which they hoarded. Tens of millions of yuan were diverted from production into the consumer market, increasing inflation. The countryside was seized by a craze for building houses and monumental gravestones, while gambling became the rage everywhere.

The campaign itself exposed the conservatives. It opened people's eyes and made them shed their illusions. What followed would be a raised consciousness, and China would move forward. This was how I saw the situation.

I also perceived a change in the intellectuals, an unprecedented change. Now, they were not content with silently resisting the campaigns that were forced on them. No, now they were beginning to voice their indignation. Others, though their numbers were small, took action. For instance, three young writers agitated for a signed letter by writers to protest against my expulsion from the Party. The plan was later dropped because only eight established writers were willing to risk signing their names; all the rest were young writers. But it is a fact that following my expulsion, many writers and reporters had stopped writing. Many veteran Party members had considered withdrawing from the Party, and some did. Young people who had been applying for Party membership changed their minds. During the February following my expulsion, political leaflets had been seen in Shandong, Zhejiang, and Shanxi, something that had happened only once in China during the last forty years, and that was in 1976.

But the conservatives kept attacking. The newly appointed provincial Party secretary of Guangdong closed down the *Shenzhen Youth News*. After the fall of Hu Yaobang, the next to fall was Zhu Houze, head of the Propaganda Department of the Central Committee, a man who was second only to Hu Yaobang in the esteem of intellectuals. After the expulsion of Fang Lizhi, Wang Ruowang, and me from the Party, a list was compiled of a second group to be expelled, sixteen people altogether, including Bao Tong, a trusted aide of Zhao Ziyang. A list of names of a third group, numbering fifty, was also being drawn up. The daily routine at the Writers' Association was completely paralyzed; since everything had to be sent to the Bureau of Artistic and Literary Affairs of the Propaganda Department of the Central Committee for approval, it was like a military takeover. Meanwhile, questions were raised about the process used to elect the governing body of the Fourth Writers' Congress held in 1984–85, implying that the elections had been rigged. A new body was formed to replace the governing body, waiting to take over. A select group of over a hundred Marxists was convened in the township of Zhuozhou in Hebei Province. Their task was to "readjust" the adjustments effected by the Third Plenary Session regarding reform. In other words, they were trying to overturn reform and the open policy and head straight back to the old order that had existed before the Cultural Revolution.

A wave of counterattacks overtook all the provinces that I had previously visited; holdovers of the Gang of Four were clamoring for reversals of their cases. The Shandong provincial papers and broadcasting station took the lead in this wave of counterattacks. A headline in one of these papers ran: "Liu Binyan is meddling in Shandong and disrupting the stable situation. We are confident that the cadres of Linyi prefecture know very well how to deal with his kind." Linyi prefecture immediately took the hint and acted on it. Various people who had been consigned to one of the "three categories" of holdovers of the Gang of Four and had been stripped of their jobs were being restored to their former positions. Some of them banded together and wrote letters of accusation against me. Even the newly appointed secretary of the provincial Party Committee, Liang Buting, who had taken up his post in 1984, was implicated. On the other hand, consternation overtook their former victims. Some left the area. In Shaanxi Province, the *Shaanxi Daily* tried to stir up public feeling and overturn the Party's decision in the case of Guo Jianying, the subject of my report "The Rights and Wrongs of Thirty-Eight Years." Meanwhile, the papers in Heilongjiang and Sichuan all carried attacks on me in an effort to discredit my criticisms and exposures.

For the past few years, the conservatives have also been busy attacking the argument of progressive journalists that "newspapers are first and foremost the voice of the people" and have tried to establish the point that newspapers are first and last the voice of the Party. We were soon to find out what was meant by the papers being the "voice of the Party"—behind their forbidding appearance, the papers had become spokesmen for local despots, corrupt officials, criminals within the party, and remnants of the Gang of Four.

People who had worked with me or people whom I had praised were now all objects of attack. For instance, in Dukou, Sichuan Province, a young reporter, Yu Yitai, who had worked with me in reporting on a major case of embezzlement and who had coauthored the report "Let History Judge," became the target of one such attack.

Following my expulsion, the provincial authorities had sent two senior reporters from the Xinhua News Agency all the way to Dukou to talk to Yu Yitai. They had tried to convince him that I had instigated everything and that he bore no responsibility. "But of course I do. I am the coauthor!" Yu had protested. "Yes, but the ideas behind it were Liu's," they had answered. "No, we talked it over together." Yu would not be led on. "Come on, you would not sympathize with an embezzler. You did not agree to shift the emphasis to things not directly related to the embezzlement case. But Liu would not listen to you. If you put this in writing, you will be completely absolved . . . ," they had argued. But Yu Yitai had refused, insisting that he had fully agreed with me regarding the article in question. Evidently, someone had had the bright idea to have one of Liu Binyan's own coauthors expose him. But it had not worked. And so they decided to make him pay the price for disobeying the Party. The Party Committee of Dukou passed a resolution that Yu Yitai must be removed from the staff of *Dukou Daily*. But that he must not move out of Dukou!

In Harbin, two thousand miles from Dukou, another young reporter, Yang Wanli, was also suffering persecution on my account.

And then there was the protagonist of "Another Kind of Loyalty," Chen Shizhong. It went without saying that he was a "pro-Liu Binyan element." For those attacking him, it was a pity that he was not a Communist, because that put him outside the sphere of the ongoing campaign. But since promotion for intellectuals was on the agenda, they soon found another way to let him feel the pinch. Chen had returned from studying in the Soviet Union in the early 1960s. Although his work had been outstanding at the Harbin Workers' Part-time University, he was not put on the list of candidates for promotion.

In many provinces, people who were not even remotely connected to me had been implicated in my case. Anybody who dared to speak up or who opposed corruption in high places was designated a "mini-Liu Binyan" or a "pro-Liu Binyan element" and was persecuted or discriminated against.

One day in April, a man in his sixties called on me at my home. His head was shaved, and his clothes were plain; he carried about him an air of dignity, calling to mind those self-styled "revolutionary cadres trained by the Party." Who would have imagined that he was the "pro-Liu Binyan element" in Ganzhou, Jiangsu Province? He had formerly been in the army and was disgusted at the special privileges and corruption he saw there. He was discharged and assigned to the Bureau of Electricity of Ganzhou, where he was deputy chief. But if he had hoped to see an improvement in morale, he was sorely disappointed. The goings-on at the bureau were beyond his wildest dreams. He tried to stamp out the corruption he saw, but was eventually labeled a "pro-Liu Binyan element," guilty of opposing the leadership of the Party.

Following my expulsion from the Party, all the "mini-Liu Binyans" were stifled, and all the "pro-Liu Binyan elements" were wiped out. It was a victory for the officials whom these people had formerly opposed; the officials were now the "positive heroes," the upholders of the Four Cardinal Principles, who now had a free hand.

Surprisingly, of all the people who had been objects of my exposure, the protagonist of my report "Let History Judge," the embezzler Qing Suqiong of Dukou, became my friend. I had interviewed her in prison, though I had not revealed my name at the time. A few years later, I received a letter from her. She reported that because of good behavior, her sentence had been reduced from life to fifteen years. She proudly announced that she had saved up her earnings in prison and donated them to the starving people in Africa. I sent her a letter of encouragement, and she sent me a souvenir she had made. After my expulsion from the Party, I assumed that she would keep quiet about our bit of correspondence. But what actually happened was that she had protested against my expulsion and had announced that she would organize a mass protest in the prison. She was immediately put into solitary confinement.

My enemies seized the opportunity. Why should a criminal whom Liu Binyan had written about take his side? There was only one explanation, they argued—that he had protected her. In my article "Let History

Judge," they said, I had shifted attention from Qing the criminal and focused on the social factors that had contributed to making her a criminal and had described many cadres of the Party as veritable criminals themselves. Wasn't that protecting Qing Suqiong?

Just as I had foreseen, the campaign against "bourgeois liberalization" ground to a halt within four months, following Zhao Ziyang's speech of May 15. At that time, Deng Xiaoping, in his conversations with visitors from abroad, stressed that the focus of attention was on leftist tendencies, which remained the main threat. This was, of course, all very nice, but seeing is believing. "Why don't you expel a couple of leftist elements from the Party?" people would ask.

In the period following the announcement of my expulsion from the Party, the *People's Daily* published an editorial under the heading "Discipline Comes Foremost Within the Party." Discipline was all right, but its coming foremost was questionable. If the Communist Party is not a fascist organization, nor a mafia, then what should come foremost is not discipline, but Marxism and the revolutionary goals as outlined in the Party program. In practice, however, discipline had indeed overruled all other considerations. During January of that same year, copies of over a dozen current publications across the nation (three in Sichuan alone) had to be destroyed because they carried articles by or about me. *People's Literature* carried a vignette of me on its cover, and so the cover had to be torn off and a new one printed. No questions asked, mind you; an order was an order. In the Chinese-literature volume of the *Chinese Encyclopedia*, the article on me was cut short, so the entire printed page that carried the article had to be destroyed, and everything redone. A few months later, I was again allowed to publish; and the article on me would not have needed to be cut at all. But the damage had been done already. Millions of yuan and tons of paper had been wasted. But nobody was held responsible. Herein lies the superiority of socialism, I suppose.

But in some cases, discipline did not work. The first 1987 number of the *Literary Review*, the journal of the Institute of Literature at the Chinese Academy of Social Sciences, had carried a short article of mine titled "On Fiction, by a Layman." Evidently, it had been too late to destroy the existing copies and put out a new issue. So they had first torn out the page with my article on it and printed a new table of contents in Chinese, deleting my article. They had simply crossed out my name and the title of my article in the English version of the table of contents. But the problem was that the end of my article had been printed on another page, and that page, of course, could not be torn out. Signs of the torn-out page stood out glaringly, which infuriated the president of the Chinese Academy of Social Sciences.

The *Literary Review* was one of the most important journals of its kind in China; both the editor-in-chief, Liu Zaifu, and his deputy, He Xilai, had published critical studies of my work. Thus, as a general rule of behavior under such circumstances, they should have rushed to denounce me to keep their own records clean. But evidently, those two thought differently. Since they had published positive comments on Liu Binyan, they argued, "We must not simply follow the crowd and repudiate him, and ourselves in the process, unless we are convinced that he is very wrong. Our names will not be linked to any blind attack on Liu Binyan in the pages of our journal." Upon saying this, Liu Zaifu left Beijing for Guangdong and stayed there for five months. Consequently, the *Literary Review* never published any articles denouncing me, and Liu Zaifu and his journal went unharmed too!

Soon, the story of how the *Literary Review* had borne up against pressure was all over Beijing. How different this was from some of those scientists, writers, and leaders of "democratic parties" who had made haste to grovel before a hand had even been lifted against them! Liu Zaifu and his associates showed their mettle as Chinese intellectuals. They showed that for them truth and conscience were foremost, not discipline.

Intellectuals from the various provinces boycotted the campaign against "bourgeois liberalization," something they had never done in former political campaigns. The Heilongjiang Party Committee sent four officials down to Heilongjiang University to gather information on my talks and activities there in 1986, but they were rebuffed on all sides. The provincial Party Committee issued orders for the teaching staff of the Chinese Department at that university to write articles refuting me, but none budged. In the south, teachers from the Wuhan Technical College of Central China and Xiangtan University in Hunan all spoke up in favor of my works in their classes, but no one interfered. Not only were they left alone; in fact, their prestige was greatly enhanced.

The affair of Liu Zaifu and the *Literary Review* proved that once a group of people decided to act with courage, they expanded their liberty; and once this expanded liberty was tacitly accepted, it would become a liberty shared by all.

China had entered a new era. Many people were not yet aware of the fact; a fraction of the population that was aware did not want to face it.

In his farewell speech to the staff of the Propaganda Department of the Central Committee, Zhu Houze had taken a strong stand. He had said at the end of his speech: "As for the merits and faults of my work here at the Propaganda Department, it is not for me to say; let history judge." The audience had applauded. Some people were predictably incensed. Later, there was a check on who had applauded. But what was the use? At the time, Deng Liqun in particular had been sitting right there on the platform. People had been aware of possible retaliation, but they had applauded Zhu Houze all the same. In fact, those people had clapped precisely to spite Deng Liqun and the power he held.

Along with a few colleagues from the *People's Daily*, I attended the Lantern Festival celebrations held by the Beijing branch of the Writers' Association. It was my first public appearance since my "disgrace in men's eyes." Many people clapped as they saw me walk in; some came forward and seized my hands. Of course, certain people didn't like this, but so what?

Every precaution was taken to limit my continuing influence. I had been invited to two meetings in Liaoning but was forbidden to enter the province by the provincial Party Committee. My name had been put up as a candidate for "people's representative" of the Chaoyang district in local elections by several groups of electors in the district, among them the Institute of Economics, the Department of Journalism of the Graduate School of the Chinese Academy of Social Sciences, as well as some commercial and neighborhood units. The authorities announced that I had been reassigned to a new unit, the Writers' Association, which was situated in another district, and so I was not qualified to stand as a candidate in the Chaoyang district. This, of course, was a lie, since the shift did not take place until a month later. And anyway, I was registered to vote in the Chaoyang district. The telephone operator at the *People's Daily* was ordered not to transfer my calls to me. The concierge at the apartment complex where I lived was ordered not to disclose my apartment number. The leaders at the *People's Daily* had contemplated moving me somewhere far away, to cut off my links with editors and reporters.

But what was the use of all these little maneuvers? My colleagues at the *People's Daily* were more cordial to me than ever. There were over two thousand staff members at the paper, most of them unknown to me, of course. But now whenever I set foot in the courtyard of the *People's Daily*,

I had to be ready to spend twenty minutes answering greetings from every side. Sometimes people would drop me a piece of inside news. Walking along the streets, either in Beijing or in the provinces, I was often recognized, even if I wore sunglasses. I would walk out to do some shopping but come back all the richer for a couple of new friends. Yaohua Middle School in Tianjin, where I had once taught, held an anniversary celebration that I attended. My name had been struck off the list of former instructors, and the authorities had not disclosed my coming, but teachers, students, and alumni bombarded me for autographs and snapshots when I appeared. It lasted from nine o'clock in the morning to three in the afternoon, until I finally had to leave. The situation was the same at all public affairs I was allowed to attend in writers' circles. The number of photographs that I had taken with people in the last three months of 1987 exceeded all the photographs that had ever been taken of me in sixty-two years.

Although my books were banned, they appeared on private bookstalls at several times their original price. I was told that tapes of my talks at Heilongjiang University were sold on the market, four tapes to a set, at forty yuan a set. Handwritten copies of my works also appeared in some places.

It was ironic that while the authorities wanted to snuff out my memory altogether, they had to allow me to appear in public as an exhibition of their tolerance. They had not taken into account another factor that no army could put down—namely, the Chinese students abroad. Twelve hundred students signed a protest against the campaign against "bourgeois liberalization." Chinese-American writers, overseas students, political activists abroad, and Sinologists in the United States and Europe issued letters of protest. Letters poured in from eminent overseas Chinese voicing their concern. In order to meet the political needs at both ends, I was removed from the staff of the *People's Daily,* but not allowed to retire. My writings were not published anymore, and those already published were taken off the bookshelves, yet I was reassigned to the Writers' Association to be a professional writer! Thus were we held up for exhibition. Fang Lizhi, though discharged as president of his university, was still a professor, while I, though a reporter no more, was still a writer! Now wasn't that sheer hypocrisy?

Soon after, another problem surfaced. I received three invitations, two from the United States and one from France. Wasn't this a chance for them to exhibit their much-vaunted tolerance? Yes, but the idea of letting me have a good time abroad was simply unbearable to them. On the other hand, if they forbade my going, their image would be further damaged.

I expected to be arrested at any moment and tried in court. This threat had hung over me throughout 1987. My offense was that my reports were "not factual," had "reversed black and white," and were full of "libel and slander." The accusation of my reports not being factual had dogged me since 1979. Of all my reports that had given rise to controversy, there had been only one investigation by the authorities, and that had been in the summer of 1980, when over a period of twenty days, one hundred people were interviewed in connection with "People or Monsters?" The conclusion was that there were a few discrepancies in minor details, but that the work as a whole had a positive value. Its main problem lay not in factuality but in a lack of thoroughness in uprooting all the problems relating to the embezzlement case of Wang Shouxin. The Heilongjiang provincial Party Committee would not accept this conclusion, since it carried some criticism of them. But when these clauses were removed, the Party Committee still found the wording of the report of the investigators unacceptable. In the end, the investigation came to nothing; its report was a waste of paper.

Since the publication of "People or Monsters?" all my reports had experienced a similar fate. I was always dogged by accusations of factual error. Although I can't say that my reports are unassailable in every single detail, they are as a whole true to the facts. I once made a comparison: suppose a building is completed, but a glazed tile falls off the wall of the lavatory; do we need to pull down the entire building to replace the one tile?

Of course the ideal would be to have every brick in place, but in a society like China, plagued as it is by bureaucratic entanglements, it is very difficult to cut your way through to the facts in cases of corruption in high places. The *People's Daily* had once reported that a county department head in Hebei Province had pocketed two thousand yuan of public money. The provincial Party Committee sent out several investigation teams, but as many as eight hundred pieces of false evidence were given, shielding him. If this was the case with official investigation teams armed with authority, how much more difficult it must be for a reporter to get at the truth single-handedly.

In fact, ignoring the truth, inflating achievements, and distorting historical events had been in practice in the media in the early fifties and reached a peak during the Great Leap Forward. The singing of praises for positive achievements and the overlooking of negative aspects prevails to this day. As I have pointed out repeatedly in my public talks, China's papers have never so much as touched on 1 percent of the negative aspects of our society. Isn't that as bad as lying? And how many papers can face up to the question: Since 1958 have you, or have you not, covered up mistakes on the part of the Party leadership as well as the disastrous effects of these mistakes? It is an established practice with us to reward the writers of such false reports; in the army, they even receive a "merit" if their articles are published in a paper of a certain status. And of those provincial leaders who have attacked me on account of factual errors in my reports, I challenge them to look closer to home—haven't they consistently encouraged their own papers to brag about nonexistent achievements and to cover up mistakes?

Following my expulsion from the Party, a wave of discrediting exposés swept the country, challenging the facts. These were, of course, not limited to attacks on my own writing. There were actually very few reporters who were writing the kind of exposés I was, not more than a handful. Even so, the conservatives of the left were uneasy. Journalists were one of the main targets of the campaign against "bourgeois liberalization," and the campaign had been intended to shake up the media in order to purge all "bourgeois-liberal" elements from the newspapers, magazines, and radio and TV networks.

In the old days, whenever I entered the courtyard of the *People's Daily* through the main gate, I had to edge in cautiously in case I was spotted by the crowd of petitioners who had come from various areas outside Beijing to petition for justice. The numbers who had besieged me at my apartment were also legion. But since 1987, I noticed when passing the main gate that these petitioners had disappeared. I remembered that the line had used to start at the gate and trail off into the main street outside. Now the registry office at the gate was deserted. I soon found out the reason why. It was not that cases of injustice had diminished. It was that a new regulation had been put in force restricting those petitioners to their own areas and prohibiting the media from taking up any petitions over cases that had been given a court verdict. Even if the petitions were not rejected out of hand, what our paper did was to relay these petitions to the units concerned. Only a fraction were pursued by our papers, and an even smaller number appeared in the pages of the *People's Daily*.

Just as the public media and publications for internal circulation in China tended to shy away from unpleasant news, efforts were also made to reduce the number of petitioners—an eyesore and an embarrassment—from the streets of Beijing. But neither the reform movement nor the Party-rectification program had reduced their numbers. The waters of the sea of adversity had swollen to the limits. What was to be done? Dams were simply set up upstream to keep the flood from Beijing. This was in keeping with the general policy of carrying out the Four Modernizations program (the program started in 1975 to modernize China's agriculture, industry, national defense, and science and technology) and ensuring an environment of peace and stability. But was stopping up all safety valves a good way to ensure peace and stability? With the waters gathering steadily, was there no fear that the dams would break?

For the last few years, one of the strongest accusations against me has been that of "disrupting the stable situation." The term *unity and stability* was concocted precisely for the purpose of upholding the existing order, the order inherited from the Mao era, a totalitarian order, one that represses human rights and protects the corrupt system, an order that regards all attempts at democracy as a threat to the unity and stability of the ruling positions. Actually, what disrupts unity and stability is the leadership's own political performance, because by their own doings, they have made the Chinese people lose confidence in the socialist system and the future of the nation. Under such conditions, some people take the law into their own hands. Hence, the eruption of violence—gunshots, bombings, arson, and railway derailments—a form of revenge for the injured and the oppressed. There has even been a bombing in front of the Mao Memorial Hall, at the gate of the Ministry of Public Security.

In 1985, I had felt the crisis gathering as never before. The campaign against "bourgeois liberalization" had been a great relief to corrupt officials and embezzlers who could proceed unhampered, while the victims and the downtrodden had been cast into despair. It was against such a background that in the province of Heilongjiang, an unprecedented string of disasters took place in quick succession. First, there was an explosion at the hemp factory, then an explosion at the gunpowder factory, then a fire in Yichun set by arsonists, then a robbery of the governor's residence in broad daylight, and finally, the great fire in the Daxinganling forest. I had lived in Heilongjiang under many different regimes, beginning with the warlord

Zhang Xueliang, followed by the Japanese occupation, and then liberation. I had never seen the like of such disasters as these.

More frightful than the disasters was the growing apathy. People voiced their own resentments, but nobody felt responsible for what was happening to the country. The whole society seemed to be falling apart. Production slowdowns, worse than open strikes, spread swiftly and widely across the nation. The young urged each other to go abroad, as if the ship of the nation were sinking fast. Could anyone blame them? Take the generation born in the sixties, for example. As far as they were concerned, was there anything in this country to hold them back? Hunger in their early years, the brutal violence of the middle sixties, then poverty, unemployment, and so few choices in life. After 1979, a new hope arose. There was more liberty and individual choice. Our country seemed more worthy of new love and loyalty. We could have kept moving forward from year to year had it not been for the "leftist" intervention. And the corruption in high places, the special privileges of the officials' children were worse than during the Cultural Revolution, while law-abiding citizens and reformers were pushed to the wall, and their personal safety was endangered. The campaign against "bourgeois liberalization" had shattered the last hopes many had had for the country. Soon after my expulsion from the Party had been announced, an overseas student, with a Ph.D. degree in mathematics, who had already made preparations to return to China, had written to me: "I'm not coming back. Those goddam swine!"

In one sense, being expelled from the Party had given me a chance to catch my breath. I had had no time to read, no time to exercise, no time to write my diary, no time even to go through the papers, no time to answer the many letters I had received.

At last I could take a break. A huge load was lifted from my shoulders. I had left so many debts unpaid—so many articles promised and not delivered, so many issues taken up and put aside. But now that it was beyond my power to act, I felt a great sense of relief. Now I could sleep more, and even play with my little grandson.

Of course, events all over the country left me very unquiet. How could one not agonize over the devastating forest fire in Daxinganling? That fire was a crime against humanity, for those trees can never be replaced; the whole ecological system has been irreparably damaged. Actually, the disaster could have been avoided. I had material in my files exposing corruption

among the forest security guards. Information on how personal connections had overridden national interests, on how absolutely unqualified
people had been smuggled into the ranks of the forest guards, and on how
upright people had been mercilessly hounded for whistle-blowing—I had
gone over this material again and again, but the attitude of the Heilongjiang provincial Party Committee made it impossible for me to do on-site
investigations. Even in the midst of that disastrous fire, underhanded deals
were going on: facts were concealed, reporters were beaten up. The public
said, "This fire has burned up everything except the corruption."

September had passed, and after all these months, my position had
improved somewhat. Thus, when Song Xiulan and her associates, who had
been fighting a losing battle against the iniquities in Daxinganling, looked
me up again, I was greatly tempted to take up my pen for their cause. But
I finally decided against it; for technically, I could never have gone on
location. Not being able to publish reports of my own, I wrote up petitions
and exposés on behalf of others and tried to get these papers sent to the
coming Thirteenth Party Congress. I also encouraged young writers to go
where I myself could not.

Thanks to the persuasiveness of Harrison Salisbury, I was given permission to leave for the United States.

Yet, I was not all that eager to leave the country. True, it had been five
years since I had last visited the United States; but I did not expect to see
much change. If my own political situation had improved, I would have
preferred to spend two years in some remote area of China, perhaps right
in the heart of Daxinganling, for during the past few years, I had spent
so little time at the grass-roots level. And it was at that level that all the
momentous changes taking place in China were most forcefully reflected,
changes that were of historical significance, since they concerned the fate
of one billion people.

I had foreseen that once I was abroad, many people would ask me
wherein the hope of mainland China lay. Since the beginning of 1988, I
had been asking everyone I knew what they saw in the life around them
that inspired confidence in the future of China. Few were optimistic.
Whether intellectuals or workers, they all had the same answer: "What's
the use?" Young writers were pessimistic about the future of Chinese
literature as well.

Finally, I received one positive response. The Shanxi writer Zheng Yi
(author of *Old Well*) talked to me on the phone just as I was about to

leave the country. He was full of hope for the future. "Our young writers are tackling more weighty works, works that surpass their former writings. I am doing the same myself. I'm not publishing anything until I have surpassed myself," he said.

"Yes, but what about the political situation?" I countered.

He answered, "I'm just as optimistic about that. Do let me tell you a piece of news. In the recent election of the people's representative for Lucheng County, all the official candidates were wiped out. It's a real anarchist vaccum there as far as government is concerned. And it happened this way: Lucheng County was scheduled to hold elections last because of the deplorable state of things there. But the delay had only helped fan the flames of democracy among the masses. With the examples of elections in other counties in which many official candidates lost before their eyes, the voters of Lucheng took matters into their own hands and broke the record by voting against all the official candidates."

That was the last piece of news I heard before I left the country.

A Finale and a Beginning

I have finally finished this book, though not entirely to my own satisfaction. The problem may lie in my life as I lived it, not in my life as I have written it. What's more, in the more than sixty years that I have lived, it is not only I but the Chinese people as a whole who have not lived life as it should be lived. In which case, what I need to change is not a book, but my life story, or even the life story of our nation.

How I wish I had life to live all over again. But then, that is also a frightening prospect. I might have been a totally different person, too clever perhaps, or overly cautious. And if there is one thing to my credit, it is that I have never been too sharp or overly cautious.

It seems that our nation is too ancient and too clever for its own good. There are too many people crouched under their individual shells of security; there are too many people who profess to see through the ways of the world and yet hold on to its pleasures. These are the clever ones. I am struck with pity as I watch them go through life without accomplishing anything. Pity for them and for our nation. In China, there are already too many talented people lying in their graves for others to throw themselves away so recklessly.

I have never tested my IQ, but judging from my youthful performance, I would guess it is not outstanding. I never was a precocious child and never at the top of my class. Science courses, in which I was not interested, were always a trial. Not that I didn't work hard. But on the whole, I had little time for study. Especially during the last thirty or more years. When there would have been time for study, I had to do manual labor. Later on, there were no books. And then, when books were available, my time was not my own. How I wish I could shut myself away and sit down to read. Even at the rate of one book a day, I could not finish all the books on my reading list.

On my visit to the United States in 1988, reading was a top priority. Yet except for a few days in September, I was not able to keep it up.

Looking back on my life, I see so many things that I have yearned for but have not been able to enjoy. I had been able to spend only a very short period of my childhood in the countryside where one could fly a kite, and I was there at the perfect age for kite-flying. After that, I never had a chance to fly kites again. In the winter of 1956, I bought a big kite for my four-year-old son; we planned to fly it the next spring. But the next spring I was so busy. And in the spring following that, I had to leave for the countryside for reform through manual labor.

Now I am able to fly kites with my grandsons, but I am an alien here in a land that does not belong to me. Besides, in Beijing the best place for kite-flying is Tiananmen Square, but no kites are being flown there. The only things being flown there now are military helicopters. Military helicopters releasing leaflets on martial law against the students' demonstration. When will I be able to embrace my two darling grandsons? That will depend on how long the military is positioned against the people.

Arriving in the United States, I was faced with two choices, to bury myself in books, or to accept the warm invitations of Chinese students to talk to them. I chose the latter. Chinese students studying abroad are hungry for news of home, and I could not disappoint them. I decided to tell them about the real state of things back home. I knew the risk I was running: if my words happened to offend the authorities, it would be impossible for me to speak out or exert any influence on the mainland, and after all, it is only on the mainland that I am in my element.

Thus, after lecturing on "Contemporary Chinese Literature and Society" at UCLA, I began to give talks at other universities on the West Coast. Later, when I joined the Nieman Foundation at Harvard, I gave talks at universities on the East Coast, in the Midwest, and in the South.

By May 1988, I had already given talks at over forty universities in the United States. Except for institutes where there were few Chinese, I usually had to speak twice—once in public and then again to several hundred Chinese students and their spouses. On our flights all over the United States, we visited many places on the East Coast, in the South and Midwest, and on the West Coast. But my wife and I rarely had time to go sightseeing. We had lived in Los Angeles for six months, had been to many universities, but had never found time to visit Las Vegas. We had been to Florida, but never saw the sea. We stayed there one night, gave two talks, and then rushed on to North Carolina.

I had planned to catch up with my reading. There were so many new developments in social science and humanities in the last century. And there is so much to learn about the USSR and the East European countries. This stay abroad was also to have been a chance for me to write a novel about perceptions of China, and all the people and events that I have come across. But I have not found the time to settle down.

In June 1988, concurrent with my visits to France and Germany, student demonstrations unprecedented in scale broke out in Burma. The first thing I did every morning was to get hold of the papers to follow new developments. The people of Burma had endured the poverty and oppression of General Ne Win's socialism for twenty-seven years, and they had had enough. There were so many people in the streets! Unarmed students and monks could effect changes of government! My heart flew to China. When, I asked myself, will the Chinese people act?

The highest rate of inflation of the last forty years had pushed down living standards in China. People knew that it was the result of the Party's bungling of the economy and abetting the bureaucratic elite in its profiteering. Why were we still enduring all this? Why couldn't the Chinese take action as the Korean students had, or as the Burmese students were doing right then? I sometimes ask myself whether the spirit so highly regarded in Chinese philosophy and medicine has been crushed out of the Chinese temperament through forty years of fear and despair. Disappointment, pessimism, and a general mood of depression prevailed, following the crackdown on the students' movement of 1986–87. But I did not believe that the Chinese people, after the new awakening after the Cultural Revolution and the newly acquired freedom of economic reform, would allow themselves to be trampled upon without offering resistance.

Even so, I never imagined that the student demonstrations following the death of Hu Yaobang would grow to such proportions and draw the eyes of the world. By late April 1989, my wife and I had decided to decline the invitation of Trinity College in Connecticut for a year's visit and leave for home. But by the end of April, Deng Xiaoping announced his determination to crush the students at any cost, and on May 20, Li Peng announced the imposition of martial law, to be followed by the massacre on June 4. Thus, we were thrice compelled to delay our return plans. And now, finally, we not only are unable to return ahead of schedule, but have ended up as exiles.

I never expected that the Deng Xiaoping ruling clique was ready to plunge the capital into a bloodbath, and I never expected the ruthless pursuit and executions that followed. The word *mad* does not adequately describe their actions. On June 4, when I first heard the news, a thought flashed across my mind: these political madmen have not stopped to consider how they are going to hold on to their rule after they do this!

Evidently, these bloodthirsty rulers stake everything on the force of arms. They have lost all ability to understand the people, whom they fear and despise at the same time. They assume that the people, in the eighties, are just as submissive as they were in the twenties and thirties to the bloody rule of the warlords of the time, or just as responsive to the rallying calls and lying propaganda of the Communist Party as they were in the fifties and sixties.

On the surface, the rulers have attained their objective. Under the all-encompassing terrorism, China seems to have been cowed into silent submission. But this will actually create a bigger nightmare for them than if they had made some compromise.

The peaceful demonstration at Tiananmen Square was crushed, but it lit a flame in the hearts of countless people. The long-suffering Chinese people, after repeatedly being bullied and cheated, have finally given up their last illusions about the Chinese Communist Party. All they have now is implacable hatred. A few days after the execution of three young "rioters" in Shanghai, a train went up in an explosion. This is a warning signal. The anger of the people will flare up in violent acts of defiance, and the anger of the people will simmer in large-scale work slowdowns. Both on an unprecedented scale. All of which will give the government no peace. It will bog down the government in political and economic crises until it is finally swallowed up in its own mire.

I gave up my youth for the Communist Party in its struggle to seize state power. And now a handful of tyrants have betrayed the Party, turning themselves into enemies of the people in the real sense of the word. My generation has thrown itself into the struggle led by the Communist Party in the hope that our children will lead a better life, and now it is precisely the best and brightest of their generation who have died at the butchers' hands, or are fugitives fleeing from arrest.

Looking forward now, I do not indulge in sentiment. The price that has been wrested from the Chinese people was inevitable, I suppose. We greeted the founding of this state with wild acclaim in 1949; we submitted so docilely to its rule from the fifties right through to the seventies. What is there for me to say? But the Chinese people have now changed. They will not tolerate this state any longer. The handful of octogenarians and the privileged bureaucratic clique whom they represent will neither change their ways nor hand over power. Thus they are doomed to destruction. Yes, the people will pay a bloody price, but in the end they will shake off this monstrous thing that is draining them of their life's blood.

This is the end of the Chinese people's adolescence and their initiation into political maturity. They are no longer waiting to be liberated; they are now ready to pay the price to liberate themselves.

I have shared all the trials, undergone all the deceptions inflicted on the Chinese people. But I do not envy my luckier compatriots who have had a smooth and easy path. Looking back, I should say that the gains outweigh the losses. As my life is nearing its end, I finally see the light breaking out of the darkness. I have at least done my part and am ready to do more. This is happiness for me.

One morning after the events of June 4, I walked across Harvard Square and saw the people sitting in the shade at an outdoor café leafing through the newspapers, and for the first time it occurred to me what a blessing peace is. My compatriots on the Chinese mainland are fleeing right and left, in danger of their lives. Then and there I suddenly rediscovered the value of freedom.

At this moment, the Chinese people are one step closer to the freedom they have dreamt of and fought for during the last hundred years.

Index

LIU BINYAN was born in 1926. He joined the Communist Party in 1944 and by the mid-1950s he was one of the prominent young journalists of China. Although purged in the antirightist campaign in 1957, Liu was rehabilitated in 1979, and became the leading investigative reporter for the *People's Daily,* until his second purging in 1987. He now lives in the United States.

TRANSLATOR ZHU HONG (whose name is only coincidentally the same as that of Liu Binyan's wife) is a research fellow at the Institute of Foreign Literature of the Chinese Academy of Social Sciences. She is author of two books on English and American literature and translator of *The Chinese Western.* Her special interests are Victorian literature and women's fiction. She lives in Beijing with her husband, M. J. Liu, a scholar in French literature.